For Yuval,
with best w

Trouble-Making Judaism

Elli Tikvah Sarah

Published by David Paul in 2012
25 Methuen Park
London N0 2JR

www.davidpaulbooks.com
info@davidpaulbooks.com

Worldwide distribution (except North America) by
Central Books, London, E9 5LN

A catalogue record for this book is available from the British Library

ISBN 978 09548482 9 3

Printed in Great Britain by Imprint Digital

Front cover illustration *Women of Jerusalem,* copyright © Jess Wood, 2008
www.jesswoodpainter.co.uk

*Elli and I spent four months in Israel in 2007. I spent many hours wandering the
streets of the Old City and trying to make sense of the multi-dimensioned fissures
within and outside Jewish life that cut through every space and moment in a city
called 'the centre of the storm of the world'. In my painting, none of the women are
connecting. Each is lost in their own world. However, the woman wearing a skull
cap in the foreground - unthinkable in modern ultra-orthodox dominated Jerusalem
– holds the disquiet and is reflective. The road that abruptly stops in Abu Dis, the
footprints from the Walk of Reconciliation in Arab-Jewish Haifa, these memories
weave with the present impasse. And the waters of life are evaporating in The Land,
now they gush – but for how long?*
Jess Wood MBE

*Jess Wood, was awarded an MBE in the New Years Honours List, for her services to
lesbian, gay, bisexual, transgender and young people. She is co-founder and director
of Allsorts, a project for LGBT young people based in Brighton.*

For Jess
and our shared and separate journeys

This book is dedicated to the memory of my parents
Edie Klempner (nee Waltzer)
3 August 1923 – 3 November 1991
and
Paul Klempner
17 October 1914 – 3 May 1998
Who bequeathed to me their weaknesses and their strengths

Zichronam Livrachah
May their memory be a source of blessing

Contents

Acknowledgements

I want to begin by acknowledging my partner, my wife, Jess Wood Sarah. It is usual for male authors to thank their wives! I want to thank Jess for spending time with me, carefully reading and proof-reading my book. But my thanks to her are, neither limited to the help that she gave me in the final stages of the preparation of *Trouble-Making Judaism* for publication, nor to the support and encouragement she has given me and always gives me. Above all, my thanks to Jess are about *who* she is, not about who she is in relation to me, and what she does for me. It is because she is an artist, who has always made painting the centre of her life, and because of her commitment to living her life fully and completely, dedicated to her work in the world, and also dedicated to her home and her garden and her inner life, that, inspired by her example, it has been possible for me to realise myself as a writer.

Virginia Woolf knew that in order for a woman to write, she needed a room of her own. I have been lucky enough to have my own study for many years, but I have not had time to write an extensive piece of work. In order for anyone to write a book, she or he needs time – and time means money. I am hugely grateful to Rabbi Danny Rich and Lucian Hudson, Chief Executive and Chair, respectively, of Liberal Judaism; and to the officers of Liberal Judaism, for generously funding my salary for one month to enable me to prepare this book for publication. I also want to express my deep thanks to my congregation for their understanding and support and for agreeing to my mini sabbatical.

To write a book is one thing, to get it published its quite another. Geela Caiden could not have known, that when I spoke about my book with her and she told me that she knew *a* publisher called David Paul, that she had helped me find *the* publisher. I am very thankful.

And so it was, just two weeks before my writing leave was due to start that, I found the website for *David Paul Books* and filled in a book proposal form. On the day that my writing leave started, I received a reply! David was interested and wanted to see a couple of sample chapters. The rest, as they say, is history. How very fortunate I have been – not just to find a publisher so easily, but to find *this* particular publisher: a committed alternative Jew, who understood where I was coming from. Enormous thanks go to David Paul, for enabling the book that had been in my head for several years to get into print, and for his careful reading of my manuscript, and thoughtful and perceptive comments.

I had long hankered for the opportunity to take some of my published articles and material I did not think would get the chance to be in print, like the piece on Miriam, which constitutes chapter 2, and put them into book form. I want to say a big thank you to my rabbinic colleagues for giving me the permission to use re-worked versions of articles that appeared in their publications: to Rabbi Sybil Sheridan, for 'B'ruria: A Suitable Case for Mistreatment' and for 'Rabbi Regina Jonas'; to Rabbis Sylvia Rothschild and Sybil Sheridan, for 'Marriage By Any Other Name'; to Rabbi Jonathan Magonet, for 'Judaism and Lesbianism: A Tale of Life on the Margins of the Text' and for 'Fräulein Rabbiner Regina Jonas'; to Rabbi Jonathan Romain, for 'Towards a New Jewish Sexual Ethic', and to Rabbi Tony Bayfield for four pieces that were originally published as essays in *MANNA*: 'The Feminist Transformation of Judaism'; 'Speaking of God Today'; 'Bridging Choice and Command' (Compelling Commitments); and 'Creating Community', and for publishing my poem, 'The Post-Modern Rabbi'.

Finally, having thanked those who made this book possible, I want to express my deep gratitude to my mentor and teacher, Dale Spender, whom I met in the autumn of 1977, when, having just graduated from LSE, I found myself in her tutor group in the English department of the Institute of Education, London University. Dale Spender, an inspirational teacher, who went on to be a prolific feminist author, and one of the founding mothers of Women's Studies, gave me and other women our first opportunities to write. Dale didn't just give me something to do when I decided that I did not want to become a secondary school teacher, she enabled me to write, and taught me, above all, to trust my own voice. She also showed me, by her example, that writing can be a joy. I shall be eternally grateful to her.

Elli Tikvah Sarah
Bishopstone, East Sussex
January 2012

The Post-Modern Rabbi

I wrote this poem in the summer of 2008, when I was going through a particularly low period, and felt the weight of my responsibility as a rabbi particularly heavily – and so, too, the weight of my *Sho'ah* legacy. Nevertheless, although, the tone is much more sombre than the spirit which resonates throughout the pages of this book, it captures my experience of working as a rabbi, and reveals the underside of my passionate commitment to developing Judaism and engendering new Jewish life.

The poem was first published in *MANNA* 104, Summer 2009.

The Post-Modern Rabbi

The post-modern Rabbi
Like her Christian counter-part is a
Multi-tasker
Minister-Pastor-Counsellor-Priest
Servant of the community
And
Spiritual Leader
Juggler extraordinaire
Rallying the remnant and the
wayfarers
From week to week
Conducting the cycle of sacred
celebrations
From year to year
Sacralising the liminal moments
of life
From birth to death

But that's not all
Teacher – by definition
(Enhanced – and regularly
updated –
by new technologies)
Curator of the Jewish heritage
Guardian of the collective
memory
Keeper of the prophetic vision
Builder of bridges to
Span the wilderness
Agent of
Redemption

And
Sometimes
(In between)

She's also an
Angst-merchant
With nothing to sell but
Emptiness and longing
So she peddles
Enthusiasm
Wholesale by the kilo
Heavy vats of
Hope
Before it turns
Sour

Never bankrupt
Nor redundant
At least
Not yet
She does a steady trade
(On the side) in
Anxiety
Anguish
Disenchantment
Despair
All the loss-leaders for
One price

The post-modern Rabbi
Dedicated disciple of the
School of meaning-making
Post-1933 – and 1938
Contains fissures
Absorbs the abyss
Like all survivors
Standing on one leg
'The rest is commentary
Go and learn'

My Journey

I am a congregational rabbi. Though I write sermons, lectures and articles for journals and newspapers – and the occasional anthology – I rarely have a clear run at a concerted piece of work. So, when I was given a precious month to work on this book, I was delighted but I should have realised what might happen.

It started very well – in under a week I had completed two chapters. So I went up to London and stayed the night with my 93-year-old Aunt Vicky and then attended, the following morning, a New Israel Fund breakfast meeting.

But the next day Auntie Vicky had a stroke. Aunt Vicky has lived alone since her husband died 13 years ago and has no children. She is one of two surviving sisters of a family of nine. My mother, who was the youngest, died in November 1991. Vicky was her closest sister – and she has been our closest aunt, since my siblings, Geoffrey and Julia, and I were children.

The same day I heard the news that my mother's oldest and dearest friend, Dita, who had been her best friend from the time that Dita came as a refugee to London in 1933, had died suddenly of a massive heart attack. Dita had always been a very special figure in our lives. So, a double blow; with very practical consequences in both cases – which included me conducting Dita's funeral.

Why am I telling you this? Because the point of beginning with my personal story is to demonstrate the extent to which what I write is an expression of who I am and of my life experience. Having time to write and edit was a gift – and in a way, having time to focus on my Aunt Vicky's needs and grieve for Dita, was also a gift. So, that month was a very special and unique time.

And then, on the last day of my writing leave two congregants died – one of whom was the president of the synagogue. The following morning, I learned that two other members were in the final stages of their lives. And, then, inevitably, as the week drew to a close, those two people also completed their life's journeys. So, more loss: for their loved ones and friends, for their fellow congregants, and, also, for me.

So what are the other aspects of my personal life and experience that are also deeply relevant to the creation of this book? It makes sense to start with my parents.[1] They had a difficult marriage. My mother was already a widow when she met my father at the age of 23 and he was a divorced man nine years her senior. They barely knew one another when they decided to get married, just two weeks after their first meeting, while my father was on a business trip to London from Johannesburg.

My parents also came from entirely different Jewish backgrounds. My mother, Edie, the youngest of nine children, and the seventh daughter, was born and brought up in Highbury, north London, where the family belonged to the Poet's Road orthodox synagogue. Her parents had met in the East End shortly after they arrived as refugees from the great empire of the czars around 1905: she from Siemiatycze, not far from Bialystok[2]; he from Czernowitz – a town known at that time for its thriving Jewish intellectual life.[3]

Edie grew up in a large loving family, but, by the age of 19, had suffered three traumatic losses that shadowed the rest of her life: the death of her beloved grandmother, Sarah, who, arriving from Russia just as she was born, ensured that *Yiddish* was her first language, and died shortly after she started going to school at the age of five; the death of her sister Vera, the second youngest, who died at the age of 15, when my mother was just 12, with whom she shared not just a

---

1 Edie Klempner (nee Waltzer), z"l, who died on 3rd November 1991, and Paul Klempner, z"l, who died on 3rd May 1998.
2 Siemiatycze is now in Bialystok province, E. Poland. 'Up to the 19th century Siemiatycze was the private property of Polish nobles; from 1807 until 1915 it was ruled by Russia. In 1905 Czarist police attacked Jewish youngsters strolling in the forest on *Rosh Ha-Shanah*, wounding ten of them and killing one. The next day young Jewish revolutionaries organized themselves into "fighting units", disarmed the police, and controlled the town for three weeks. Jewish self-defense units were set up in Siemiatycze (see: www.jewishvirtuallibrary.org/.../ejud_0002_0018_0_18478.html).
3 Czernowitz is the German name. The Polish name is Czerniowce and it is called Chernivtsi in Ukrainian. 'The city is situated on the upper course of the River Prut, a tributary of the Danube, in the northern part of the historic region of Bukovina, which is currently divided between Romania and Ukraine. Historically, as a cultural and architectural centre, the city was known as "Little Vienna" and "Jerusalem upon the Prut"' (see: http://en.wikipedia.org/wiki/Chernivtsi).

bedroom but also a bed; the death of her first husband Max, a Czech Jew, who served as an officer in the British Army and was killed in action just six months after their wedding, when she was just 19. She was pregnant at the time, but having contracted tuberculosis of the bowel, had to have an abortion. My mother never recovered from these losses, and even the birth of her three children, whom she adored, could never fully assuage her deep feelings of grief.

My father, Paul, on the other hand, came from Vienna, the middle child of three in an affluent Jewish family, who became *Bar Mitzvah* at a progressive synagogue. Born with a hole in his heart, his cure had been sport, and he became a fantastic athlete – excelling in swimming, diving and skiing. But his parents favoured his elder sister, Hedi, and younger brother, Hansi, sending the young Paul away from home to live with his bachelor uncle, because he was seen as a bad influence on Hansi. He became an angry young man, and refusing to go to work in his father's tie factory, in 1936 at the age of 22, he went to South Africa. It was an impulsive decision, but it saved his life. Had he remained in Vienna, he would, no doubt, have shared the fate of his father, who was incarcerated in Dachau after *Kristallnacht*, from 13th November 1938 to 19th January 1939.[4]

But my father's flight to South Africa did not just save him from the clutches of the Nazis. Thousands of miles away in South Africa, he managed to organise domestic permits for his parents, which enabled them to flee to England, together with his sister and brother, just before war was declared. Apart from two cousins, who had converted to Catholicism after attending convent schools and also came to England, the remainder of the wider family were murdered.

As a child, I was aware of living in the midst of a clash of Jewish cultures – my mother's love of *Yiddish* and Hebrew; my father's love of fine things and Richard Tauber – and of the incompatible person-alities of my parents. However, it did not occur to me until I was an adult, that my father's tyrannical behaviour and fits of terrifying temper may also have been influenced by his up-bringing, and by being a stranger in a strange land, twice removed, while his imme-

---

4 I have in my possession a copy of a document, headed, *Stiftung Bayerische Gedenkstatten, KZ – Gedenkstatte Dachau*, which states that my grandfather, Julius Klempner, born 26.11.1885 in Wien (Vienna), a merchant, a Jew, and an Austrian, entered Dachau on 13.11.38, where he was given a number 31372, and was released on 19.01.39.

diate family experienced the horror of the *Sho'ah* at first hand.

Born a Jew, heir to the combined legacy of Eastern European and Central European Jewish experience, I nevertheless chose to be a Jew. I say, 'nevertheless', because not all Jewish children of my generation have actively embraced Jewish life. I didn't make the choice to be a Jew all at once. I remember, as a child, thinking it was really great to be Jewish on Friday nights when my mum sung *Yiddish* and Hebrew melodies after dinner that tore my heart out. I also remember lying in bed one afternoon, hardly able to contain my excitement, in anticipation of staying up really late that evening because my family were going, as we usually did each year, to my Aunt Vicky and Uncle Bernard, for the *Pesach Seder*, (my usual bedtime was 7pm right up until the age of twelve).

My childhood experiences as a young Jew were not all positive. The most memorable incident of one of the most memorable holidays I had as a child – going away to a three-week summer camp next to Beachy Head – was one early morning before breakfast, when, bespectacled eight-year-old that I was, I managed to fell a tall 12-year-old, who had made anti-Semitic comments. I also recall my puzzlement and pain and fierce anger when a school acquaintance informed me that the Jews had killed Jesus. Even at the age of nine, I knew it wasn't true and the injustice of it made me wild.

One of my strongest memories was at the age of twelve: it was the time of the Six-Day War in June 1967. My mother was an ardent Socialist Zionist, but my father certainly wasn't. In fact, when I wanted to put up a poster of General Moshe Dayan on the wall of the bedroom I shared with my sister, Julia – because that's what my Jewish friends were doing – he shouted that the picture of a 'warmonger' was 'not going up on any wall' in his house. Nevertheless, in the face of the existential threat to the Jewish state, just twenty-two years after the end of the *Sho'ah*, both of them – and my older brother, Geoffrey, too – went to give blood at the synagogue, where my brother had become *Bar Mitzvah*, three years earlier.

My parents had friends who were Israelis, Ofra and Henry, and I remember sitting with them in their flat glued to the news on the TV. The war, famously, lasted less than a week, but it was enough time for me to stand on a desk in the classroom and give a speech during break-time about the valiant Israelis, and have our form teacher, Mrs Webb, her face reddening, walk in and command me to 'get down, at once!' Not long after that, she called one of my Jewish classmates, Ronald, a 'lazy Jew', because he wrote 'G-d' in R.E. and, after getting everyone in the class to sign a petition, I went down to the headmaster, Mr Savage, to insist that she got the sack. A terrifying man, with huge hands, he didn't fire Mrs Webb, but he did make her apologise to Ronald in front of the whole class. Of course, she hated me after that ....

My clearest memory of anti-Semitism as a young adult was when I was involved, in the mid-70s, in the Hampstead branch of the Anti-Apartheid movement with my husband, Robert. Every Saturday afternoon we used to have a stall at the front of the market at the top of Hampstead High Street where we held up placards and gave out leaflets. On one occasion, out of nowhere, a passer-by, a man, who looked to be in his 60s, his face contorted with rage, came up to me, and hissed in my face, 'they should have gassed you all.' That was the first time I was really aware that I *looked* different; that a complete stranger could tell that I was Jewish. I was deeply shaken and it made me feel frightened – but it also made me feel defiant, although I didn't express that defiance at the time.

There were other moments when my experience of anti-Semitism, underlined the sense that I was different – a sense that I always had, and which, when I was a child, I put down to having a father who spoke with a foreign accent, and a mother who insisted on talking to people in the street and in shops – and interfering, on occasion, with what they were doing. Like the time she told a mother, who was standing at the bus stop with her baby, that her baby wasn't wrapped up properly against the wind and then proceeded to show her how to do it (very embarrassing, of course, when you're a child).

But *feeling* different is not the same as *choosing* to be. I remember the day I decided to make that choice. Aged 19 and a first year sociology student at LSE, I was sitting at lunchtime in the refectory. An active member of the International Marxist Group, at that time, I started flicking through one of the far-left papers that lay strewn across the tables – I think it was the Workers Revolutionary Party rag. I remember noticing an article about Israel – about how it was 'a puppet of Western imperialism' – and thinking, 'I can't do this anymore'. So, still a Marxist, I stopped being an IMG activist, and decided that first and foremost, I was a Jew.

But then, shortly after I graduated in 1977, I discovered Feminism, and my choice to be Jewish got overtaken by my enthusiasm for being part of the Sisterhood. I went to Israel for the first time in July 1978 for a holiday, and was so taken by the experience, I went back the following November and stayed on a small kibbutz on the Lebanese border for seven months. But when I returned to England I had other priorities, not least finding a place for myself as a lesbian, which wasn't an option for me in Israel at that time.[5] So, I became active in the Women's Liberation Movement, got involved in writing, editing and historical research[6] and joined the Lesbian Line collective, a helpline service by and for lesbians.

Not long after participating in the first Jewish Feminist conference in London in January 1982, and starting to get involved in Jewish

---

5 When I lived in Israel in 1978-79, the Law of Return, which was enacted by the government of Israel in 1950, to establish the right of all Jews living in the diaspora to immigrate to Israel, was being interpreted in such a way that lesbian and gay Jews were excluded. During the 1990s, as lesbian and gay Jews began to come out in Israel, and the first lesbian and gay pride marches were held, openly lesbian and gay Jews were able to make *aliyah* – literally, 'go up' – that is, immigrate to Israel.

6 Having met the educator and feminist writer, Dale Spender, who was my tutor at the Institute of Education, 1978-9, I joined the writing group of feminist teachers, which she convened at that time. The outcome of our endeavours was a book, which I co-edited with her, *Learning to Lose – Sexism and Education*. (The Women's Press, London, 1980). This book became a standard text for teacher education during the 1980s, and as a result, a revised edition was published in 1988, with a new introduction by Pat Mahony, a lecturer in teacher education at Goldsmiths College, London University. While involved in the writing group, I also became Assistant Editor of a new journal, founded by Dale Spender in 1978, *Women's Studies International Quarterly* - which later became, *Women's Studies International Forum*, when it expanded to 6 issues per year. In this role, having begun research at the Fawcett Library into the early feminist movement in Britain, I edited a special issue of WSIF, *Reassessments of First-Wave Feminism*, which was subsequently published as a book (Pergamon Press, 1982). During this period, I also co-edited with Scarlet Friedman, *On the Problem of Men: Two Feminist Conferences* (The Women's Press, 1982), which includes my article, 'Female Performers on a Male Stage: The First Women's Liberation Movement and the Authority of Men, 1890 to 1930.' Another article, reflecting my research, 'Christabel Pankhurst: Reclaiming Her Power' was published in *Feminist Theorists. Three Centuries of Women's Intellectual Traditions*, ed., Dale Spender. (The Women's Press, 1983). I also became a member of the Women's Research and Resources Centre collective, and, during 1983, worked at Onlywomen Press, where I was involved in the mechanics of printing, as well as in publishing.

Feminism, something else happened, the Israeli invasion of Lebanon. In the aftermath, not just the Marxist press, but the Feminist press, too – specifically, the *Women's Liberation Movement Newsletter*, the magazine, *Spare Rib*, and the black feminist paper, *Outwrite* – got whipped up into the frenzy of anti-Israel sentiment, which included the depiction of the Israeli Prime Minister, Menachem Begin, as Hitler. Soon afterwards, two Jewish lesbian groups formed and I joined one of them. A year later, I became part of an initiative to establish the Jewish Feminist magazine, *Shifra*.[7] I also started reading lots of Jewish books, including a couple by Emil Fackenheim. Disagreeing with Fackenheim's approach to Jewish empowerment and the exercise of Israeli power, I was, nevertheless, deeply affected by what he had to say about what he called the 614th commandment, 'Thou shalt not give Hitler posthumous victory.'[8] I felt that the additional commandment was directed to me, personally: I couldn't give Hitler a posthumous victory. That meant that being a Jew wasn't enough; I had to actively engage in *my* Judaism, too – and do what I could to contribute to the continuity of Jewish life after the *Sho'ah*.

So, I decided I wanted to be a rabbi for two main reasons: in order to do what I could to thwart any posthumous victories for Hitler; and in order to do what I could to make Jewish life more egalitarian and inclusive. Perhaps, because of my own personal experience, the emphasis in my rabbinate has always been on enabling individuals to make Jewish choices, engage with the Jewish heritage and realise their own ways of being Jewish.

Being a lesbian is fundamental to my rabbinate – and to how and what I write. My experience as a lesbian living in a hetero-normative society has shaped everything: how people have treated me and responded to me – both on an institutional and an individual level; how I have made sense of my role and purpose and tasks as a rabbi; how I have related to and grappled with my Jewish inheritance – and how I read and teach and write about that inheritance; how I

---

7 *Shifra* was first published in December 1984. The *Shifra* collective: Jane Black, Bev Gold, Linda Bellos, Marilyn Fetcher, Riva Krut, Libby Lawson, Scarlet Pollock, Leah Ruth, Elizabeth Sarah and Sheila Saunders.
8 See *The Jewish Return into History. Reflections in the Age of the Auschwitz and A New Jerusalem* by Emil L. Fackenheim (Schocken Books, New York, Chapter 2, The 614th Commandment, pp. 19-24)

relate with others – my congregants, my colleagues, those who come to see me to talk about their journeys; all the different people I meet, both inside and outside the Jewish community, as I go about my work.

And the experience of being a lesbian, who is a rabbi, has not just been about my experience of living and working in a, largely, hetero-sexual environment. How my family and friends responded when I first told them has also been a factor. My immediate family – my mother, my father, my sister and my brother – were shocked when I broke the news that I was applying to the Leo Baeck College.[9] They had got around to accepting that I was a radical feminist lesbian, but selling out and joining the Jewish establishment was a different matter!

Progressives in the widest sense of that term, my parents had never participated in Jewish communal life, apart from being members of a Reform synagogue for as long as it took for my brother to prepare to become *Bar Mitzvah*, because they saw the organised Jewish community as too narrow, monolithic and conformist, so I had quite a lot of explaining to do. I will never forget our first *Erev Shabbat* meal together after I learned that I had been accepted onto the rabbinic programme (although my parents never attended *shul*, *Erev Shabbat* candle-lighting and a special meal had always been part of our family life). Would I eat roast chicken (Sainsbury's best)? And what about having whipped cream with desert? As the daughter of a Viennese father, I was (and remain) addicted to cream. I ate the chicken but didn't have the cream – and reassured everyone present that I didn't mind *them* enjoying it. I also patiently explained how I balanced a progressive approach to *kashrut* with the fifth Command-ment about honouring one's parents.[10]

When I decided to train for the rabbinate, my parents assumed that I had 'got religion'. I hadn't. A socialist, a radical lesbian femi-nist, my journey into Judaism, was a journey of discovery and reclamation, in which everything I encountered – the ancient narra-tives of the *Torah*, rabbinic literature, liturgy, theology, the ethical

---

9 Founded in 1956, following the death of Rabbi Dr Leo Baeck (2nd November 1956), the leading Rabbi of German Jewry, who survived incarceration and came to London after the end of the Second World War, Leo Baeck College was for fifty years the only progressive rabbinic seminary in Europe.

10 Exodus 20:12; Deuteronomy 5:16.

codes and ritual practices – created opportunities for learning, growing and making meaning. I did not find God in a dramatic moment of revelation.

In fact, to this day, I have never found God in the sense in which so many people speak of a transcendent Being. Rather, my experience of exploring and engaging with my Jewish inheritance, enlivened and brought together all the different parts of myself, emotionally, spiritually and intellectually, in a way that enabled me to open myself to the multiple layers of existence, both material and mysterious, that I had hitherto ignored or misunderstood. I didn't find answers when I decided to become an observant Jew. I wasn't looking for answers. I was on a quest for a way of living that would entangle me with challenging questions, and challenge me to forge connections within myself, with Jewish existence, past and present, and with the ineffable that I could not name or contain.

I didn't lose my family – either, when I came out as a lesbian, or, when I came out as an observant Jew. In fact, although my domineering father struggled with his independent lesbian daughter, when I got divorced in 1980, and chose my middle name, Sarah, as my last name, he was the first one to write me a letter addressed to Elizabeth Sarah.

But I did lose some friends: some lesbian 'sisters', who would cross the street, rather than talk with me, after they heard that I had decided to train for the rabbinate. The context is very important. When I made the decision to become a rabbi and get involved in the Jewish community, I was a lesbian separatist – which means I had virtually nothing to do with men, apart from my father and my brother. The issue at stake revolved round how the Women's Liberation Movement that I was a part of grappled with those 'sisters', who also had other allegiances. The Women's Liberation Movement did, eventually give way to the new mood of what has been called 'identity politics', which emerged fully in the 1990s. I'm very sorry about that. I still see myself as a radical feminist, and I regret that a vibrant and vital feminist movement splintered into a variety of fragments: Jewish feminists, Jewish lesbian feminists,[11] black feminists,

---

11 I attended the first Jewish feminist conference, which took place in north London in January 1982, and then two further Jewish feminist conferences in Leeds and Oxford during the next couple of years. In 1982 two Jewish lesbian groups were formed in London – and I became a member of one of

black lesbian feminists, feminists living with disabilities, and so on. In my view, this wasn't inevitable.

There is no doubt, however, that in addition to all the other pressures – the impact of Thatcherite individualism, to name just one – the Women's Liberation Movement did not manage to become creatively pluralist. But although it did fracture and splinter, as it happens, the various feminisms that emerged, not only became strong and vibrant in their own right, they have persisted to this day – not least, Jewish feminism, which has become a major force in the Jewish world, as is apparent throughout this book.

What is more, in addition to all the different feminisms, which are a feature of contemporary multicultural society, an internationalist perspective has emerged, as part of the developing global consciousness, so that, in fact, in its broadest sense, despite the re-emergence of reactionary, patriarchal, forms of religion, a burgeoning Women's Liberation Movement across the world is now challenging patriarchy in all those places that the original 1960s to 1980s western-situated Women's Liberation Movement failed to reach.

So what difference did being a lesbian make to my experience of becoming a rabbi and then working as a rabbi?

When I went through the interview process at the Leo Baeck College in February 1984, like the other lesbian applicant,[12] I had two interviews to assess my psychological aptitude – not just one. From the moment I entered the Leo Baeck College, the usual probation period of one year was extended to five, for both of us; and we were informed, that at any time, we might be asked to leave – although no one could say in advance, what particular behaviours would warrant expulsion. If it hadn't been for the support of Rabbi Barbara Borts,[13] who had sponsored my application to the college,

---

them. In 1984 I was part of a group of Jewish feminists, who created a new Jewish feminist magazine, *Shifra*, which was launched in December 1984. The first issue included my article, 'Knowing No Bounds, or, What's a Nice Jewish Lesbian Doing Holding the *Sefer Torah?*' which explored the emergence of my Jewish consciousness, and why I had become religiously engaged and decided to study for the rabbinate. See the Introduction to Part Two.

12 Sheila Shulman, who, after ordination, became the first Rabbi of the congregation she founded, *Beit Klal Yisrael*.

13 I met Rabbi Barbara Borts in the autumn of 1983, when she was Rabbi of Hampstead Reform Synagogue. When she became Rabbi of Radlett and

and Rabbi Lionel Blue, who became my tutor, I don't think I would have survived. Because of concerns that our presence as lesbian rabbinic students might upset congregations and their members, instead of spending our third year in Israel, we undertook apprenticeships with the senior rabbis of two Reform synagogues,[14] before being launched on congregations, solo, in our fourth and fifth years. As it happens, our apprenticeships went well – but the degree of anxiousness about the two lesbian rabbinic students was reflected in how difficult it was to find congregations and rabbis prepared to have us.

More than anything else, perhaps, the fact that we were treated together, as 'the lesbian students', despite being very different individuals, with different experiences, qualities, aptitudes and attitudes, constituted another constraint for both of us. Even after ordination in July 1989, when it was clear that both of us were going to work in congregations within the Reform Movement, the Reform Assembly of Rabbis decided to hold an unprecedented one-day meeting to discuss whether or not to accept us as members of the assembly, even though, usually, the only qualification for membership of the Assembly of Rabbis, is being appointed rabbi of one of the constituent Reform synagogues. Fortunately, the assembly decided in our favour. Fortunately, also, working in very different congregational environments meant that, from that point onwards, our experiences as 'lesbian rabbis' became more individual.

My first job was as the first full-time rabbi of a small Reform congregation. I got off to a good start because I had done my fifth year student placement there, and so the congregation already knew me. But it was not by chance that I had worked there as a fifth year student. The other lesbian rabbinic student had gone there in her fourth year and the sky hadn't fallen in. When it came to my placement, a meeting was arranged in advance with some of the key players in the congregation. Convened, by the executive director of

---

Bushey Reform Synagogue, I followed her there, becoming a teacher in the *cheder*, and subsequently, a junior warden.

14 I was apprenticed to Rabbi Henry Goldstein of South West Essex Reform Synagogue (which has since been renamed, the South West Essex and Settlement Reform Synagogue, following an amalgamation of SWERS with the Settlement Synagogue), and Sheila Shulman was apprenticed to Rabbi Jeffrey Newman of Finchley Reform Synagogue.

the RSGB at the time, the meeting was an opportunity to discuss the best way to proceed with the appointment of an 'out' lesbian rabbi.

So, I had the best possible context to begin my rabbinate – and, overall, the five years I served the congregation, following my ordination, went very well. But during that time, two things happened, both motivated by homophobia, which had a deep impact on my developing rabbinate, indeed, they have shaped my rabbinate ever since.

The first began quite insidiously. A couple had adopted two girls from another country. I oversaw their Jewish adoption, via the Reform *Beit Din*.[15] Everything seemed fine, but then the couple let it be known that they did not want me to tutor their children, because they were fearful that I might molest them. Their issue with me was conveyed to me by one of the congregation's lay leaders, who was keen to reassure me that, of course, no one else felt like that. I felt reassured – but also very troubled – that anybody could believe that just because I was a lesbian, I might molest their children.

This made me feel terrible. Intellectually, I knew it was nonsense. The 'facts' make it clear that sexual abuse of children is overwhelmingly committed by heterosexual men. Nevertheless, from that moment onwards – long before the development of 'child protection' policies became the order of the day – I made sure that I avoided any physical contact with children. All those gestures that adults used to do very readily, like putting an arm round the shoulders of a child in distress, I tried not to do. In fact, I didn't just refrain from these innocent acts, the effect of not acting naturally towards children made me stiffen up and become a little formal. As a consequence, the children and young people I have encountered have always known that I took them seriously, but not that I can be easygoing and fun.

The second experience of homophobia during my first appointment as a rabbi was much more blatant, and became such a problem, that the chair of the Reform Movement[16] was called in to

---

15 *Beit Din* – literally, 'House of Judgement' – the name given to the Rabbinic Court, which presides over conversions, adoptions and issues related to Jewish status.

16 At that time called, the Reform Synagogues of Great Britain. Since, renamed: the Movement for Reform Judaism.

arbitrate. It began in a very small way. One *Erev Shabbat*, since we were such a small group, I suggested that we might all sit in a circle – including me. When it came to reciting the *Sh'ma*, I suggested that we remain seated, explaining that the words of the *Sh'ma* teach us that they may be said when we 'lie down' and when we 'rise up', and that is why the *Sh'ma* is recited in the evening and morning services, but not in the afternoon service. No one raised an objection. A week or so afterwards, the chair of the congregation, who was very supportive of me, showed me a letter he had received from the previous chair, who had been in the congregation on that *Erev Shabbat*. In this letter he claimed that I was agitating for change and promoting a feminist and lesbian agenda.

Unfortunately, he wasn't a lone voice. But there were others on the council, not least the chair, who totally disagreed with this view. For a while, it remained an internal issue amongst the core of the congregation – and it was during this time, that the council called on the arbitration services of the Reform Movement. But the issue simmered on. In the end, it was only resolved at the AGM when my chief detractor called on people to stand up if they felt I should no longer be the rabbi. Only a half dozen people did so – the great majority of the gathering of well over 150 people, remain seated.

That was the end of the matter – but it affected me very deeply. Despite the fact that so many people had shown me positive support, this experience of active persecution entered my soul, combining with the earlier experience to make me feel afraid and insecure. In October 1994, not long after the matter was resolved, I left the congregation to become Director of Programmes for the Reform Movement. Although working in an office was completely new to me, it felt much safer not to be in a congregational setting.

Ironically, I became so comfortable in my new environment, and felt so safe that within two years of being there, I made an error of judgement, which changed my rabbinate forever. The Assembly of Rabbis had recently established a working party to work out Reform policy towards lesbian and gay Jews and same-sex commitment ceremonies. Shortly afterwards, in February 1996, in my capacity as RSGB director of programmes, I participated in an edition of Joan Bakewell's BBC1 programme, 'Heart of the Matter', exploring religious attitudes to lesbian and gay people. By the autumn, invited to be guest preacher at the Reform congregation where I had begun my journey to the rabbinate,[17] I thought the time was right to bring the issue into my *Kol Nidrey* sermon. I was wrong. The sermon was about how the Jewish concept of *b'rit*, 'covenant', might be related to people's lives.[18] At the point in the sermon when I mentioned that I was going to officiate at a 'Covenant of Love' ceremony for two women, one man stood up and started shouting, 'It's an abomination', and four people walked out. I asked the other 700 or so people gathered there if they would like me to continue; the consensus was that I should. But there were clearly very mixed feelings. After the service, a few people approached me. A group of young people, whom I had taught at the synagogue a few years earlier, came up to me together to express their support and three other people expressed their anger.

I made a mistake – but soon that mistake was played out in an even larger public arena. The *Jewish Chronicle* got hold of the story, and it was all over the front page the following Friday.[19] I had to give public apologies to the RSGB board, the RSGB council, and the assembly of rabbis. Perhaps, that's the sort of thing that happens when you occupy a senior post, and speak out of turn. But unfortunately, the whole incident unleashed the most appalling homophobia. I received hate letters from members of Reform congregations. The Northern Region Reform Conference was coming up and the programme included me leading part of the *shabbat* morning service. But there were voices in the northern congregations that objected and threatened to walk out. With assurances from the RSGB northern office, that there was plenty of support for me too, my appearance was not cancelled. I cannot put into words what went through me that morning when I stood in front of that congregation, waiting for something to happen. In the end, the service passed without incident, but I felt completely shattered, and afterwards, I returned to my room and burst into tears. That was a particularly low point, but as the months passed, the problems around my continuing employment within the Reform Movement did not go away. In March 2007, I resigned. Everyone was very relieved.

---

17 Radlett and Bushey Reform Synagogue.
18 See Appendix
19 27th September 1996. The 'story' continued to be reported in the JC the following week (04.10.96).

I knew when I decided that I wanted to be a rabbi I would face difficulties as a lesbian. I was determined to make a place for myself, and overcome any obstacles that I encountered. I also wanted to do what I could to make Jewish life more inclusive, so that other lesbian and gay Jews could find a home within the Jewish community. Since the shattering events of 1996, my experiences as a lesbian rabbi have been, on the whole, quite positive, despite an initial hiccup. The morning that the *Jewish Chronicle* reported my resignation as the lead story on the front page,[20] the then executive director of the Liberal Movement phoned me to invite me to join the Liberal Rabbinic Conference.[21] I accepted, gratefully. But then, when a vacancy came up at Brighton and Hove Progressive Synagogue, just as I was leaving my job in July 1997, and I applied for the post, the synagogue council decided not to interview me. It was very disappointing. So, without a congregation to go to, I began to work freelance and also taught at the Leo Baeck College. And then, in June 1998, Leicester Progressive Jewish Congregation, the community I had visited once a month when I was a fourth year rabbinic student, invited me to become their first rabbi – albeit, on a very part-time, once a month basis. It made all the difference to my morale.

From that moment on, things began to improve. In 2000 the Liberal Rabbinic Conference set up a Working Party on lesbian and gay Jews and same-sex commitment ceremonies, on which I served. After a positive interview process in July 2000, in December 2000, I started working as rabbi of Brighton & Hove Progressive Synagogue. By December 2005, when civil partnership became law, a positive inclusive policy towards lesbian and gay Jews had not only already been accepted by the Council of Liberal Judaism, but the working party's anthology of ceremonies and same-sex relationships, was published to coincide with the act.[22]

In March 2006 my partner, Jess Wood, and I had a *chuppah* in my synagogue, following our civil partnership ceremony, which was attended by over 100 congregants, as well as our family and friends

---

20 28th March 1997 – headline: 'Gay weddings' Rabbi quits top Reform Job.'
21 Rabbi Dr Charles Middleburgh – who was Executive Director of the Union of Liberal and Progressive Synagogues (ULPS) at that time; ULPS has since been renamed, Liberal Judaism.
22 *B'rit Ahavah – Covenant of Love. Service of Commitment for Same-Sex Couples.* edited by Rabbi Mark Solomon, Liberal Judaism, London, 2005.

– and at the party afterwards, we were presented with gifts from the congregation, including a beautiful silver *kiddush* cup and a very generous cheque. We also received dozens of cards – most of which had 'wedding' and 'marriage' messages – both from members of the congregation, and from members of the wider Jewish community in Brighton and Hove. One of the most significant aspects of this experience was the way in which the synagogue council carefully planned for it. Not only did they invite members to donate money for a gift, but the president wrote a wonderful article in the monthly magazine in which he generously extolled our virtues![23]

More recently, in December 2010, my congregation celebrated my 10th anniversary with them by organising a special *kiddush*. Receiving, again, another very generous cheque, I was overwhelmed by everyone's warmth, and was particularly moved by the tributes paid to me by ten different people, each of whom had joined the congregation during one of the previous ten years.

So, finally, I feel that being a lesbian rabbi in the Jewish community is becoming a blessing for me and for others. Slowly, lesbian and gay Jews, and lesbian and gay people looking for a home within Judaism, are finding their way to my congregation. And the impact of a policy of inclusion is also being felt in those other Liberal congregations that are willing to offer a warm welcome to lesbians and gay men. Just as important, since I was a student there, the Leo Baeck College has developed a non-discriminatory policy towards lesbian and gay applicants, and consequently, there are now several lesbian and gay rabbis working within the Jewish community. On a personal level, one of the most heart-warming experiences I have on an almost daily basis is when I'm talking with a congregant – mostly over the age of 75 – either on the phone or in person, and they invariably ask after my partner and send their best wishes to her.

Of course, in addition to the specific experiences associated with being a lesbian rabbi, I also get to suffer some of the trials that heterosexual women rabbis endure. Sometimes, on those few occasions when, engaged in my wider rabbinic role, people meet me for

---

23 The president of my synagogue, Ivor Miskin, *zichrono livrachah*, may his memory be for blessing, sadly died on the last day of my writing month. He wrote an article about my partner and me, and our forthcoming civil partnership and *chuppah*, in the February/March issue of the synagogue magazine.

the first time, who don't know that I'm a lesbian, I am treated to the ordinary range of offensive behaviours to which women rabbis are subjected. For example, the uninvited touching and kissing, which I first experienced as a student rabbi; being sidelined in cross-communal gatherings; people – even (older) women – telling me, in voices expressing great surprise, how well I have done! And on occasion, when I have introduced myself as a 'rabbi', I have been corrected, and called a 'rebbitzin'! It's humiliating and unacceptable, of course. But sometimes, I welcome sharing experience, even of such a negative kind, that is in common with my other female colleagues. It has been quite a burden being a lesbian rabbi pioneer!

A Guide to Trouble-Making Judaism

This selection of essays, sermons and talks reflect the key areas of Jewish life with which I have concerned myself since receiving *s'michah* (ordination) more than two decades ago: in particular my desire to make Jewish life more egalitarian and inclusive, to seek new ways of engaging with congregations and individuals to make vibrant communities, and to show how it is possible to be an advocate of both Israel and Palestine.

Progressive Judaism has many concerns[1] only some of which are described here, but wherever one looks Judaism appears to be trouble-making, troubling and troubled. And so the writings I have chosen are intended to provoke Jewish and non-Jewish readers alike to think about the role of trouble-making in Jewish life and to understand the ways Jews can make a unique contribution to contemporary issues. I believe that by taking new journeys into our sacred texts and re-examining our history and the people who shaped it, we can better engage with our inheritance and participate in the vital issues of Jewish life today.

It will not be a surprise to learn that since I made the decision in 1983 to become a rabbi and get involved in the mainstream Jewish community I have been seen as a trouble-maker within Jewish life – and that I have also seen myself in this way – and that, above all I have been troubling with and troubled by, both Jewish life and my Jewish inheritance.

The Legacy of the Prophets

So, what is 'Trouble-Making Judaism'? In recent years, an irreverent, group of Jewishly-committed young Jews has made its presence felt in the Jewish community by making as much trouble as possible. Calling themselves by the provocative name of 'Jewdas', they have

---

1 See the following leaflets published by Liberal Judaism for a presentation of a liberal Jewish perspective on a number of contemporary issues not included in this book. For example: The Environment; Animal Welfare; Ethical Eating; Genetic Research. Liberal Judaism leaflets are available from The Montagu Centre, 21 Maple Street, London W1T 4BE. See also: www.liberaljudaism.org.

challenged what they have seen as Jewish communal conservatism and narrow-minded parochialism by being as shocking and disruptive of the communal status quo as possible. Perhaps their most audacious activity has been the mass distribution of a hoax e-mail, which appeared to come from the Board of Deputies of British Jews, informing recipients that a pro-Israel rally arranged for the following week had been cancelled.[2] But as this action indicated, while determined to shock the mainstream Jewish community, their intent is very serious – and not just on a political level. Jewdas has organised wonderfully creative Jewish study opportunities and edgy cultural events. One of my first contacts with the group entailed sitting round a fire on Brighton's shingle beach getting drenched on a wet and windy summer evening discussing Leviticus and my approach to Jewish sexual ethics.[3] Jewdas has also arranged extended study marathons. I was involved in one in London with a host of speakers. And they haven't just been interested in engaging Jews. At the festival of *Sukkot* (Tabernacles) in 2010, Jewdas organised a week-long activity around the *sukkah*, temporary shelter, they set up by the East London mosque.

Creative, irreverent, engaged and crossing boundaries, Jewdas is one answer to the question, what is trouble-making Judaism? A narrative related in the First Book of Kings provides another answer, which reminds us that, actually, at its heart, Judaism is about – is supposed to be about – trouble-making. We learn here that 'Ahab, the son of Omri, became king of Israel in the thirty-eighth year of Asa, King of Judah' – that is, in the middle of the 9th century BCE. Ahab married Jezebel, the daughter of the King of Tyre, an idol worshipper, and while the two of them consorted to worship Baal, Jezebel went about killing off the prophets of the Eternal One[4]. But when 'the word of the Eternal' comes to Elijah[5], Ahab soon finds

---

2   Jewdas later apologised in the pages of the *Jewish Chronicle* (22.01.09), saying that they had not intended "to offend, be malicious or even prevent people from attending the rally... Our reasons, which we stand by, were to make a political point, both in criticism of the rally and of the current conflict." For more on Jewdas, see www.jewdas.org

3   See Chapter 9: "Towards an Inclusive Sexual Ethic" where I examine the subject.

4   I Kings 16:31-32.

5   ibid.18:13

that he has met his match – and what the text tells us, when Ahab confronts Elijah, is very instructive:

> When Ahab caught sight of Elijah, Ahab said to him, 'Is that you, you troubler of Israel?' He retorted, 'It is not I who brought trouble on Israel, but you and your father's house, by forsaking the commandments of the Eternal, and going after the ba'alim. Now summon all Israel to join me at Mount Carmel, together with the 450 prophets of Baal and the 400 prophets of Asheirah, who eat at Jezebel's table.'[6]

Yes, Elijah certainly was 'a troubler of Israel' – *ocheir Yisrael* – the noun/verb 'troubler', *ocheir*, based on the root, *Ayin Kaf Reish* meaning to 'trouble', as in, 'stir up', or 'disturb'. That was the role of the prophets in their societies. The prophets were the hecklers; the sacred wordsmiths who barraged the kings and the priests, with criticism, tormenting them with threats of punishment for their sins and misdeeds. Their only responsibility was to speak out. As Brian Klug puts it: 'as a breed, the Hebrew prophets were intent on making trouble; trouble was their trade. They gave offence to ruler and to people alike, discomforting them to the core'.[7] And that is what the prophetic message is always meant to do: trouble, disturb, stir up the status quo.

In Jewish liturgical practice established by the rabbis almost 2000 years ago, on *Shabbat* and festivals, congregations throughout the Jewish world, read both a portion from the *Sefer Torah*, and a section from the second part of the *TaNaKh*,[8] the Hebrew Bible, known as *N'v'im*, Prophets, which begins with the Book of Joshua, and includes all the prophetic books. This second reading is called the *haftarah*, which means, 'conclusion'.[9] So, week in and week out, and

---

6 I K 18:17-19
7 See Brian Klug, *Offence: The Jewish Case*, p. 61 (Seagull Books, 2009).
8 *TaNaKh* = *Torah* ('Teaching' – the Five Books of Moses'), *N'vi'im* (Prophets) and *K'tuvim* (Writings) – the three sections of the Hebrew Bible
9 All Hebrew verbs, nouns and adjectives, are based on three letter 'roots'. The root for *haftarah* is *Pei Teit Reish*, meaning, 'to conclude'. The last three verses of the *Torah* portion are known as the *maftir* from the same root, meaning 'concluding' – that is, the concluding verses. In traditional liturgical practice, after the whole portion has been read, the scroll is covered and a version of the *Kaddish* is recited – the *Chatzi* ('half') *Kaddish* – and then the three

as the cycle of the year turns, congregants are made familiar, not only with the books of Genesis, Exodus, Leviticus, Numbers, and Deuteronomy, but also, with the rousing words of the prophets.

The prophets – chief among them, Isaiah, Jeremiah, Amos, and Micah – spent a good deal of their time berating, both the secular rulers of their day and the people; admonishing them for their failure to keep the commandments, most particularly, the ethical injunctions. The rabbis, engaged with the task of reconstructing Jewish life after the destruction of the Temple by the Romans in 70 CE, declared that the age of prophecy was dead.[10] Nevertheless, by developing the practice of reading sections from the prophetic books each *Shabbat* and festival, they ensured that those who participated in worship services were made directly aware of key prophetic messages. Irrespective of the precise reasons and context in which the *haftarah* was introduced, the impact remains.[11] By taking the trou-

---

concluding verses, the *maftir*, are read again. The person called up to preside over the reading of the *maftir*, will also recite the *haftarah*, thus creating a link between the concluding words of *Torah* and the conclusion of the scriptural reading, taken from the *N'vi'im*.

10 In the Babylonian *Talmud*, tractate *Bava Batra* 12a, we read: 'Rabbi Abdimi of Haifa said: Since the day when the Temple was destroyed, the prophetic gift was taken away from the prophets and given to the Sages. Is a Sage not also a prophet? What Rabbi Abdimi meant to say was this: Although prophecy has been taken from the Prophets, prophecy has not been taken from the Sages. Amemar said 'A Sage is even superior to a Prophet, as it says "And a Prophet has the heart of Wisdom" (Psalms 90:21). Who is usually compared with whom? Is not the smaller compared with the greater?"'

11 The origin of the inclusion of passages from the prophetic books in these services is shrouded in mystery. The prevailing theory is that the practice was introduced during the period of the persecutions instigated by the Selucid Emperor, Antiochus IV Epiphanes in 167 BCE, when the Temple altar was desecrated and the Jewish people were prohibited from reading the *Torah*, observing the Sabbath and other key practices, like, circumcision. Ismar Elbogen, in his authoritative work, *Jewish Liturgy. A Comprehensive History*, first published in English in 1993 by the Jewish Publications Society (Philadelphia – Jerusalem), writes (p.143): 'In the absence of any information from the ancient period, we must resort to conjectures. The reading from the Prophets is surely later than the reading of the *Torah*, but it must necessarily be earlier than the closing of the canon of the Prophets. The Prophets are not read in order, as is the *Torah*, but by freely chosen selections.... The books used for the reading from the Prophets are not subject to the stringent regulations that apply to *Torah* scrolls. The *Torah* that is used for reading must be complete and must contain all five books, while for the reading of the

ble to read the Bible for her/himself, the ordinary 'Jew in the pew' gets to hear the words of the prophets.

The significance of this experience is nowhere more evident than on *Yom Kippur*. Even as a rabbi, who is more than a little familiar, with the liturgical structure of Jewish worship, I always experience a jolt when I read the prophetic passage that is set aside for the morning of *Yom Kippur*, from Isaiah chapter 57 to 58.

Just imagine it: congregations of Jews, the world over, are gathered in their synagogues on *Shabbat Shabbaton*, the 'Sabbath of Sabbaths', the most sacred day of the Jewish calendar, the day set aside for the confession of our transgressions and misdeeds, and a gruelling journey towards atonement. By the time we get to the *haftarah* in the morning service, we have probably already fasted for at least 16 hours. Our stomachs are rumbling. However, that's not really a problem, because we feel we are engaged in something really important, and it is satisfying to know that we are observing all the important rites, established by our ancestors. But then, as if the prophet is present among us, and knows exactly how we are feeling at this point, he takes the opportunity to taunt us: 'Is this the fast I have chosen, a day for humanity's self-denial? To bow one's head like a bulrush, to grovel in sackcloth and ashes? Is this what you call a fast, a day the Eternal One would accept?' (58:5) The prophet is not saying that we should *stop* fasting; he is simply intent on reminding us *why* we are fasting: 'Is not this the fast I have chosen; to loosen the fetters of evil, to untie the straps of the yoke, to let the oppressed go free, and whatever the yoke, to break it? / Is it not sharing your food with the hungry and bringing the homeless into your home; when you see the naked, to clothe them, never hiding from your own flesh and blood?' (:6-7)

Prophets it is enough to have the book that is being read. All this permits the conclusion that when the *haftarah* was introduced, the Prophets were not yet considered to be a closed canonical work. In any case, it is certain that the *haftarah* was introduced in pre-Christian times, because the earliest Christian sources already know the prophetic reading as an absolutely fixed institution (Luke 4:17; Acts 13:15). Also, the *Mishnah*, whose contents regarding this are much older than the date of its redaction, speaks about the reading of the Prophets in language that compels the conclusion that the institution had long been in existence.'

The words of the unknown prophet[12] are a powerful reminder for all those who are inclined to forget that, as Brian Klug puts it, 'being Jewish' is about 'doing justice'.[13] The rabbis chose to highlight this message on the most sacred day of the Jewish year; a day set apart from all the other days of the Jewish year, when the observant Jew relinquishes every aspect of ordinary life and the daily routine: eating, washing, anointing, sex. So: a day devoid of any connection with any other day. And yet, the rabbis took this totally exceptional day, and taught us, through the words of the unknown prophet, that this day is, in fact, inextricably linked with all our days; that the whole point of observing *Yom Kippur* is for us to acknowledge our misdeeds and resolve to go out into the world and put things right.

If it were not for the rabbis, Jewish life would have come to an end when the Temple was destroyed by the Romans in 70 CE, and with it, the system of sacrificial worship, involving the presentation of offerings, the substance of this agricultural people's labour on the land. The work of the rabbis in reconstructing Jewish life generated the new era of Rabbinic Judaism. But they did much more than rebuild Jewish life out of the ashes and rubble of the Temple. Keen to establish a seemingly seamless continuity between Temple Judaism and Rabbinic Judaism, the rabbis, nevertheless, transformed Jewish life, creating new rituals and practices and investing ancient Jewish practices, including the festivals, with new meanings. If the catastrophe they faced was happening now, and a group of scholars came along and completely reinvented Jewish life, we would call them revolutionaries. So, why don't we regard the first rabbis in this way? Because, actually, their interventions were much more subtle and sophisticated than the kind of actions we associate with disruptors of the social order. Knowing that the future of the Jewish people lay in their hands, they presented their innovations as the 'oral law' that was also given to Moses on Sinai, alongside the 'written law'. In

---

12 This is the unknown prophet referred to as Deutero-Isaiah, the 'Second Isaiah', to whom the later chapters of the Book of Isaiah (chapter 40, onwards) are attributed. He lived and prophesied in the 6th century BCE, during the period of the Babylonian exile.

13 See Brian Klug's book, *Being Jewish and Doing Justice – Bringing Argument to Life* (Vallentine Mitchell, London, 2010)

this way, the rabbis established the authority for their reinvention of Jewish life.[14]

So, while the age of prophecy had ceased, the rabbis ensured that the prophets continued to speak to each succeeding generation of the Jewish people. It is significant to note in this respect, that the first paragraph of *Pirkey Avot*, the 'Sayings of the Sages', which is appended to the first rabbinic code of law, the *Mishnah*, edited around 200 CE, opens with this concise chronology, creating the link between the heritage that the rabbis were receiving, and their own work (*Pirkey Avot*, 1:1):[15]

> Moses received *Torah* from Sinai and handed it on to Joshua, Joshua to the elders, and the elders to the prophets. And the prophets handed it on to the members of the Great Assembly. The latter said three things: be deliberate in judgement; raise up many disciples; and make a fence around the *Torah*.

In view of the fact that a great portion of the *Torah* is devoted to the rules and regulations governing the priesthood, with Aaron, Moses' elder brother occupying the position of the first High Priest,[16] and given that the rabbis were involved in regenerating Jewish life after the destruction of the Temple, the absence of the *priests* from this chronology seems incredible. But here it is. According to the rabbis, the prophets handed the *Torah directly* to the members of the Great Assembly, the semi-mythic body that is regarded as the first institutionalised expression of rabbinic leadership.[17] And so, one might

---

14 Rabbinic Judaism is defined by the belief that when God revealed the *Torah* to Moses, during the forty days and nights he sojourned on Mount Sinai, Moses received two parts: the 'written' *Torah* and the 'oral' *Torah*. The oral *Torah* was later committed to writing: in the *Mishnah* and the parallel work, the *Tosefta*, both edited around the 2nd century CE; in the *G'mara*, the commentary on the *Mishnah* that together with the *Mishnah*, forms the *Talmud* – which is in two versions: the *Y'rushalmi*, the Jerusalem *Talmud*, and the *Bavli*, the Babylonian *Talmud*, and also in the various collections of *Midrashim* (Hebrew, meaning, 'Interpretations').

15 The *Mishnah* consists of six 'orders'. *Pirkey Avot* is appended to the fourth order of the *Mishnah*, *N'zikin*. See the Judaica Press seven volume edition, edited by Philip Blackman (Gateshead, 1983).

16 See, especially, the Book of Leviticus, which outlines the system of worship during the second Temple period

17 The Great Assembly, *K'nesset G'dolah*, also known as, *Anshey K'nesset Ha-*

say, that the rabbis were engaged in, both, ensuring the continuation of Jewish worship[18] in the context of establishing a new framework for the observance of the commandments, and with ensuring that the legacy of the prophets would be kept alive. They achieved this, practically speaking, as we have seen, through the practice of the *haftarah* reading. However, it could be said that, while the rite of the *haftarah* reading is, indeed, integral to *Shabbat* and festival observance throughout the Jewish world, it is not evident that the congregations who listen to the *haftarah* week in week out, actually pay attention to the proclamations of the prophets. There may be quite prosaic reasons for this. In most Orthodox and traditional congregations, the *haftarah*, like the *Torah* portion, is read only in Hebrew, which most congregants don't understand. But it's not just that most congregants can't make sense of the language. The very nature of the rite of the *Torah* and *haftarah* readings may serve as a bar to people taking notice of what the texts being read with such ceremony, actually say. While every effort is generally made to ensure that all aspects of the ritual associated with the *Torah* service are performed correctly,[19] the content of the read-

---

G'dolah, 'The Men of the Great Assembly'; according to tradition, an assembly of 120 scribes, sages and prophets, in the period from the end of the Biblical prophets to the time of the development of Rabbinic Judaism, marking a transition from an era of Prophets to an era of Rabbis. In *Avot d'Rabbi Natan*, 1:1, the parallel collection to *Pirkey Avot*, the first paragraph states: 'Haggai, Zechariah, and Malachi received from the Prophets; and the men of the Great Synagogue received from Haggai, Zechariah, and Malachi.' Haggai, Zechariah and Malachi were the last of the prophets, and so understood as involved in directly passing on the tradition to the rabbis. The Great Assembly is mentioned elsewhere as being responsible for specific innovations. For example, the Babylonian *Talmud*, *B'rachot* 33a states, in the name of R. Yochanan:'The men of the Great Synagogue instituted for Israel the blessings and the prayers, as well as the blessings for *Kiddush* and *Havdalah*'; and in tractate *M'gillah* 17b, we find: 'R. Yochanan said that, according to some, a *baraita* taught that one hundred and twenty elders, including some prophets, instituted the *Sh'moneh 'Esreh*, the 'Eighteen Blessings.'

18 With the Temple destroyed, and with it *Avodah*, the 'service' of God through sacrifice, the rabbis instituted *Avodat ha-lev*, 'service of the heart'. We read in the Babylonian *Talmud*, *Ta'anit* 2a: '" … love the Eternal your God, and serve him with all your heart and with all your soul." (Deuteronomy 11:13). What is this service of the heart? You must say: it is prayer!'

19 The rite of the *Torah* reading includes the following practices: *Aliyah* (Plural: *Aliyot*), from Hebrew root, *Ayin Lamed Hei*, to 'go up', which means, in the

ings may be overlooked. It's a triumph of form over substance – which is, precisely, the theme of the *Yom Kippur* morning *haftarah*.

Perhaps another reason why, despite having access to the words of the prophets, via the *haftarah* readings, congregants seem to fail to be troubled or disturbed or stirred up, is to do with the establishment of the liturgical convention of the *haftarah*. This involved, not only identifying particular passages for reading on *Shabbat* and the festivals, which, for the most part, bear some relation to a theme in the *Torah* portion,[20] but also, selecting those passages that end on an upbeat note, and, in some cases, manipulating the passage, by appending a few verses from elsewhere at the end, to fulfil this purpose. In this way, however challenging the message, the *haftarah* invariably concludes with words of comfort and consolation, and so may be seen as a homiletical device. The concluding scriptural passage completes the reading of the sacred Scriptures within the service, by soothing any disturbance they may cause.

So, the troubling messages of the prophets are contained and confined – but why? It is important to remember that when the rabbis were creating a new system of worship for post-Temple Jewish existence, they were rebuilding Jewish life following an enormous catastrophe, characterised by trouble and disturbance. In this context, reassuring the people, and providing an orderly, secure framework for their lives was paramount.

To a significant extent, despite upheavals, persecutions and exiles, the framework for Jewish life created by Rabbinic Judaism held sway throughout the Jewish world, right up until the collapse of the *ancien regime* ushered in by the French Revolution of 1789. But then that

---

context of the synagogue service, to go up to the *bimah* – platform, where the *Torah* scroll is read – and recite the blessings connected with the *Torah* reading; *G'lillah*, from the root, *Gimmel Lamed Lamed*, to 'roll', which refers to the undressing and dressing of the *Torah* scroll; and *Hagbba'hah*, from the root, *Gimmel Beit Hei*, to 'lift', which refers to the raising of the scroll – before the reading in Sephardi, that is, Spanish/Portuguese tradition, and after the reading, in Ashkenazi, that is, German/Northern & Eastern European tradition.

20 While the majority of the *Shabbat haftarot* (plural for *haftarah*), connect with the theme of the weekly *Torah* reading, in the three weeks leading up to the fast of *Tishah B'Av*, which commemorates the destruction of the Temple by the Babylonians in 586 BCE, there are three '*haftarot* of affliction', followed by seven '*haftarot* of consolation', during the seven weeks from *Tishah B'Av* to *Rosh Ha-Shanah*, the Jewish New Year.

revolution led to another one. With the birth of Progressive Judaism, just over 200 years ago, a positive response to Enlightenment and the emancipation of the Jews of Europe from a segregated ghetto existence, was combined with a determination to re-emphasise the ethical teachings found in the *Torah* and expressed by the prophets.[21] This response involved sitting up and taking notice of what the *haftarah* reading – read now in the vernacular – had to say. It also meant taking the trouble to re-engage with the words of the prophets outside of a liturgical context, to make connections with the issues of the day.

In more recent years, the Jewish world has experienced another cataclysm, which has also generated a massive transformation. However, unlike the liberating explosion of Modernity, which generated new possibilities for Judaism and for Jewish life, like the Jewish community following the destruction of the Temple, Jews today are still living, at least partially, in the shadow of our own catastrophe – the *Sho'ah*.[22]

Nonetheless, many would argue that the time has come for 'troublers' and a disturbance of the collective peace. And indeed, since the 1970s new 'troublers of Israel' have been making their presence known: Jewish women challenging a rabbinic tradition that confines them to the domestic arena, marginalises and silences them; lesbian and gay individuals, couples and families searching for a home within Jewish life, and the right to participate fully in the synagogue, and celebrate their lives and their relationships on equal terms; Jews of conscience, both in the diaspora and in Israel, like the prophets of old, calling upon the leadership of the Jewish state to put the fine words of the declaration of Independence into practice, by ensuring

---

21 See *Response to Modernity. A History of the Reform Movement in Judaism* by Michael A. Meyer (Oxford University Press, 1988), for the most comprehensive account of the development of Progressive Judaism in the 19th century.

22 *Sho'ah* – meaning, 'devastation' or 'catastrophe' - a noun, with biblical origins, from the root *Shin Aleph Hei*, to 'crash into ruins'. *Sho'ah* is the term preferred by Jews. The word 'Holocaust', which has much greater currency, is a translation of the biblical Hebrew word, *olah*, 'burnt offering'. In the Bible, a burnt offering was a form of sacrifice. The notion that the murder of the Jews might be considered a sacrificial offering to God is highly problematic, and does not represent a Jewish understanding.

that all Israeli citizens enjoy equal rights,[23] and urging the government to 'pursue', as a matter of urgency, the Jewish values of justice and peace in relation to the on-going conflict with the Palestinians.[24]

The significance of the individual

So far, I have focused on the ethical domain of Jewish life, and the importance of disturbing the status quo in order to ensure that justice is served. But there is also, another less obvious aspect to being a 'troubler'.

One of the characteristics of the *halachah*, the Jewish legal system that regulates Jewish practice, is that it determines and constrains, both, the life of the community and the life of individuals. Progressive Judaism inspired by Enlightenment values, and the empowerment of the individual, as a citizen of her or his country, to make choices and decisions in his or her own right, has, since its inception, enabled individuals to make informed choices concerning how to live their Jewish lives.

Nevertheless, the empowered individual is not, simply, a product of the Enlightenment. While the *halachah* controls and constrains individual action, *aggadah*, the narrative tradition, which begins with the stories of the Jewish ancestors related in the *Torah* – and includes the rabbis' imaginative interpretations,[25] presents us with individu-

---

23 Israel's Declaration of Independence of May 14th 1948, states in paragraph 13: 'The State Of Israel will be open for Jewish immigration and for the Ingathering of the Exiles; it will foster the development of the country for the benefit of all its inhabitants; it will be based on freedom, justice and peace as envisaged by the prophets of Israel; it will ensure complete equality of social and political rights to all its inhabitants irrespective of religion, race or sex; it will guarantee freedom of religion, conscience, language, education and culture; it will safeguard the Holy Places of all religions; and it will be faithful to the principles of the Charter of the United Nations.'

24 Deuteronomy 16:20, states: 'Justice, Justice you shall pursue.' Psalm 34:15, proclaims: 'Turn away from evil and do good; and seek peace and pursue it.' See chapters 5, 6, 7, 8, 9 and 15

25 The main collection of rabbinic *aggadah* is *Midrash Rabbah*, which encompasses *aggadic* commentary on the five books of the *Torah* - Genesis, Exodus, Leviticus, Numbers, and Deuteronomy – and the five books included in the third part of the Bible/*TaNaKh*, known as the *Chameish M'gillot*, the Five Scrolls, which are read in connection with particular commemorative dates in the Jewish year: the Song of Songs at *Pesach*, Ruth at *Shavuot*, the Festival of 'Weeks', Lamentations at *Tishah B'Av*, Ecclesiastes at *Sukkot*, 'Tabernacles',

als, acting on their own volition.[26] So, when individuals ask questions, as we explore the texts, when we trouble Jewish teachings and traditions because we are troubled by them, we find powerful role models in the texts themselves. Some examples: the first woman, who questioned the prohibition against eating the fruit of the tree;[27] Abraham, who argued with God concerning the fate of Sodom and Gemorrah;[28] Rebecca, who, troubled by the contest going on within her womb, took the initiative to enquire of God;[29] Jacob, who, on the eve of his reunion with the Esau, wrestled with an unknown man or himself, and wrested a blessing and a new name from the encounter;[30] Moses, who demanded that the Eternal One demonstrate the Divine presence;[31] Miriam, who challenged her younger brother's special relationship with God.[32]

However, identifying connections between our lives and challenges and those of the characters we discover in the narratives of the *Torah*, and in the rest of the Hebrew Bible, is only one dimension

---

and Esther at *Purim*, the Feast of 'Lots'. The term *Rabbah* was first applied to the *midrash* on Genesis, which dates to 400CE. The *Rabbah* to Lamentations, Esther and Leviticus are also dated to the earliest period of 400 to 600 CE, while the *Rabbah* to the Song of Songs, Deuteronomy and Ruth are dated between 650 and 900 CE. Exodus *Rabbah* came later, between 900 and 1000 CE, and Numbers *Rabbah*, later still, during the Middle Ages. The ten volumes of *Midrash Rabbah* are available from Soncino Press. Louis Ginzberg's seven volume, *The Legends of the Jews* (Jewish Publication Society of America, 1909), which has been reprinted many times, is the most accessible and comprehensive collection of *aggadah*.

26 See Abraham Joshua Heschel, 'A Time for Renewal'. Address delivered at the 28th World Zionist Congress in Jerusalem on January 19, 1972 and published in *Midstream* 18/5 (1972), pp. 46–51 for a compelling description of the difference between *halachah* and *aggadah*: '*Halachah* teaches us how to perform common acts; *aggadah* tells us how to participate in the eternal drama. *Halachah* gives us knowledge; *aggadah* exaltation. *Halachah* prescribes, *aggadah* suggests; *halachah* decrees, *aggadah* inspires; *halachah* is definite, *aggadah* is elusive... the interrelationship of *halachah* and *aggadah* is the very heart of Judaism. *Halachah* without *aggadah* is dead, *aggadah* without *halachah* is wild.'

27 Genesis 3:1ff. See Chapter 1
28 Gen. 18: 23-33
29 Gen. 25:22
30 Gen. 32:23-33. See the Introduction to Part Three
31 Exodus 33:12-23
32 Numbers 12. See Chapter 2

of the experience of engaging with the source texts of Judaism. Exploring the sources, also involves grappling with passages that we find challenging or difficult or troubling, and insinuating ourselves and our questions into them, refusing to be satisfied with simple readings, and allowing our assumptions concerning what any particular text is teaching, to be disrupted as we engage with it. In the following pages, you will find some examples of this method: in my approach to Leviticus chapters 18 to 20;[33] in my imaginative reconfiguration of the narrative following the Revelation at Sinai;[34] and in my *aggadic* interpretation of Miriam's problem with Moses.[35]

And there is something else. Of course, the empowered, choosing, individual Jew may choose to opt out of Jewish life – and, sadly, since the *Sho'ah*, many have chosen not to identify as Jews.[36] At the same time, as my experience as a congregational rabbi demonstrates, increasing numbers of previously unaffiliated Jews are choosing to engage with Judaism, connect with other Jews, grapple with the Jewish source texts, interrogate what they say, and trouble the texts to discover new meanings that speak to their own individual lives and struggles.

The third part of the book, The Struggle with Trouble, rooted in my congregational experience, explores the nexus between the individual Jew on her or his own journey, the challenge of commitment, and the development of enabling forms of Jewish community that far from constraining individuals, are, increasingly, providing a context for individuals to express their diverse struggles and ways of being Jewish.[37]

While Part Three focuses on the British context, Part Four – preceded by an analytical reflection on the connections between Justice, Truth and Peace in Chapter 14 – addresses the thorny issue of the conflict between Israel and Palestine, which, still unresolved, impacts, not only on Israelis and Palestinians, but also on individual Jews and Jewish communities throughout the diaspora.

---

33 See Chapter 9
34 See Ch. 11
35 See Ch. 2
36 The Jewish population in Britain in 1945 was 450,000. Today it stands at c. 265,000
37 See, in particular, Ch. 10 and 11

The Legacy of the Rabbis

To conclude this introduction, a reminder of the first paragraph of
Pirkey Avot, 1:1:

> Moses received *Torah* from Sinai and handed it on to Joshua,
> Joshua to the elders, and the elders to the prophets. And the
> prophets handed it on to the members of the Great Assembly.
> The latter said three things: be deliberate in judgement; raise up
> many disciples; and make a fence around the *Torah*.

If it had not been for the vision of the rabbis and their determination to rebuild Jewish life after the destruction of the Temple,
Judaism would have died. Their efforts ensured the continuation of
Jewish life, and should also remind us that the future of Judaism
cannot be taken for granted. It requires effort to reinvent Jewish life
to meet the needs of each new generation – particularly, in the aftermath of catastrophe.

And there is more to learn from the example of the rabbinic revolution, which makes the legacy of the rabbis much more complex.
Despite their determination to reconstitute Jewish life in such a way
that there was a secure 'fence around the *Torah*', engaged with generating *aggadah*, as well as *halachah*, they could not resist generating
multiple meanings and troubling the *Torah* to tell many, many tales
as they explored every word, investigated the gaps, and prodded the
hints.[38]

So, to continue the analogy: while building a fence, they also
made of each panel in the fence, a door, which each Jew today may
choose to open or to close. What is more, the rabbis saw themselves
as the inheritors of the prophetic tradition – and so should we: as the
prophets were 'troublers of Israel', exhorting the people of their day
to examine the distance between the ethical values expressed in the
Torah, and the social reality of iniquity and injustice all around them,
so, we, too, need to be troublers, as we move between our sacred
texts, and the broken world, we are summoned to repair.[39]

---

38 See Chapter 1 for a brief account of the rabbinic hermeneutical method
known as PaRDeS: *P'shat* – the search for the 'plain' meaning; *Remez*, the
exploration of every 'hint' in the text; *D'rash* - the 'interpretation' of what the
text does and does not say; *Sod* – the mystical meaning of the text.

39 Repair – *Tikkun*. The expression, *tikkun olam* is first used in the Mishnah;
mip'nei tikkun ha-olam 'for the sake of *tikkun* of the world'. See Glossary.

PART ONE

Trouble-Making Precedents:
The First Woman and Other Female Firsts

One of the problems with the progressive view of history is the tendency to assume that societies always improve over time, and that social conditions today represent an improvement upon social conditions of the past. Another aspect of this assumption is to imagine that our forebears were more 'primitive' than we are, or less intellectually and spiritually developed.

While there is no doubt about the way in which technology has progressed over time, any student of history will know that past societies grappled with the challenges they faced in ways no less sophisticated than our own. Equally, the human species has not evolved to any significant extent for tens of thousands of years, and when it comes to human conflict, and the realm of the tumultuous human emotions, we are just as 'primitive' as our ancestors were.

And so, although this book focuses on some key contemporary issues and developments in Jewish life over the past four decades, it begins with an exploration of what I have called, 'trouble-making precedents' within the Jewish story.

This exploration begins with my re-reading of the creation stories in Genesis[1]. The Genesis account of the creation of humanity is a very well-known story, first popularised by the King James translation of the Hebrew Bible. How you read it will depend on your perspective, whether you see yourself as religious or secular, and whether or not you are Jewish or Christian. From a feminist perspective, the way in which the story of the genesis of human life is presented in the *Torah*, represents trouble-making on an audacious scale – and there have been many feminist analyses of the text we find in Genesis chapters 1 to 3.[2] My approach to this provocative tale, drawing on the framework of rabbinic exegesis, troubles with the Hebrew in a slightly different way to draw out my own particular interpretation.

---

1 This chapter originated as a lecture I gave at The Divinity School of Cambridge University in 1990, as part of a series entitled, Women's Voices in Religion, which was organised during 1990 to 1991. The series of lectures was subsequently published as an anthology: *Women's Voices – Essays in Contemporary Feminist Theology* edited by Teresa Elwes. (HarperCollins, London 1992). I later extended the lecture, for one of the Bible and Literature Seminars, held at the Sussex University Meeting House in March 2002. The text included here is, largely, that expanded version.

2 See, for example, footnote 10 in Chapter 1.

Having explored the story of the first woman and man, the rest of Part One is devoted to my study of exceptional women, who were the first of their kind: Miriam the elder sibling of Aaron and Moses, the first female leader of the Jewish people; B'ruria, the only woman scholar of the early rabbinic period, whose story survived, not only through the pages of the *Talmud*, but in later commentary; and Fräulein Rabbiner Regina Jonas, the first woman to be ordained as a rabbi.

Although I have written brief articles about Miriam, and included her in sermons and talks[3], I have never said everything that I wanted to say about Miriam. The 'untold story' I present here has been in my consciousness for many years, and takes the form of *aggadah*, the storytelling method for explicating the *Torah* created by the first rabbis.

The chapter on B'ruria explores the rabbinic treatment of women by way of a study of the teachings and experience of an exceptional woman, who lived in the 2nd century CE[4], and the chapter on Rabbi Regina Jonas investigates the story of the first woman rabbi, ordained in Germany in 1935, and her mysterious 'disappearance'[5]. In the cases of, both, B'ruria and Rabbi Regina Jonas, as my treat-

---

3 I spoke about Miriam most recently in a talk I gave about Women as Agents of Change at Brighton & Hove Interfaith Contact Group Women in Faith Dialogue Event, held at my synagogue in March 2009.

4 This is the text of the lecture I gave at the Leo Baeck College in February 1989, a few months before I was ordained, as part of a term-long series, The Sayings of the Mothers – the first lecture series at the college to give expression to a feminist approach to Jewish life and tradition. The lecture was later published in *European Judaism* (Vol. 26, No.2, Autumn 1993), and subsequently included in the first collection of the writings of women rabbis published in Britain in 1994, entitled, *Women Rabbis Tell Their Stories*, edited by Rabbi Sybil Sheridan. (SCM Press, London), and dedicated to the memory of Rabbi Regina Jonas.

5 *Hear Our Voice* also includes 'Rabbi Regina Jonas, 1902-1944: Missing Link in a Broken Chain', which I wrote following a brief period of research into her life and work. Earlier in 1994, I was honoured to give the first public lecture about Rabbi Jonas at the Leo Baeck College, entitled, 'The Discovery of Fräulein Rabbiner Regina Jonas: Making Sense of Our Inheritance', which was subsequently published in *European Judaism* (Vol. 28, No.2, Autumn 1995). The chapter included here, is the text of that lecture, which I delivered again at a gathering of the Jewish Historical Society of Brighton and Hove on 23rd February 2010, with some revisions to acknowledge subsequent research.

ment of each exceptional woman reveals, two things are clear: that they were extremely troubling to the men of their times, and, that as a result of their exceptional forays into the exclusively male rabbinic arena, they were, in different ways, punished for their audacity – although in the case of B'ruria, the punishment she received was much more blatant.

CHAPTER ONE

Making Trouble from Day One: Re-Reading the Creation Stories in Genesis

Making trouble from Day One, I am beginning at the beginning with the troubling beginning of the Bible: the tales of the beginning of Creation, the tales of the Creator-God, the tales of the relationship between God and His Creation, and the tales of the creation and differentiation of humanity into two forms. I have used the plural word 'tales' repeatedly because when we read the first two chapters of the book of Genesis we find that there are two Creation stories. Why two? I will return to that question later.

As you will see from the pages that follow, beginning at the beginning is no easy matter. The Genesis tales are too well-known - and have been too misused to justify the subjugation of women - to allow for anything other than a thorough treatment. In order to understand what is going on, we need to embark on a painstaking and careful analysis of these narratives. They not only inform Jewish and Christian teaching but have become an integral part of popular mythology and culture. And so, let us begin.

My framework of interpretation is influenced by the approach of the early rabbis who lived between 200-500 CE. The tale of the 'Fall' and 'Original Sin' is not my story. According to rabbinic tradition, the first woman and man transgressed the Divine prohibition when they ate the fruit of the forbidden tree, and so discovered their limitations as human beings, subject to God. When they left the Garden of Eden, they became fully human in both the physical and the spiritual sense – not only mortal and vulnerable to pain and hardship, but morally responsible for their own actions and capable of 'good' and 'evil'. I am saying this in order to distinguish between the mainstream perspectives of Judaism and Christianity on the story of 'Adam and Eve'.

My method of reading the text is based on an examination of the Hebrew and reflects an awareness of the different modes of traditional rabbinic exegesis: *p'shat*, the search for the plain meaning; *remez*, the sensitivity to hints, the sub-text, *d'rash*, explaining the anomalies, the gaps, the silences in the text; *sod*, exploring the hidden meaning – the mystical interpretation. The mystical approach, which developed in the Middle Ages into a distinct branch of Jewish study and practice, known as *Kabbalah*[1], is less relevant to my elucidation of the difficulties in the *Torah's* tales of the creation of humanity, so my analysis draws on *p'shat*, *remez* and *d'rash* – but not on *sod*.

Schooled in traditional exegesis, I am also a progressive rabbi, who was taught by my teachers at the Leo Baeck College in London,[2] to read the *TaNaKH*, the Hebrew Bible,[3] both from the standpoint of critical scholarship and as a work of literature. From the perspective of Progressive Judaism, the Bible is a human document, written by God-inspired people - even the sacred core, the Five Books of Moses, is the work of human hands and minds. A product of European Enlightenment, Progressive Judaism does not accept the traditional view that the *Torah* is *min-hashamayim*, 'from heaven' – dictated by God to Moses on Mount Sinai.

When I read the text, I am responding specifically to the interpretation of the text by Jewish male scholars over the centuries. From my perspective, despite the carefully crafted methodology of rabbinic exegesis, in reading the text, the rabbis sacrificed *p'shat* – the search for the plain meaning – in favour of explanations which served to legitimate the subordination of woman to man. According to Jewish tradition, Adam, the first human being was a 'man'. We read in *The Legends of the Jews* – a collection of rabbinic interpretations of the

---

1 The foundational text of *Kabbalah* is the *Zohar*, meaning, 'splendour' or 'radiance', a collection of books which offers a mystical commentary on the *Torah*, as well as other mystical insights. The *Zohar* was first published by Moses de Leon in Spain in the 13th century. Moses de Leon attributed the text to the 2nd century sage, Rabbi Shimon ben Yochai, who, according to legend, spent 13 years living in a cave studying the *Torah*, and was inspired by the prophet Elijah to write the *Zohar*.

2 See 'My Journey', note 9. Since my ordination in 1989, I have maintained a continuous connection with Leo Baeck College, where I have taught Classical Hebrew, Spirituality and Progressive Judaism, served as a rabbinic tutor and mentor, chaired the Rabbinic In-Service Training team, and continue to contribute sessions to the Practical Rabbinics programme.

3 For an explanation of TaNaKH, See: A Guide to Trouble-Making Judaism, note 8.

Bible – that after creating the first man, God made two attempts to create a wife for him:[4]

> To banish his loneliness, Lilith was first given to Adam as wife. Like him she had been created out of the dust of the ground. But she remained with him only a short time, because she insisted in enjoying full equality with her husband. She derived her rights from their identical origin. With the help of the Ineffable Name, which she pronounced, Lilith flew away from Adam, and vanished in the air....

> The woman destined to become the true companion of man was taken from Adam's body.

This *midrash* ('interpretation') is a response to the fact that the *Torah* includes two accounts of the Creation of humanity, and as such, is an attempt to make sense of the two tales. Interestingly, it also reflects an awareness that there were other versions of the Creation story, and that the tales in the *Torah* may include survivals of these other versions.

A number of Jewish feminist scholars have investigated the tales of 'Lilith' and argued that the first account of the creation of humanity in Genesis chapter 1 includes a remnant of the Lilith story.[5] My approach is slightly different. While the Bible reflects diverse literary and oral sources – the Bible is a literary whole. I have chosen to read the text as we find it in the Bible. As a feminist, who was an active participant in the Women's Liberation Movement, which began in the 1960s, I understand that the Bible as a literary product is the

---

4 See: *The Legends of the Jews.* Vol.1. From the Creation to Jacob edited by Louis Ginzberg. The Jewish Publication Society of America, Philadelphia,1968, pp. 65, 66).

5 See, for example, 'Lilith' by Barbara Borts in Sybil Sheridan, ed., *Hear Our Voice. Women Rabbis Tell Their Stories* (SCM Press, London, 1994); *Women and Judaism, Myth, History and Struggle* by Roslyn Lacks (Doubleday & Co. Inc., Garden City, New York, 1980); 'The Goddess in Judaism – an Historical Perspective' by Asphodel Long in Alix Pirani, ed., *The Absent Mother, Restoring the Goddess to Judaism and Christianity.* (HarperCollins, London, 1991). *In a Chariot Drawn by Lions: The Search for the Female in Deity* by Asphodel Long (The Crossing Press, Freedom, CA, 1993); 'The Genesis of "The Sphere of Redemption": The Theme, and Power, of Lucifer – and the Creative Presence of the Shekhinah and Lilith' by Fay Pomerance in Alix Pirani, ed., *The Absent Mother* (as above).

work of male scholars and storytellers, reflecting the experience and understandings of men and the reality of patriarchal social structures.[6] Starting from the premise that the redactors of the Bible were men crafting the tales from a male standpoint – although there is evidence of female authorship of particular texts[7] - I am concerned not simply to reveal male bias, but to demonstrate that the tradition of male rabbinic interpretation does not do justice to the text we find in Genesis chapters 1 and 2. It is easy to read the Bible from a feminist perspective as simply, patriarchal. My re-reading challenges traditional interpretations by restoring the *p'shat*, the plain meaning of the text, and discovering how the Hebrew Scriptures are infused with a consciousness which is not simply patriarchal – it is a specifically Hebraic consciousness, which includes both patriarchal, and what I will call 'holistic' elements. Adopting the method, if not the content, of traditional exegesis, let us go back to the beginning.

Why does the Bible, a carefully crafted literary work, include two accounts of Creation? The question will answer itself – once we investigate what the text tells us about the two principal players in the Creation stories – God and Humanity.

God

The *Torah* is a theological document written by human beings that defines and describes God by telling God's story – of Creation, of humanity, of a particular family, of a particular people. God is one of the characters in the drama and interacts with the other characters. God both frames the narrative and is part of it. God is centre-stage. But first, right at the beginning of this epic tale, God creates the stage.

So, we begin God's story at the beginning - with the first verse of *Torah*. But when we do, we discover that this is not *the* beginning:

In beginning, God created the heavens and the earth.

Although standard translations read, 'In *the* beginning', the Hebrew

---

6 *The Israelite Woman: Social Role and Literary Type in Biblical Narrative* by Athalya Brenner (JSOT Press, Sheffield, 1985); *Discovering Eve: Ancient Israelite Women in Context* by Carol L. Meyers (Oxford University Press, 1988); 'Gender Roles and Gender 3:16 Revisited' by Carol L. Meyers in Athalya Brenner, ed., *A Feminist Companion to Genesis* (Sheffield Academic Press, 1999).

7 See, for example, 'The Song of Solomon's Wife' by Sybil Sheridan in Sybil Sheridan, ed., *Hear Our Voice*.

b'reishit does not include the definite article, 'the'. If it did, the Hebrew text would read *ba-reishit*. So the verse does not tell us *when* God created the world, but rather suggests that creating the world was the *beginning* of God's creative activity. According to Jewish tradition, God's creativity *continues* and so we read in the *Yotzeir*, the blessing of Creation in the liturgy of the morning service that 'God renews the work of creation continually day by day'. The beginning of the *Torah* tells us as much about God, the Creator – the Creating God – as it does about Creation.

We encounter God in the very first verses of the *Torah* – that is, we, the *readers* of the text – encounter God. There is no evidence of interactive encounter in the text (Genesis 1:1-2):

> In beginning, God created the heavens and the earth. / Now the earth was formless and void, and darkness was upon the face of the deep; and the wind of God was hovering over the face of the waters. / And God said, 'Let there be light.' And there was light.

What is 'the wind of God'? The word for 'wind', *ru'ach*, also means 'spirit': 'The spirit of God'? God is present – but how to describe God? Is this an attempt to convey an elusive mystery? The noun, *ru'ach* (wind), linked with the verb, *m'rachefet* (hovering), which is in the feminine singular form, led Martin Buber to see in this description, a great mother-bird hovering over her young in the nest.[8] Perhaps God is this too. But such a suggestive, intimate portrait

---

8 'We should note that *Elohim* is named only at the beginning of the creation story – it is the undivided intentional totality of the work of creation that is assigned to *ru'ach*, not the individual actions in the world's becoming or even the entirety of them. Not even where the divine breath is blown into Adam is *ru'ach* named, although (as is clear from 6:3) it is *ru'ach* itself that expands in him into the breath of life ... Both accounts of creation – the account of the making of the world (1:1-2:4a) and the account of the making of human beings (2:4b-25), the primordial legend of nature and the primordial legend of history ... In the first, *ru'ach* maternally spreads her wings to shelter the totality of the things that are to be; in the second, unnamed and enigmatic, she is infused into the being destined for existence in history, to be present for his decision and to share his fate.' ('People Today and the Jewish Bible: From A Lecture Series' by Martin Buber (November 1926) pp. 4-21 in *Scripture and Translation by Martin Buber and Franz Rosenzweig*, translated by Lawrence Rosenwald with Everett Fox (Indiana University Press; Indianapolis,1994).

of God's immanent presence is belied by the word for God – *Elohim* – a masculine plural noun signifying omnipotence and transcendence. With the phrase, "And God said, 'Let there be Light.' And there was light", the reader confronts the spectre of an all-powerful super-Sovereign, masterfully creating a world out of 'formlessness and void' in an orderly manner, administering a series of separations: creating both the heavens - sun, moon and stars - and the earth - vegetation, creeping things, fish, animals, and, finally, humankind, stage by stage.

In the first twenty-five verses of the book of Genesis, God has no identity except that of 'Creator' and is entirely separate from His creation. God creates by a set of declarative decrees: 'Let there be light' (: 3); 'Let there be a firmament in the midst of the waters, and let it divide the waters from the waters' (: 6); 'Let the waters under the heavens be gathered together to one place and let dry land appear' (: 9) and so on. God declares and then God creates and names each element and each creature within His creation.

The creation of humanity

It is only when God creates the animals and speaks to them directly, blessing them with 'fruitfulness', that an encounter takes place between God and His Creation (: 22). But it is not until God creates humanity that a *relationship* between Creator and created is indicated. We read at verses 26a and 27:

> 'Let us make a human being (*Adam*) in our image, according to our likeness.... /'. So God created the human being in His own image, in the image of God He created it (*oto*); male and female He created them (*otam*).

Throughout this first chapter of Genesis, Divinity is encapsulated by the Hebrew word *Elohim* – as I have already indicated, a masculine plural noun. As God is singular and plural - literally all in one - so humanity created 'in the image of God' (*b'tzelem Elohim*) is singular and plural. Hebrew has no 'neutral' gender - all nouns and adjectives are either masculine or feminine forms. For this reason, I translate the word *oto*, denoting the singular human being, as 'it' rather than 'him'. It is only when the one human being becomes two that male (*zachar*) and female (*n'keivah*) forms of the human being emerge.

God creates humanity in His own image, both singular and plural. But what does it mean for humanity to be 'according to' the 'likeness' (*d'mut*) of God - to be *like* or *similar* to God? We read at verse 26b:

> 'And let them have dominion (*v'yirdu*) over the fish of the sea, and over the fowl of the air, and over the cattle, and over all the earth, and over every creeping thing that creeps over the earth'.

And then at verse 28:

> And God blessed them; and God said to them: 'Be fruitful and multiply and fill the earth, and subdue it (*v'chivshuhah*); and have dominion (*u'r'du*) over the fish of the sea, and over the fowl of the air, and over every creeping thing that creeps upon the earth.'

God blessed the animals with reproductive capacity, but the human being is set apart to be *like* God, omnipotent and masterful.

But that is not the end of the matter. There are two accounts of Creation. In the second (Genesis 2:4ff), the image of a transcendent Sovereign Creator-God is supplemented by the image of God - now given the name YHWH - as an artist/artisan, forming (*yotzeir*), the human being (*ha-adam*), out of the dust of the ground (*adamah*). And a picture of tangible intimacy is heightened when this artisan parent-like God infuses the human being with 'the breath of life'. We read at chapter two, verse 7:

> Then YHWH God formed the human being of the dust of the ground, and breathed into its nostrils the breath of life (*nishmat chayyim*); and the human being became a living being (*nefesh chayyah*).

Here, not only is God, God - *Elohim* - with all that designation infers but, God has a *name*, a name formed from the consonants *Hei Yud Hei* which describe God as 'being'.[9] And so God is a 'Being' in

---

9 The consonants YHWH are a form of the root *Hei Yud Hei*, to 'be'. Traditionally, God's name must not be pronounced, so a substitute word is used, which is translated, Lord – although the substitute, *Adonai*, means, literally, 'my lords' (the 'ai' ending – the vowel *kamatz* plus a *yud* - is the possessive suffix for a plural noun in pause). In the printed version of the Hebrew Scriptures, the vowels of *Adonai* are added to the consonants, YHWH, to indicate how the word should be pronounced. Unfamiliar with this substitution, some read the consonants with the vowels as *Y'hovah* – hence, Jehovah's Witnesses.

the world, and is now knowable by those who are not God. This 'Being' 'forms' the human being - and the human being feels the kneading touch of God. This 'Being' infuses the human being with 'the breath of life' - and the human being feels the breath of God in its nostrils. And it is not only the human being whom YHWH God forms out of the ground - but the animals, too (2:19a). The transcendent Deity who creates the world by commanding it into existence also goes down to the ground and gets His hands dirty.

So, if we put the two pictures of God side by side, the omnipotent Sovereign, separate and intangible, and a 'Being' tangibly connected with His creation, God is a dichotomy. And yet there is something else *between* these two images: the 'wind' or 'spirit' sweeping over the waters – *both* Buber's mother-bird (intimate presence) *and* elusive mystery (absolute otherness). God is both transcendent *and* immanent *and* utterly other. So how can humanity be *like* God?

God forms humanity and the animals *alike* 'out of the dust of the ground'. But still, the relationship between God and humanity is unique. In the first account, God creates humanity 'in our own image, according to our own likenesses'. And being 'like' God is about subduing the rest of God's creation - indeed, all the earth - and having dominion over it. In the second account, God infuses humanity alone with the 'breath of life'. But, paradoxically, in the second account, instead of revealing more about how like God humanity is, the text sets boundaries between God and the human being. Indeed, in place of 'dominion over all the earth', God, having formed the human being out of the ground, a particular part of the earth set aside for cultivation - a *cultural* rather than a *natural* space - puts the human being into a garden, a distinct, boundaried section of the ground 'to work it and to tend' it (*l'ovdah u'l'shomrah* - 2:15) - to be the first gardener, so to speak. What is more, even the boundaried garden is not the human being's unrestricted domain. We read in the following verses (: 16-17):

> And YHWH God commanded the human being saying: 'Of every tree of the garden you may freely eat; / but of the tree of the knowledge of good and evil, you shall not eat of it; for on the day that you eat of it you shall surely die.'

So much for the human being's license to dominate and subjugate the rest of Creation. Contrary to what chapter 1 implies, the human being is not like God at all. The text already indicated as much when it related that 'YHWH formed the human being out of the dust of the ground' (2:7). Unlike God, the human being is mortal and subject to God's commands. At the end of the Creation story, having transgressed the boundaries set by God and eaten of the forbidden tree, the first woman and man forfeit companionship for strife (3:16), and cease to live in harmony with the rest of Creation (: 15; 17-18). Most significantly, the human being (male and female) learns, finally, what it means to be a human being. We read in chapter 3, verse 19:

> In the sweat of your face you shall eat bread, till you return to the ground; for out of it you were taken; for dust you are, and to dust you shall return.

The human being (*ha-adam*), intimately connected with God is not like God - but rather like the ground (*ha-adamah*) from which it came, with which it must struggle, and to which it shall return.

So, what is God like? Utterly transcendent in Genesis chapter 1, tangibly immanent in Genesis chapter 2, God is an omnipotent, omniscient, male-like being, creating, forming, looming large over His Creation: *Super*man, perhaps. Or as traditional Jewish liturgy puts it, both 'king' and 'father' – reflecting a time when kings – however just - had absolute power over their subjects, and fathers – however loving - had absolute power over their children.

But what about that elusive aspect of God – between the transcendent and the immanent? After the first woman and man eat from the fruit of the forbidden tree, they suddenly become aware of God's presence (Genesis 3:8):

> And they heard the voice of YHWH God walking in the garden in the wind of the day.

Note the description: 'The voice of God *walking*'. The verb form, *mit'haleich* is reflexive not simply active - suggesting that the only reference point for God's action is God. A literal meaning would be 'walking Himself'. But how does a voice 'walk'? God's voice is not simply a *sound* they can *hear* - it is a moving presence. And yet, unlike the actual presence of a physical being walking on the ground, it moves around, in its own dimension, in the *wind* of the day – rather like a *spirit* (*ru'ach*). The reader can imagine the couple sensing the air changing, the leaves rustling. Here is the spirit of God hovering so close, they can feel it and yet, totally mysterious, beyond reach.

Humanity: male and female, woman and man

Having conducted an analysis of what Genesis chapters 1, 2 and 3 say about God and humanity, I shall now turn to the heart of the issue: the *Torah's* account of the first man and the first woman. Everybody has heard the story about the first man and woman. First, God made a man called Adam. Then He made a woman called Eve from one of Adam's ribs. While this story is based on *one* of the accounts of the creation of humanity set out in the *Torah*, it is not exactly the tale that the *Torah* tells. The story is an interpretation of the text, an interpretation learned so well by generations of readers, Jewish and Christian alike, that, it can be readily re-told and identified as 'what the Bible says'.

Well, what does the Bible say? If we return to the account of Creation in Genesis chapter 1, we read that there is no mention whatsoever of a man called Adam and a rib-to-woman called Eve. We read (: 26-27):

> Then God said, 'Let us make a human being (*adam*) in our image, according to our likeness; and let *them* have dominion over the fish of the air, and over the cattle, and over all the earth, and over every creeping thing that creeps upon the earth.' / So God created the human being (*ha-adam*) in His own image, in the image of God created He it (*oto*); male (*zachar*) and female (*n'keivah*) He created them.

Adam - a *human being* - not a man called 'Adam'. As I have already pointed out, the Hebrew language expresses everything in gendered terms. Clearly, the singular human being is genderless - hence the translation 'it'. God creates a singular human being in two forms, male and female. Because the text is so succinct, it is easy to miss the significance of the switch from one being to two *different* forms of that being. The Hebrew words for 'male' and 'female', *zachar* and *n'keivah*, express the *difference* between these two types of human being in sexual terms. The word *n'keivah* is particularly explicit. It is based on the root, *Nun Kuf Beit*, meaning 'to pierce'; a female is a being with an orifice.

The significance of the use of these two words, *zachar* and *n'keivah*, becomes clear in the next verse (: 28):

> Then God blessed them; and God said to them: 'Be fruitful and
> multiply, and fill the earth, and subdue it; and have dominion
> over the fish of the sea, and over the fowl of the air, and over every
> living thing that creeps on the earth.'

God has differentiated humanity into male and female forms for the
purpose of reproduction. While the words *zachar* and *n'keivah* could
not be more explicit concerning sexual difference, the relationship
between them is completely egalitarian: God creates one human
being, then two sexually differentiated human beings, and then
commands *both of them* to 'be fruitful and multiply'. What is more,
together, both male and female human beings are to 'subdue' the
earth and exercise 'dominion' over it.

Of course, I'm not the first feminist to draw attention to the sexual
equality evident in these verses.[10] But sexual equality is not all there
is to it. The gratification I feel as a woman reading this egalitarian
account of the creation of humanity is under-cut by the image of
humanity the text describes. After creating the world stage by stage,
God arrives at the pinnacle of creation, humanity, created 'in the
image of God', in the image of an all-powerful, super-Sovereign, with
a God-given license to subjugate and dominate the rest of the earth.

But as I indicated earlier, the second account of creation tells quite
a different tale. The locus of the rib-to-woman story, it may be seen,
on one level, as little more than a male-defined myth, explaining
and justifying, the subordination of women to men.[11] However,
while the account certainly serves this purpose, the *p'shat* - the plain
meaning - of the Hebrew text, is, as we shall see, both more straight-
forward and a lot more complicated.

In the first account of creation, humanity - male and female - is
God-on-earth with seemingly unlimited power over the rest of
creation. God creates the human being, *ha-adam*, which means that
ha-adam is not God, but it is not clear if there are any limits to *ha-
adam*'s power. This is one of the problems, which the second account
of creation addresses. But the second creation story is not simply an

---

10 *God and the Rhetoric of Sexuality* by Phyllis Tribble. (SCM Press, London,
   1978).
11 *Women and Judaism, Myth, History and Struggle* by Roslyn Lacks (Doubleday
   & Co. Inc., Garden City, New York, 1980).

answer to, or embellishment of, the first extremely condensed account. It provides an *alternative* perspective. First, the relationship of *ha-adam* to the earth is totally different. We read (2:5-8; 15):

> No shrub of the field was yet in the earth, and no herb of the field had yet sprung up; for YHWH God, had not caused it to rain upon the earth and there was no human being (*adam*) to till the ground (*adamah*); / but a mist went up from the earth and watered the whole face of the ground. Then YHWH formed the human being (*ha-adam*) of the dust of the ground (*adamah*), and breathed into its nostrils (*b'apav* - literally: 'his nostrils') the breath of life; and *adam* became a living being. And YHWH God planted a garden eastward, in Eden, and there He put *ha-adam* whom He had formed. / ... And YHWH took *ha-adam* and put him in the Garden of Eden to work it and to tend it (*l'ovdah u'l'shomrah*).

In the first 'seven day' hierarchical account of creation, vegetation appears on the third day (1:11-12), and we learn later that vegetation is what the living creatures - including humanity – eat. It is a source of food without a life of its own (1:29-31). In the second version, an implicit connection is made between the human being (*ha-adam*) and the plant life which grows out of the ground (*adamah*). Both *adam*, a masculine noun, and *adamah*, a feminine noun, derive from the same root, *Alef Dalet Mem*. God forms the human being out of the dust of the ground for the purpose of ensuring the growth of plants which cannot flourish without the work of the human being. *Ha-adam* is one with *ha-adamah* – almost – differentiated from the ground solely in order to tend it. The 'almost' is 'the breath of life', *nishmat chayyim*, the breath of God. *Ha-adam* formed by God out of *adamah* becomes a 'living being', *nefesh chayyah*, with God's breath. And as a 'living being', *ha-adam* is also at one with every other living being described in the initial 'order' of creation (1:20-28) – which upsets the hierarchical presentation of that order somewhat.

Ha-adam is to work the ground, nurturing the plant life, but this second account of Creation is far from complete. *Ha-adam* is still *singular*, and there has not, as yet, been any mention of the animals. Unlike Genesis chapter one, where, Creation unfolds, stage by stage, here the order is not 'evolutionary' and serves other purposes. Just as the purpose of *ha-adam* as a tiller of the ground is crucial to the growth of plant-life, so the need of *ha-adam* for companionship explains the formation of other living creatures - also 'from the ground'. Rather than being the *pinnacle* of creation, the human being is at the *centre*. Here we have a view of the world, which is circular, not linear. We read (2:18-20):

> And YHWH God said: 'It is not good for *ha-adam* to be alone, I will make it a helper, corresponding to it (*eizer k'negdo*)' / Then out of the ground, YHWH God, formed every beast of the field, and every bird of the air; and brought [them] to *ha-adam* to see what it would call [them]; and whatever *ha-adam* would call every living being, that was to be its name. / And *ha-adam* gave names to all the cattle, and to the birds of the air, and to every beast of the field, but for *adam* there was not found a helper for it.

Ha-adam needs 'a helper corresponding to it', *eizer k'negdo*, an awkward way of describing a being who is both a 'support' and an equal - the word *neged* denotes the *eizer* as one who is 'opposite' in a spatial sense, a being *apart*, and on the same level. For those who insist on translating the masculine noun *adam* as a *male* human being, a 'him' rather than an 'it', it is as well to note that the word *eizer* is also a masculine singular noun. Not surprisingly, gendered readings of the text ignore this side of the equation! More logically, as I remarked earlier, the singular human being is genderless. The significant piece of information in this text is that, in naming the animals, *ha-adam* establishes their identities as living beings of another, unequal kind, and exerts power over them. And so *ha-adam* cannot find an *eizer k'negdo* among the animals.

Which brings me to the infamous, misconstrued, rib-to-woman story. We read (2:21-23):

> And YHWH God caused a deep sleep to fall upon *ha-adam*, and it slept; and He took one of its *sides*, and closed up [the] flesh in place of it. / And YHWH God built the side which He had taken from *ha-adam* into a woman (*ishah*); and He brought her to *ha-adam*. / And *ha-adam* said, 'this is now bone of my bone, flesh of my flesh; she shall be called Woman (*ishah*) because she was taken out of Man (*ish*).'

Here issues around gendered language are compounded by a gendered commentary, which is part of the text. To recap. The word *adam* is a masculine singular noun. The word *adamah*, the ground, out of which God forms *ha-adam*, is a feminine singular noun. And yet in its singular state, it is clear that *ha-adam* is not a man - or, indeed, a woman. Interestingly, this second account of the creation of humanity, portrays the first singular human being with characteristics which patriarchal culture identifies both as feminine – for example, nurturing – and as masculine, for example, naming. In relation to plant life *ha-adam* is presented in traditional feminine terms, in relation to the animals, *ha-adam* is presented in traditional masculine terms.

Unlike the first account of the creation of humanity in which differentiation into male and female forms is described simultaneously with the creation of *ha-adam*, in the second account, differentiation is the outcome of a long process which begins by establishing the relationship of *ha-adam* to other forms of life, as well as to God. It is only once the identity and purposes of the human species have been clarified that the differentiation of *ha-adam* takes place. And it is against this background, that the account of the formation of woman (*ishah*) and man (*ish*) should be understood. But the Hebrew text abandons the logic of the account thus far, halfway through, and standard English translations, following the new logic of these verses, opt to change the meaning of *ha-adam* right from the very beginning of the second creation story. According to the *p'shat*, the plain reading of Genesis 2:21-22a, the first new being which God separates from the singular form of *ha-adam* is a *woman*. My interpretation – *d'rash* – of what follows, made in the light of this observation, draws on the hints – *remez* – in the text. Let us now examine the verses in more detail, and see how the transformation of *ha-adam* into 'man' takes place:

First, God takes one of the sides of *ha-adam* while *ha-adam* is in deep sleep (: 21). The root *Reish Dalet Mem*, conveys sleep, which is extraordinary and full of foreboding - like the vision-filled sleep of Abraham,[12] or the dead sleep of Jonah in the bowels of his ship-of-flight.[13] The word for 'side', *tzeila* – a feminine noun – is used variously in the Bible to denote: the 'sides' of the Ark,[14] the 'sides' or

---

12 Genesis 15:12
13 Jonah 1:5
14 Exodus 25:12 and 26:26-27

'planks' of cedar, which paneled the Temple walls,[15] and the 'slope' of a hill.[16] So far, so good.

Then God builds (*va-yyiven*) the 'side', which He has taken out of *ha-adam* into a woman (*ishah*), and brings her to *ha-adam* (: 22). What is the identity of *ha-adam* at this point? With one side removed, and the flesh closed up again (: 21), logic dictates that the remaining side needs to be 'built' into a man (*ish*). But this is not what the text says. The remaining side - minus woman - is still *ha-adam*. *Ha-adam* is undergoing a transformation of a different kind.

And thirdly, *ha-adam* identifies the new being as 'bone of my bone and flesh of my flesh', and calls her 'woman' (*ishah*) because she was taken out of man (*ish*) (: 23). But *ishah* was not taken out of *ish*. God 'built' one of the sides of *ha-adam* into *ishah*. The words *ishah* (plural: *nashim*) and *ish* (plural: *anashim*), based on the root *Aleph Nun Shin*, meaning to be 'social', are equivalent terms denoting a social relationship characterised by equality and interdependence. Clearly, they are used here for the first time to describe the *outcome* of the differentiation of *ha-adam* - just as the words *zachar* and *n'keivah* are used in the first account of the creation of humanity to express the differentiation of *ha-adam* into two 'sexes' for reproduction. However, while the words *zachar* and *n'keivah* emphasise sexual *difference*, the words *ishah* and *ish* draw attention to the *similarity* between 'woman' and 'man' as social beings. Indeed, it is not clear from the use of the words *ishah* and *ish* alone, that these two forms of *ha-adam* correspond to 'female' and 'male' respectively - although the word *ishah* is a feminine noun (remember: the word *eizer*, 'helper', is a masculine noun). All we know from the *context* is that because 'It is not good for *ha'adam* to be alone' (2:18), God has split *ha-adam* in two. On the one hand, the two beings are two halves of one whole; on the other hand, they are two separate selves *k'neged* – opposite – one another. The difference between them derives from the fact of *separation*, not from sexual difference.

If one follows a standard English translation, one might make the mistake of thinking that the problem in the text derives from the use of the word 'rib'. The Hebrew text tells a different story. *Ha-adam* remains – minus one side – and in the same mould as *ha-adam* who

15 I Kings 6:15-16
16 II Samuel 16:13

named the animals. The logic of the account has faltered. The transformation of *ha-adam* into *ishah and ish* is incomplete, and by staying in the picture *ha-adam* has not only become identified with 'man', but identified 'woman' *in relation to himself*. And so we read: (2:24-25):

> Therefore shall a man (*ish*) leave his father and his mother, and shall cleave to *his woman*, and they shall be one flesh. / And they were both naked, *ha-adam* and *his woman*, and were not ashamed.

On the one hand the account of the creation of humanity has come full circle: one human being, then two, then one again. On the other hand, this concluding homily on the preceding text underscores a transmutation of the logic of both creation stories. The new human being is a *man* and the woman is *his other half*.

The woman and the man in the garden
Two human beings inhabit the garden – and they are not alone: a serpent speaks to the woman (3:1-4); God moves about 'in the wind of the day' (3:8-9) and addresses them both. There is no mention of the other living creatures; the woman and the man – in that order; the serpent and God – in that order. And the garden, a haven of trees dominated by two special specimens, the Tree of Life and the Tree of Knowledge of Good and Evil (2:9) – both off-limits (2:16).

So who is this talking serpent? At the end of chapter 2, we learn that, 'They were both naked (*arummim*), *ha-adam* and *his wife*, but were not ashamed' (: 25), and at the beginning of chapter 3 we read, 'Now the serpent was more cunning (*arum*) than any beast of the field which YHWH God had made' (3:1a). Although there is no etymological connection between the adjective *arummim*, based on the root *Ayin Vav Reish*, and the adjective *arum*, based on the root *Ayin Reish Mem*, clearly we *hear* a connection when we read the two words, which underlines the paradox of the juxtaposition of the two verses. Nakedness without shame is a sign of innocence; the serpent, by contrast is cunning, crafty, full of guile. But, again, who is the serpent? The woman who talks with the serpent (*nachash* - a masculine noun) has clearly been aware of the trees, which God has prohibited. In fact, her responses to the serpent, as we shall see, suggest that she has been extremely curious. Naked, she may be, but not entirely innocent. Perhaps, rather than introducing us to a talking animal, the text, as Benno Jacobs suggested,[17] is externalising the woman's own internal conversation with herself? Let's see if this interpretation works, by setting out the 'conversation' between the woman and 'the serpent'. The words in square brackets are a straight substitution for 'the serpent', and there are no other adaptations to the text (3:1-6):

> And [the woman's inner voice] said: 'Has God really said: "You shall not eat of any tree of the garden?"' / And the woman said to [herself]: 'Of the fruit of the trees of the garden we may eat; / but of the fruit of the tree which is in the midst of the garden, God has said: "you shall not eat of it, neither shall you touch it, lest you die"'. / Then [the woman's inner voice] said to the woman: 'You shall not surely die; / For God knows that in the day you eat of it, your eyes will be opened, and you shall be like God, knowing good and evil.' / And when the woman saw that the tree was good for food, and that it was a delight to the eyes, and that the tree was to be desired to make one discerning, she took of its fruit and ate, and she gave also to her man (l'ishah) with her, and he ate.

Re-reading the dialogue between the woman and the serpent as an internal monologue, we understand better the words attributed to the woman in the text: 'Of the fruit of the trees of the garden we may eat; / but of the fruit of the tree which is in the midst of the garden, God has said: "you shall not eat of it, neither shall you touch it, lest you die"'. So preoccupied with these forbidden trees has the woman been, that she has conflated 'the tree of life in the midst of the garden, and the tree of the knowledge of good and evil' (2:9b). What is more, God told ha-adam, the singular undifferentiated human being, concerning the tree of the knowledge of good and evil: 'for on the day that you eat of it you shall surely die' (17b), but the woman enlarges the prohibition - 'neither shall you touch it'. Touching comes before eating; the forbidden trees coalesced into one have

---

17 Born in Breslau, where he studied at the Rabbinical Seminary and University, Benno Jacob was a Reform rabbi in Germany until World War Two. Before leaving Germany, he produced a monumental commentary on Genesis: *Das Erste Buch der Tora: Genesis*. (Schocken Verlag, Berlin 1934; Neudruck, 1999). Condensed English translation: *The First Book of the Bible: Genesis* (Ktav, New York, 1974).

been at the centre of her garden-world – how often has she reached out her hand and drawn it away again?

As an interesting counterpoint to the image of 'ha-adam and his wife' (2:25) at the end of Genesis chapter 2, here we encounter the woman, taking the fruit and eating it before giving it 'to her man with her' (3:6). Whatever we make of the serpent, the woman takes the initiative. Of course, later, 'her man' uses this to protect himself and blame her – and she, indeed, blames the serpent rather than take responsibility for her actions (3:12-13). Contrary, to the homiletic image of 'ha'adam and his wife,' being 'one flesh' (2:24b), they are individuals who act separately from one another – even before their eyes are 'opened' (3:7).

The woman and the man, differentiated for the purposes of repro-duction (Genesis chapter 1) and companionship (Genesis chapter 2), realise a potential that God has tried to deny them. They have acted independently from, and, against, God's will. But after eating from the tree, God still exerts power over them (:8):

> And they heard the voice of YHWH God walking in the wind of the day; and ha-adam and his wife hid themselves from the pres-ence of YHWH amongst the trees of the garden.

They think they can hide, God knows they cannot, so God's question - 'Where are you?' (Ayyekkah?) - is more than it seems. This becomes apparent when the man, alone, answers (: 10):

> 'I heard your voice in the garden, and I was afraid, because I was naked, and I hid myself.'

They both hide. The man answers – for himself. God's additional questions again request information that God already knows, and invite the man to focus further on his own individual predicament (11):

> Then He said: 'Who told you that you were naked? Have you eaten from the tree concerning which I commanded you that you should not to eat?'

The man duly complies (: 12):

> 'The woman whom you gave to be with me, she gave me from the tree, and I did eat.'

The relationship between God and *ha-adam* broken, God's questions help to rupture the relationship between the now self-conscious man and woman. Aware of their nakedness, they hide together. Exposed by God's questions, they try to protect their individual selves. But they do not lie – or do they? Certainly, the woman did give the fruit to 'her man'. But when God turns to the woman for her response, is the serpent an excuse for her own act of defiance? We read (13-15):

> Then YHWH God said to the woman: 'What is this you have done?' And the woman said: 'The serpent deceived me, and I ate.' Then YHWH said to the serpent: 'Because you have done this, cursed are you from among all the cattle, and from among all the beasts of the field; upon your belly you shall go, and you shall eat dust all the days of your life. / And I will put enmity between you and the woman, and between your descendants and between her descendants; they shall bruise your head, and you shall bruise their heel.'

Like a 'how things began' tale, we learn how serpents came to be creatures that slither on the ground. And this curse introduces the punishments, which follow (more of this in a moment). But the place of the serpent in the story may owe itself more to the woman's failure to admit what she has done than to its own culpability – a possibility which is reflected in what God says to her next (: 16):

> To the woman He said: 'I will greatly multiply your pain and your labour; in pain shall you bring forth children; and your desire shall be to your man, and he shall rule over you.'

Is this a rationalisation for patriarchy, as part of God's 'grand scheme'? Or, more parochially, a fitting rejoinder to an uppity woman, who took the initiative and acted independently? The woman's 'punishment' may also be understood as a response to her cowardice when challenged. How might God have responded if the woman had taken responsibility for her actions? Certainly, God chastens the man for listening to his woman, *as well as* for eating from the forbidden tree (: 17-19):

> Then to *Adam* He said: 'because you have listened to the voice of your woman, and have eaten of the tree, concerning which I commanded you saying: "You shall not eat of it", cursed is the

ground for your sake; in toil shall you eat of it all the days of your life. / Thorns also and thistles shall it bring forth for you; and you shall eat the herb of the field. / In the sweat of your face shall you eat bread, till you return to the ground; for out of it you were taken; for dust you are, and to dust shall you return.'

Ha-adam, humanity, – 'the man' – and at the point that God 'punishes' him, also *Adam* – a man called *Adam*. Everything, with the exception of the forbidden trees, was available to humanity in the garden, but now *Adam* must work hard for a living. But not only *Adam*. The relationship between woman and man broken, humanity's relationship with the ground is also ruptured. But this scene of conflict and struggle is also the locus of humanity's coming of age. Unless the first human beings leave the garden, how will they be in a position to 'be fruitful and multiply and fill the earth'? In the next verse, we read: 'Then *ha-adam* called his woman's name *Chavvah* for she would be the mother of all the living'(: 20). As the undifferentiated human being named the animals and so established a position of domination over them, so now the new man, names 'his woman' and in this way removes the last vestiges of 'companionship' from their relationship. And yet, the woman, *Chavvah*, has a power the man cannot control: the 'living one', she will bring forth life, and become 'the mother of all the living'. The extreme pain of labour, even the power he now has to rule over her, will not change that basic fact. When God drives the first human beings out of the garden (3:22-24), equipped with the knowledge of good and evil, they begin to live in the world. And one cannot help feeling that for all the hardship they must endure, individually and together, the suffering of their Creator is even greater. God, the parent who tried to keep humanity under His control – innocent, safe and near – has lost His children.

Conclusion
Classical feminist readings of the biblical creation tales, applaud the egalitarian treatment of the differentiation of humanity in Genesis chapter 1, and reject the image of male supremacy presented in chapter 2. Troubling our assumptions about what the two versions of the creation of humanity teach us, my re-reading suggests that by focussing on the ways in which God appears and acts in these tales,

and identifying the differing objectives of the two accounts of the differentiation of humanity, we become aware of the patriarchal aspects of the first and the holistic aspects of the second. And so, we discover in Genesis chapter 1, a linear, hierarchical order of creation, with humanity, created in the image of an omnipotent deity, at its apex. And, by contrast, when we read Genesis chapter 2, we enter a holistic world, with the earth and humanity at its centre, in which the human being starts life as a humble gardener, formed by an artisan out of the dust of the ground, not to dominate creation, but to tend it and serve it. While the differentiation of humanity into separate male and female forms serves the purposes of reproduction in the first account, in the second, differentiation is the outcome of the single human being's long search for companionship. The two creation narratives may be understood as alternative visions of humanity, and they also belong together and complete one another. It is only in the process of the splitting of humanity into two that the first human being becomes synonymous with the first man, and the first woman, consequently, becomes his unequal other half.

CHAPTER TWO

Why Miriam Spoke Against Moses:
An Untold Story

What do we know about Miriam? If you are familiar with the Bible, you will probably know the story quite well: Big sister helps her mother to save her baby brother, whose life is threatened by the Pharaoh's decree condemning Hebrew baby boys to death ...[1]

Then, not another word about her until she turns up very briefly, after the slaves have fled Egypt. Named 'Miriam, the prophetess, the sister of Aaron', she leads the women in a dance with song and timbrels after the crossing of the Sea of Reeds ...[2]

Again, nothing more until a curious less well remembered story, during the second year of their journey in the desert, about how Miriam – and, to a lesser extent, middle sibling, Aaron – challenge the authority of their younger brother ...[3]

The next thing we learn is that Miriam has died ...[4]

That is it – twenty-nine verses in all in the whole of the *Torah* – plus a reference to Miriam in a passage dealing with civil and criminal law in Deuteronomy 24 in the context of an injunction concerning the plague of 'leprosy'[5] - more of that later - and a chronology at Numbers chapter 26,[6] which is very telling:

> ...the family of the Korachites: K'hat begot Amram. / And the name of Amram's wife was Yocheved, the daughter of Levi, who was born to Levi in Egypt; and she bore to Amram, Aaron and Moses, and Miriam their sister.

Miriam was, indeed, the sister of Aaron and Moses – their *elder*

---

1 Exodus 2:1-10.
2 Ex. 15:20-21.
3 Numbers 12:1-16.
4 Num. 20:1.
5 Deuteronomy 24:8-9.
6 Num. 26:58-59.

sister. And yet, the *Torah* narrative relegates her to third place, and provides the reader with only brief snippets of her life. Nevertheless, the few verses where Miriam appears, speak volumes.

Let me begin at the end of the story with the account of Miriam's death at Numbers chapter 20, verse 1:

> The Israelites, the whole congregation, came into the wilderness of Tzin, in the first month; and the people dwelt in Kadesh; and Miriam died there, and was buried there.

Thirty-eight years have elapsed. A gaping lacuna in the *Torah* narrative and this is all that the *Torah* has to say about the death of one of the three sibling leaders of the Exodus, the elder sister of Moses! The brevity of the passage is made all the more apparent when we compare it with what the *Torah* says about the death of Aaron, just a few verses further on in the same chapter. Eight verses[7] are devoted to an account which includes a description of Aaron's preparation for death, his death at the top of Mount Hor, and the reaction of the people. When Aaron dies, the *Torah* tells us:[8]

> When all the congregation saw that Aaron had expired, they wept for Aaron thirty days, the whole house of Israel.

A formal period of mourning, as one might expect, where the death of a leader is concerned. Similarly, when Moses dies, the *Torah* relates in Deuteronomy chapter 34, verse 8:

> The Israelites wept for Moses in the plains of Moab, thirty days.

So, what about Miriam? Why no thirty-day mourning rite for her? Significantly, no sooner has Miriam died and been buried, then we read in the very next verse:[9]

> There was no water for the congregation: so, they assembled themselves together against Moses and against Aaron.

The sages, who first commented on the *Torah*, puzzled by the absence of any reference to mourning rites for Miriam, made a connection between these two events: the death of Miriam and the

---

7 For the account of Aaron's death see Numbers 20:22-29

8 Num. 20:29.

9 ibid. 20:2.

lack of water. From this crucial conjunction emerges the legend of Miriam's Well, which sustained the people, providing them with the water they needed to survive, throughout the forty years that they wandered in the wilderness. For example, in the *Talmud*, tractate, *Ta'anit*, which deals with 'fasts', which were frequently related to drought, we read: 'Israel had a well in the desert in Miriam's merit'.[10]

But the legend of Miriam's Well is more than a *d'rash*, more than an exegetical interpretation that arises from the curious conjunction between Miriam's death and the lack of water. It also reflects a rabbinic response to the *Torah*'s treatment of Miriam as a whole. If Miriam was, as the *Torah* relates, both the elder sister of Aaron and Moses, who became one of the sibling leaders of the Exodus, and, even more significantly, a *n'vi'ah* - a prophet[11] – why does the *Torah* say so little about her? The rabbis found evidence of Miriam's powers of prophecy, in the way that she waited by the reeds of the River Nile – after Moses' mother had placed her baby son in a basket there – 'to know what would be done to him.'[12] According to rabbinic interpretation, Miriam foresaw the future redemption of the people.[13]

The rabbinic sages filled in the missing pieces of the Miriam story, and brought out the significance of the role she played, as a leader, in the Exodus and wilderness narratives. However, they were limited by their own imagination, and the *midrashim* concerning Miriam, fail to do justice to the key text at the heart of the *Torah*'s account of

---

10 *Ta'anit* 9a. Another tractate in the *Talmud*, *Shabbat* 35a, has this: 'If one wishes to see Miriam's Well, s/he should go up Mount Carmel and look toward the sea where one will witness something that looks like a sieve amid the sea and that is Miriam's Well.' Rashi comments: 'Miriam's Well: This is the well that would follow Israel through the desert by virtue of Miriam's merit, as it is written, "And Miriam died there." The very next verse says, "And there was no water for the community."' Rashi is an acronym for Rabbi Sh'lomoh Yitzchaki – Solomon ben Isaac. Rashi was born in France in 1040, where he spent most of his life. He died in Worms in the Rhineland in 1105. He is famous for his commentaries on both the TaNaKh, the Hebrew Bible, and the *Talmud* comments. See also *Legends of the Jews*, Vol. III edited by Louis Ginzberg (Jewish Publications Society of America, Philadelphia, 1968) for a compilation of all the *midrashim* related to Miriam's Well (pp. 50-54). The notes (119-135), with the references, are in Vol. VI, pp. 20-22.
11 Exodus 15:20.
12 Ex. 2:4.
13 *Midrash* concerning Miriam's powers of prophecy: Who are the seven prophetesses? Sarah, Miriam, Deborah, Channah, Abigail, Chuldah and

Miriam, which we find in the *parashah, B'ha'a'lot'cha,* in one short chapter – Numbers 12, which I will now quote in full (:1-16):

Esther (*M'gillah* 14a). She prophesied and said, "My mother is destined to bear a son who will redeem Israel" (*M'gillah* 14a). When Moses was born, the whole house was filled with light. Her father kissed her on her head and said, "My daughter, your prophecy has been fulfilled." (*M'gillah* 14a). On the tenth of Nissan, Miriam the prophetess died (end of *M'gillat Ta'anit*. (In Exodus 12, the tenth of the month was the day each household was instructed to take an unblemished lamb (:3), which was then to be killed on the 14th at dusk (:6), with its blood placed on the door-posts (:7) – the Israelites' first sign that they were prepared to participate in their own liberation). Amram acted on his daughter's advice. When Pharaoh decreed, "Every son who is born you shall be cast into the Nile" (Exodus 1:22), he rose and divorced his wife and all of Israel followed his example. "Father", said his daughter, "your decree is harsher than Pharaoh's. Pharaohs decree is directed only against the males, whereas yours by preventing the birth of new children is directed against the males and the females" (*Sotah* 12a). Miriam was six years old at the time. Yet when her father heard her words, he brought her before the Sanhedrin. They said to him, "Amram, it is you who forbids marriage, and it is you who must permit it." "What do you advise?" asked Amram. "Shall we remarry quietly?" They replied, "Then who will make it known to all Israel?" (*Pesikta Rabbati* 43:27). Amram took back his wife and seated her in a palanquin for the wedding procession. Aaron and Miriam sang and danced before her happy that the saviour of Israel would be born to their mother when married to their father (*Maharsha*) (*Sotah* 12a; *Bava Kama* 120a). The Hebrew midwives (Exodus 1:15) were Yocheved and [her daughter] Miriam. Miriam, who was only five years old then, went with Yocheved to assist her. She was quick to honor her mother and to serve God (*Eitz Yosef*), for when a child is little its traits are already evident. The name of the second (i.e., Miriam) was *Puah* (ibid.) for she gave the newborns wine and restored the babies to life when they appeared to be dead, she lit up Israel before God by teaching the women, she presented her face before Pharaoh, stuck up her nose at him, and said, "Woe is to the man (i.e., Pharaoh) when God punishes him!" Pharaoh was filled with wrath and would have killed her, but Yocheved appeased him, saying, "Will you pay attention to her? She is only a child, she has no understanding" (*Shemot Rabbah* 1:13). Why did Miriam stand from afar to see what would become of the baby Moshe? Because she prophesied, "My mother is destined to bear a son who will redeem Israel." When the baby was thrown into the Nile, her mother slapped her on the head and said, "My daughter, where is your prophecy?" (*Shemot Rabbah* 1:22). Betzalel's wisdom was in Miriam's merit. It is written, God made them houses (Exodus 1:21), the priesthood and the monarchy. Miriam received wisdom. She produced Bezalel, and from her issued David (*Shemot Rabbah* 48:4). See *Legends of the Jews*, Vol III, pp. 255-261 – and the references for the notes (488-498) in Vol. VI, pp. 90-92.

Miriam – and Aaron – spoke against Moses because of the Ethiopian woman whom he had married: for he had married an Ethiopian woman. / And they said, 'Has the Eternal indeed spoken only by Moses? Has He not spoken also to us?' And the Eternal heard it. / Now the man Moses was very meek, above all the men who were upon the face of the earth. / And the Eternal spoke suddenly to Moses, and to Aaron, and to Miriam, 'Come out you three to the tabernacle of the congregation.' And the three came out. /

And the Eternal came down in the pillar of the cloud, and stood in the door of the tabernacle, and called Aaron and Miriam: and they both came forward. / And he said, 'Hear now my words: If there be a prophet among you, I the Eternal will make myself known to him in a vision, and will speak to him in a dream. / My servant Moses is not so, who is faithful in all my house. / With him I speak mouth to mouth, plainly, and not in dark speeches; and he beholds the likeness of the Eternal: why then were you not afraid to speak against my servant Moses?' / And the anger of the Eternal burned against them; and he left. /

Then the cloud withdrew from the tabernacle; and, behold, Miriam was stricken with leprosy, white as snow: and Aaron looked at Miriam, and, behold, she was leprous. / Then Aaron said to Moses, 'Alas, my lord, I beseech You, account not to us the sin which we committed in our folly. / Let her not be as a still-birth, which emerges from its mother's womb, with half its flesh eaten away!' / So Moses cried to the Eternal, saying, 'Heal her now, O God, I beseech You'. / And the Eternal said to Moses, 'If her father spat in her face, should she not bear her shame for seven days? Let her be shut out from the camp seven days, and after that let her be received in again.'

So, Miriam was shut out from the camp seven days: and the people did not journey on until Miriam was brought in again. / After that the people moved from Hazeirot, and pitched in the wilderness of Paran.

Before examining this fascinating passage, or, rather, by way of an introduction to my commentary on Numbers chapter 12, let me tell you a story – my own *aggadah* – that encompasses what the *Torah* tells us about the death of Miriam and what happened afterwards. Let me remind you of the text in the *Torah*:[14]

> The Israelites, the whole congregation, came into the wilderness of Tzin, in the first month; and the people dwelt in Kadesh; and Miriam died there, and was buried there. / There was no water for the congregation: so, they assembled themselves together against Moses and against Aaron.

My story introduces two fictional women, named Deborah and Rebecca, in tribute to two powerful biblical Jewish women,[15] and another female character, called Acheret. I have named her Acheret – a feminine form of the Hebrew word for 'other' – because my story of Acheret and Miriam constitutes another, utterly *other* way of making sense of the texts about Miriam that we find in Numbers chapters 12 and 20 - and the gap between them. Like the first rabbis, I am responding to the text of the *Torah* and making sense of it by imagining Miriam's untold story:

The death of Miriam – An Untold Story

Acheret turned in her sleep towards her lover. But as skin touched skin, she felt icy cold. The shock woke her: 'Miriam? Miriam! Miriam!' The question became a howl and then a deep moan. She wrapped her body around the frozen form, trying to encompass her completely. Rocking. Rocking. Rocking. Miriam. Miriam. Miriam.

Acheret did not know how long she lay there, curled tight around her love: rocking, shivering, whimpering quietly. Suddenly, a great light entered the tent, and then a shadow bent over her: 'Miriam? Acheret? What's wrong? Miriam? Acheret?' Deborah knelt down beside the trembling mound. Trembling herself now, she reached out a hand and began to pull back the covers, slowly, gingerly: 'Miriam? Acheret?' Deborah saw the top of Acheret's head, and then her eyes, and screamed: 'Miriam!'

Acheret felt Deborah's body encircling her – warm, so warm – and her hands reaching around her, trying to peel away. But she couldn't move. Her body felt heavy. Frozen. Locked. And then, there were

---

14 Numbers 20:1-2 and 3-13.
15 The *haftarah* reading for the *Torah* portion, *B'shallach* which includes Miriam leading the women, is Judges, chapters 4 and 5, which tells the story of Deborah, a prophet and leader of the people.

more shadows and more voices and more hands. And she was stroked and cradled and unclenched and lifted up and carried away.

'Where is Miriam?' Moses faced Deborah squarely. 'Where is she? I want to see her. I must see her. She's my sister.'

'You will see her, Moses. The women are preparing her body.'

Moses didn't ask about Acheret. He wanted to. He couldn't. They had not spoken in years, not since Miriam's terrible outburst … As Moses turned away from Deborah, he stumbled – stiff, mute with grief. She reached out a hand to steady him.

'Where is Aaron?' She asked.

'In his tent. He wants to be alone.'

'Go to him. He needs you. You need each other.'

But Moses couldn't go to Aaron yet. He wandered around the camp. It was deserted. Where is everybody? He knew where the women were. But where were the men? Eventually, he stopped outside his brother's tent. It was so quiet and still. He put out his hand to pull back the flap, but it dropped loosely beside him. Moses stood there motionless. And then, he raised both hands and, slowly he began to pull at his clothes, and then to tear them, his nails catching in the course cloth, scratching his skin. His movements became faster, frenzied. He opened his mouth and heard himself gasp, 'Where are you? Mysterious One, where are you?!'

Sitting huddled in his tent, Aaron listened and wept.

As the sun began its steady descent and the mountains turned to flame, the entire camp gathered to bury Miriam. Acheret stood as best she could among the women, held up by Deborah and Rebecca. Moses and Aaron walked towards the lifeless form of their sister, shrouded in white, lying next to the open grave, and waited.

Seven women came forward. They lifted Miriam's shrouded body, and then lowered her gently into the emptiness. Acheret followed. At the edge of the grave, she knelt down amidst the sand and stones and began to gather handfuls which she, alternately, spilled over her head and over the body of her love.

The silence, thick with grief, began to break as the wind rose, moaning with the mourners, swirling the landscape into a dance of grit and dust. Deborah and Rebecca moved towards Acheret, and, gathering her up in their arms, drew her away. Slowly, one by one, the women came forward, and then the men. Each one, bending down to gather their own stony handfuls.

Finally, Aaron and Moses, the brothers of Miriam, knelt down, filling their hands also, until the burial place of Miriam had become one with the desert.

'We should mark the grave with a stone', Aaron whispered to his brother, 'by morning we won't know where it is.'

'No, Aaron', Moses responded, staring into the wilderness, 'tomorrow we will journey on, and we will never return.'

When they stood up again, Aaron spoke out loud for the first time that day. His voice sounded strange to him, strangled and sticky inside his mouth. Although he knew what he had to say, the words he spoke shocked him, making little sense: 'Tomorrow we will take up the camp and journey on.'

The people murmured in astonishment. The entire assembly looked up as one at the darkening sky, and then across the plain towards the centre of the camp. The cloud still covered the Tabernacle. The wind became stronger, carrying their murmurings into the night. But the cloud remained dense and still.

As night fell, the people, too, became still. Some standing, some sitting, some lying down in the dust, they encircled the grave in a mass of grief.

With the blue-grey light of dawn, the women began to dance – slowly, haphazardly, at first. And then, as the men stood back, making space for the wordless memorial, the dancing became more rhythmical – circle within circle within circle. And Acheret, too, rose and joined the dance – slow and mournful, around and around – until the sun rose, smothering their mourning in heat and light.

In the scorching heat, the murmurings of the people became more intense. We will not move on. We will observe the rites of mourning. Thirty days. They became angrier and angrier, and in the noonday sun their murmurings against Moses and Aaron became a huge howl of loss as they realised that, with Miriam's death, the well of water that had travelled with them for almost forty years, had dried up.

Soon, the howling mourners had become a mob, desperate with grief and thirst. 'Miriam has died, and now we will die too. Give us water! Give us water! Give us water!' The demand became a challenge as the people clamoured around Moses and Aaron.

The sister-less brothers took refuge at the door of the Tent of Meeting, where they fell on their faces and waited for the voice of the Eternal. Before long, Moses pulled his brother up: 'The Mysterious

One has spoken to me. We must assemble the people before the rock nearest to Miriam's grave, and take the rod which parted the waters – it will make water flow from the rock.'

As he looked into the mob, Aaron at his side, all Moses could see was one face. The face of Acheret – the 'other '… 'Miriam! Miriam! Miriam!'

Moses heard the insistent voices, and his heart pounded to their demand: Miriam! Miriam! Miriam!

Miriam! Help me, please. As he made his silent plea, Moses opened his mouth and emitted a sound so loud, the people became still: 'Hear now, you rebels, shall we bring you water out of this rock?'

Silence. Moses lifted his rod and struck the rock. He saw Miriam's face: why was she smiling? A little boy once more, all alone, wild with terror, he struck the rock again.

The water gushed and the exhausted mob drank, drowning their sorrow.

Why did Miriam Speak Out Against Moses?

Is that how it was? Who knows? I am offering a contemporary *aggadic midrash*, an interpretation of the narrative in Numbers chapter 20, which also links it with the narrative in Numbers chapter 12. So, what's the link? Let me remind you:[16]

> Miriam – and Aaron – spoke against Moses because of the Ethiopian woman whom he had married: for he had married an Ethiopian woman. / And they said, 'Has the Eternal indeed spoken only by Moses? Has He not spoken also to us?' And the Eternal heard it.

Most translations, simply, say: Miriam and Aaron spoke against Moses …

But the verb is in the feminine singular: *Va-t'dabbeir* – 'she spoke' – suggesting, that it was *Miriam*, who took the lead in the protest – and, the fact that she was the prime mover is underlined, when it is Miriam, not Aaron, who is punished - with temporary leprosy.[17]

So, why did Miriam feel moved to speak out against Moses? The text offers two reasons: because Moses had married an Ethiopian woman; and because Moses had an, apparently, exclusive relation-

16 Numbers 12:1-2
17 Num. 12:9

78

ship with the Eternal. Was the first reason a pretext for the second, more fundamental grievance? There is no doubt that Miriam, even more than Moses, had reason to be aggrieved by Moses' special relationship with the Eternal. After all, like Moses, she is called a prophet – *n'vi'ah* – while the *Torah* designates Aaron as the High Priest, responsible for conducting the sacred rites. But, interestingly, as if to emphasise the exceptional position of Moses, when the *Torah* mentions Miriam by name for the first time, after the rabble of ex-slaves passed through the Sea of Reeds on dry land, she is referred to as 'the sister of Aaron'. In a crucial sense, the two verses we find here, tell the reader everything we need to know about Miriam, her leadership, and her position vis-a-vis Moses. We read:[18]

> Now Miriam, the prophet, the sister of Aaron, took a timbrel in her hand; and all the women went out after her with timbrels and with dances. / Then Miriam sang to them: 'Sing to the Eternal, for He is highly exalted: both horse and rider He has thrown into the sea.'

Significantly, these two short verses appear after the much longer song, led by Moses.[19] The *p'shat*, the 'plain' meaning of the text is that Miriam is a prophet, but her leadership position is alongside Aaron, rather than as Moses' equal. After the congregation has sung, she leads the women in dances with timbrels. The leader of the women then? Yes, but actually, a *remez*, a small 'hint' suggests that she was, in fact, one of the leaders of the whole congregation. Not only does she echo, in brief, the congregation's song of triumph, she sings to the whole congregation. How do we know this? Because the text says: 'Then Miriam sang to *them*' – *la-hem* – masculine plural; not *la-hen* – feminine plural. The difference in the Hebrew is in just one consonant: *mem* – 'm' – instead of *nun* – 'n'. If Miriam had only sung to the women, the feminine form would have been used. The convention of the *Torah* is that unless a specific mention is made of the women, the masculine plural form indicates *both* men and women. So, while Miriam led the women in dances with timbrels, she, indeed, sang *la-hem*, 'to them' – to the whole congregation.

Clearly, Miriam was a leader of the Exodus. So, why does the *Torah*

---

18 Exodus 15:20-21.
19 Ex. 15:1-18.

say so little about her? Why, in the rest of the wilderness narrative, is she completely absent until the passage we find in Numbers chapter 12, in the fourth book of the *Torah*, which describes events in the second year of the wilderness wanderings?[20]

Interestingly, that passage relates the first of a series of rebellions, that are narrated in the next two portions of Numbers: the rebellion of the leaders of ten of the twelve tribes, sent out to reconnoitre the land beyond the river Jordan,[21] and the rebellion led by Korach, another member of the K'hat family, and a first cousin of the three sibling leaders.[22] It is as a result of the rebellion of the ten tribal leaders, that the congregation is condemned to wander in the wilderness for a total of forty years – one year for each of the forty days spent checking out the land.[23] And, intriguingly, it is after all three rebellions that the narrative of the wilderness wanderings goes silent – for thirty-eight years – only resuming once more, with the account of the death of Miriam and the clamouring for water.[24]

So, where does Miriam's rebellion fit in with this rebellious chain-reaction? Significantly, she is the first to speak out – and while the other rebels challenge both Moses and Aaron, Miriam speaks out against Moses, specifically. Like cousin Korach, and Datan, Aviram, and On, members of the tribe of R'u'vein, the firstborn of Jacob with Leah, that had been displaced by the tribe of Levi, Jacob and Leah's third born, Miriam had good reason to feel marginalised. Of course, Aaron, despite his special priestly role, may also have felt upstaged by Moses. But, when Miriam says, 'Has the Eternal indeed spoken only to Moses? Has He not spoken also to us?' (12:2), her grievance, as a prophet, is very particular and so the message she receives is also especially for her.

According to Numbers chapter 12 (:5-8), Miriam may be a prophet, like Moses, but Moses is an *exceptional* prophet, with whom God speaks, 'mouth to mouth'. So, Miriam is put firmly in her place – and by saying this, I am not simply rehearsing an over-used cliché: punished with a temporary dose of leprosy, rendering her ritually unclean, Miriam is excluded from the camp for seven days. But that

20 See Numbers 1:1
21 Num. ch. 13-15.
22 Num. ch. 16-18.
23 Num. 14:34.
24 Num. 20:1ff.

is not all. Miriam is not just a sister, as an unmarried woman, she is also, a daughter, subject to her father. And so, when Aaron and Moses plead with the Eternal on Miriam's behalf, the text has the Eternal reminding Moses of the patriarchal law concerning daughters: 'If her father spat in her face, should she not bear her shame for seven days? Let her be shut out from the camp seven days, and after that let her be received in again' (:14).

Miriam was put in her place – but only temporarily: 'the people did not journey on until Miriam was brought in again (:15). The people could not, would not, journey on without Miriam – and so it was for the remainder of their long sojourn in the wilderness.

But that's not the end of the matter. Uncomfortable with her unmarried status, the rabbis married Miriam off to Caleb,[25] who together with Joshua, did not join in the rebellion following the tribal leaders' reconnoitre of the land.[26] But there is no evidence that Miriam was married – which brings me back to the initial reason for her rebellion (:1):

Miriam – and Aaron – spoke against Moses because of the Ethiopian woman whom he had married: for he had married an Ethiopian woman.

Who was the Ethiopian woman? And why did Miriam – and to a lesser extent – Aaron protest against Moses' marriage to her?

Moses was already married, of course, to Tzipporah, the daughter of the priest of Midian, whom he had met, after killing a taskmaster

---

25 Caleb, son of Chetzron, fathered children by Azubah his wife, and Jerioth (I Chronicles 2:18). Azubah (lit., 'forsaken') is Miriam, whom all the young men forsook at first and would not marry because she was sickly (Rashi). She is also called y'ri'ot (lit., 'sheets') because her face was white as a sheet so sickly was she (Rashi). Two wives, Helah and Naarah (I Chronicles 4:5). Miriam was like two women, at first she was helah (lit.,' sickly') and finally she became na'arah (lit., 'young girl'). And the sons of Helah, Zohar (ibid. v. 7), her face became as radiant as the sun at noon (Sotah 12a). Azubah died, and Caleb married Ephrath (I Chronicles 2:18). Miriam, who is called both Azubah and Ephrath fell ill with leprosy and was treated as if dead. Caleb, too, left her. After she was healed, he remarried her and seated her in a palanquin for the wedding procession in his great rejoicing over her. Then the Holy One, Blessed is He, restored her youth, and she bore him children (Shemot Rabbah 1:17).

26 See Numbers 13:30 (Caleb); Num. 14:6-9 (Joshua and Caleb).

and fleeing Egypt, at the beginning of the Exodus story.[27] For the rabbis, the Ethiopian woman was Tzipporah.[28]

Meanwhile, some contemporary commentators, focussing on the fact that the Ethiopian woman was black, have made the point that Miriam was being racist, and was punished for her racism.[29]

Let me offer you an alternative interpretation.

Why Miriam Spoke Out Against Moses' Marriage to the 'Cushite Woman': Another Untold Story

Miriam felt lonely. She always felt different – was this why she felt lonely? And what made her so different? Her daring and courage? How many other sisters had saved their baby brothers from Pharaoh's decree? Was it, perhaps, her dreams? For as long as she could remember, Miriam had known that the day of liberation would arrive – and she had even seen the great river turned to blood, the frogs, the lice, the swarms of flies, the pestilence that would afflict the herds and flocks, the boils, the hail, the locusts that would eat every shred of vegetation, the suffocating darkness, the death of all the firstborn of Egypt. Miriam's friends had laughed at her. Her parents had cautioned her to keep quiet, saying: 'so you think you're a second Joseph?' They were anxious that she would bring disaster upon them. Even her brother Aaron, who had hardly left her side since Moses went to live with Pharaoh's daughter, had no patience to listen to her tales of a new life of freedom in the desert.

But that wasn't all that made Miriam different. As she got older, and her friends became preoccupied with the young men on the periphery of their lives, and became flirtatious whenever they encountered a male who wasn't a family member, Miriam knew that she wasn't like them. Astonished by their readiness to leave their

---

27 See Exodus 2:15-21; 4:24-26.

28 All the *midrashim* assume that the 'Cushite woman' was Tzipporah - see, for example, *Avot d'Rabbi Natan* 9:39; ARN, 43:122; *Sifre* Numbers, 99; *Talmud Mo'eid Katan* 17b, *Targum Y'rushalmi* on Numbers 12:12. *Targum Y'rushalmi* on Numbers 12:1-2, sees here an allusion to the 'queen of the Ethiopians, whom Moses was forced to marry while fleeing from Pharaoh' – which is a legend related by Josephus, the 1st century Jewish historian in his Antiquities, Volume II, pp.10-11. Louis Ginzberg discusses the legend in note 80 of the section on 'Moses' in Volume V of his *Legends of the Jews*, pp. 407-410.

29 If you Google Miriam's response to the Cushite woman, you will find scores of items, which regard Miriam as 'racist'.

homes to become a servant to a stranger and his family, all she wanted to do was go on living in the company of the women and girls she had known all her life, forever – and to become a wife, only if she too could find a wife.

Eventually, after most of her friends had already married, Miriam did find what she was looking for. By then, the desert wanderings had already begun, and the woman she had set her heart on was one of the 'mixed multitude' of slaves, who had made a dash to freedom with the Hebrews. Tall and beautiful, her skin shimmering like ebony, before they had even met, the unknown stranger had returned Miriam's gaze. From that moment on, even though they had not yet spoken, Miriam called her Acheret, 'other', convinced that, so different in the way she looked, she was also, like Miriam, different in another way – another kind of woman, who was also in search of a wife ....

What gave Miriam the courage to approach Acheret? In the end, it was simply that she could no longer stand the constant nagging of her parents and her brothers – forever trying to match her up with this man or that one. 'You are so choosy', her indulgent father would say, half exasperated, half laughing. 'Don't you know that before too long, you'll be unable to find anyone who is prepared to marry you', her mother would chide, 'Look at you! Soon you'll be too old to have children!' Miriam did look at herself and she looked at Acheret – also, still unmarried; and she decided.

For a few months, the two women met secretly under cover of darkness. But then, one night, Moses caught Miriam and Acheret at the edge of the camp, lying in each other's arms under the stars. At first, they didn't notice him – and he didn't take in what he was seeing. But then he heard his sister's laugh – such an unmistakable sound: 'Miriam? Is that you? Who are you with?' The two women tried lying perfectly still, hoping he would go away – but then, Miriam felt her brother's breath on her face, as he knelt down to examine the tangle of bodies on the ground. And then, it was over: 'What is this?' Ignoring Acheret, half-stumbling over her body, Moses grabbed Miriam, and pulled her up. Miriam tried to struggle out of her brother's grip. By the time, she had broken away, and could look around, Acheret was nowhere to be seen.

Where had Acheret gone? Tasked by Moses to watch his sister, day and night, Aaron did his job so well Miriam did not have a moment to look for her. And then, out of nowhere, the shocking announcement, one morning, as the family sat at breakfast: 'I've decided to take another wife – the Ethiopian woman. We will marry tomorrow night.' 'Why, Moses?' his mother asked; 'Tzipporah is such a good wife to you.' 'Why, Moses?' his father echoed; 'one wife has always been enough for me.' Aaron, usually so ready with words, knowing full well, 'why', looked down at his feet. Taking her opportunity, Miriam fled outside.

But she didn't find Acheret. Moses had made sure that his sister wouldn't have a chance to get to his new wife-to-be – at least before the wedding. All that day and the next, concealing herself behind rocks at the edge of the camp, Miriam raged. Then, as the sun began to set on the second day, realising that the wedding was imminent, Miriam stole back to the camp – and just caught a glimpse of Acheret, as Moses led her into his tent.

But before she could retreat once more, Aaron stood before her: 'Miriam, I'm sorry, but what's done is done.' She pushed past him into the night. 'So, our baby brother is able to do whatever he likes', she hissed, when he caught up with her. 'No, of course not …' Aaron's voice trailed off. 'Well, I've had enough', Miriam continued: 'What would Moses do without you speaking for him and dealing with the people. And what would he do without me? He wouldn't even be here if it wasn't for me!' I'm going to get some rest now – but tomorrow, I'm going to tell him what I think!' Will you join me?'

So (Numbers 12:1-2):

> Miriam – and Aaron – spoke against Moses because of the Ethiopian woman whom he had married: for he had married an Ethiopian woman. / And they said, 'Has the Eternal indeed spoken only by Moses? Has He not spoken also to us?' And the Eternal heard it.

Another Chapter in the Untold Story

You think this is a tall story? Perhaps you should take a look at what the rabbis made of the *Torah* narratives and the tales they told to make sense of the sacred text. But, yes, this is one story they could never have come up with. The sages spoke out of their experience, I speak out of mine. And yet, heir to their legacy, I am engaged in the same process – the process of exegesis, 'reading out' from the text.

84

My *midrashim*, like theirs, are also rooted in the *Torah*. But that is, actually, not the main point. We cannot change the *Torah*. We cannot change millennia of patriarchal history, but we can find ways of enabling the *Torah* to speak to us today. By taking the trouble to wrest new meanings out of the *Torah* narratives about Miriam, I am creating an opportunity for lesbian and gay Jews to engage with a tradition that seems to exclude them. By troubling the *Torah* to speak with new voices, I am also trying to model how readers of today might create a bridge between their experience and experience of our ancestors. Not content to accept the *Torah* as it is, or the traditions of interpretation as they are, I am engaged in generating a *living* Judaism; a Judaism that lives in and through our lives, by relating to, and reflecting our lives, just as the rabbis did before us.

Finally, what about those thirty-eight lost years? The *Torah* is silent, allowing the reader to be as inventive as she or he likes. And so, taking up where I left off:

Acheret didn't stay with Moses. Gradually, first Miriam, and then Acheret, began to speak with the other women, who were, after all, their friends. As a result, not only did the women begin to accept their relationship, but some of them, emboldened by Miriam and Acheret's example, also found love with one another. With the passing years, as more and more partnerships between women – and then, between men – emerged, the community in the desert became more inclusive. They remembered that when their parents and grandparents and great grandparents came out of Egypt, they created a community in the inhospitable wilderness by bringing their varied gifts together, by contributing in their own ways, as their hearts moved them.[30] Sadly, Moses could never bring himself to speak to Acheret again, and he ignored Miriam as much as was decent, given that she was his elder sister. But while the breach of trust between them was never fully repaired, the community in the desert managed to function, nonetheless. As the people clamoured in their grief against Moses and Aaron, Miriam's death certainly threatened the hard-won stability, but the moment of danger passed, and, in any event, by then the wilderness wanderings were drawing to a close.

I sense voices of protest. Surely, this is *isegesis*, 'reading in', rather than *exegesis*, 'reading out' – to the level of absurdity? What can

---

30 See Exodus 25:1-8 – and my *midrash* on this text in Ch.11.

possibly justify making sense of the missing *Torah* narrative through the lens of the concerns and values of the early 21st century? Well, there is no text to read out from for a start ... so, yes, this is isegesis – 'reading in', from my perspective, pure and simple – in order to connect the two *midrashim*, and to get readers thinking that, yes, there were women, who loved women, and men, who loved men, back then, too. And they may even have got married. As it happens, the rabbis were aware of the possibility,[31] although, of course, they disapproved – and, of course, as far as they were concerned, that kind of thing only happened among non-Jews ....

So, Miriam, the prophet, the sister of Aaron and Moses was, together with her brothers, a leader of her people, who sustained them through their wilderness wanderings. And: 'unmarried' Miriam, the wife of Acheret – an inspiration to all the women.

What do you make of Miriam – and of those lost years? How would you fill the gaps and tell her story?

31 See *Sifra* on Leviticus 18:20 – explored in Ch. 7

CHAPTER THREE

B'ruria: A Suitable Case for Mistreatment

B'ruria is the only woman whose learned teachings are recorded in rabbinic literature, as if she too, had been part of the scholarly debates.[1] She is an anomaly, a token, an exceptional case which proves the rule. I am going to examine the exceptional case of B'ruria with the aim not only of recovering what she said, but more importantly, of exploring why her 'sayings' do not form part of our inheritance as Jews, and why we have not got the 'sayings' of our mothers.

I shall begin, not with B'ruria, but with *Pirkey Avot*, the 'Sayings of the Sages' or rather to be more precise: 'The Chapters of the Fathers', whose legal debates and decisions over more than 200 years constitute the *Mishnah*, the first post-biblical code of Jewish law, edited around the end of the 2nd century. *Pirkey Avot* is a sort of appendix to the *Mishnah*, a 'Who's Who' which sets out the 'generations' responsible for transmitting *Torah* (God's teaching), and records their philosophical attitudes. The 'authority' of the generations of fathers is established in the first chapter, which opens by tracing the chain of tradition back to Moses, and then sets out the line of transmission

---

1 There are other women who are included in the *Talmud*. In particular, Imma Shalom and Yalta – both of whom were very well-connected. Imma Shalom, born c. 50 CE, is identified as the wife of Eliezer ben Hyrcanus, head of the Academy at Lydda and sister of Gamaliel II, the Nasi, the head of the *Sanhedrin*. She was brought up by her brother, and is sometimes cited as his daughter - *Sanhedrin* 39a and 90b. See *Written Out of History: Our Jewish Foremothers* by Sandra Henry and Emily Taitz. (Biblio Press, New York, 1983) as an early example of Jewish feminist retrieval of our foremothers. Their chapter on 'Daughters of the Law', also includes, B'ruria. Since that landmark publication, there has been much more research, and the establishment of the Jewish Women's Archive has also made this research available to a wide audience. See http://jwa.org/encyclopedia/article/yalta for a short article by Judy Hauptman on Yalta, identified as the wife of Rabbi Nachman, c. 250 CE. Yalta is mentioned a few times in the Babylonian *Talmud*. The most telling reference to her concerns the story that she broke four hundred jugs of wine when slighted by a guest, who made barbed comments directed at her – and women in general (*Talmud B'rachot* 51b).

through to the period of the early rabbis responsible for the survival of Jewish learning in the aftermath of the destruction of the Second Temple in the year 70 CE. The actual chronology of the period up to the turn of the era is uncertain and there are huge gaps, but this is beside the point: the whole aim of the exercise is, simply to establish the 'authority' of the 'fathers' as links in the chain of tradition, as 'receivers' and 'transmitters' of the *Torah* which 'Moses received from Sinai'.

Before we go on to investigate the 'sayings' of our mother, B'ruria, it is important for us to be clear that we are not engaged in the first stage of some sort of 'anthologising' exercise with a view to eventually collecting and distributing the 'Sayings of the Mothers' as a handy companion to *Pirkey Avot*. *Pirkey Avot* is much more than an anthology put together by an enterprising editor, well-versed in the wise adages of the sages. It is a statement, a statement of the reality of the 'chain of tradition' as a chain of *men*, formed by the relationships between 'teachers' and 'pupils', from Moses onwards. Traditionally studied on *Shabbat* afternoon, *Pirkey Avot* is a brilliant, sometimes inspiring, collection of rabbinic wisdom, providing the reader and student with insight into their concerns and values. It also includes a host of valuable teachings – three of which I have drawn on in this book.[2] Nevertheless, *Pirkey Avot* also establishes the authority of the 'fathers' with one simple message: the transmission of *Torah* is quite literally in their hands.

So where were the mothers? What were the vast majority of women doing while the 'fathers' busied themselves with the task of receiving and shaping and handing on the tradition? The combined scholarship of the *Mishnah* and the *G'mara* gives us some clues. In tractate *B'rachot* (17a), we read:

> "Rav said to Rabbi Hiyya: 'With what do women earn merit? By making their sons go to the House of Assembly to learn scripture, and their husbands to the House of Study to learn *Mishnah*, and waiting for their husbands until they return from the House of Study.'"

---

2 Indeed, I have explored one of the sayings in *Pirkey Avot*, in different contexts several times – namely: 'The world stands on justice, truth and peace' (1:18). See chapters 10, 13, 14 and 15.

Rabbi Hiyya belonged to the last generation of *tanna'im* - 'teachers', whose teachings were edited into the *Mishnah*, and whose 'sayings' were recorded in *Pirkey Avot*. Rabbi Hiyya's pupil, Rav, who died in 247 CE, was one of the leading scholars of the first generation of *amora'im*, literally 'speakers', who gave themselves the task of clarifying the *Mishnah*. The simple expression, 'Rav said to Rabbi Hiyya', makes us aware of the extent to which the *Mishnah* and its *amoraic* commentary (the *G'mara*),[3] reflect the conversations, the debates, between study partners and colleagues, between pupils and their teachers: Rabbi Hiyya is Rav's 'teacher', and Rav 'speaks' back to him, adding his own understanding to the tradition, indeed establishing his own authority to continue the process of transmitting *Torah* after the *Mishnah*.

When Rav 'speaks' to his teacher, he asserts his obligation, and also his right, to go to the House of Study, *Beit Ha-Midrash*, and learn the *Mishnah*. But what else does he say? He makes it clear that the House of Study is a male preserve. Study of the tradition is for boys and men, but not for women. Women occupy another sphere, the private sphere of the home, where as 'mothers' and 'wives' they 'earn merit' by ensuring that their sons and husbands get together in the synagogues and study houses to learn, while they 'wait' for them at home.

Rav's comment reflects his understanding of the separate spheres and roles assigned to men and women. The *halachic*, legal, arguments for the exemption of women from the study of *Torah*, are given elsewhere, in tractate *Kiddushin* (29a;b). Commenting on a *mishnah* which begins, 'All the obligations of the son upon the father, men are bound, but women are exempt', Rav Judah (ben Ezekiel), a second generation *amora*, and a pupil of Rav, explains (29a):

'All obligations of the son' [that is, those] which lie 'upon the father' to do to his son, 'men are bound, but women are exempt'.

---

3 The *Talmud* consists of the *Mishnah*, the work of the *tannai'm*, edited by Judah ha-Nasi, 'the Prince', the leading sage of his day, around 200 CE, and the *G'mara*, the work of the *amora'im*, the sages, who expounded the *Mishnah*. The *amora'im*, who remained in the land of Israel, completed the *Y'rushalmi* – the Jerusalem *Talmud* – c. 400 CE – the *amorai'm* in Babylon (present day, Iraq) – completed the much longer *Bavli* – the Babylonian *Talmud* – c. 500 CE.

One of the obligations of a father towards his son, from which a mother is exempt, is 'to teach him *Torah*'. The *G'mara* explores the implications of the obligation of a father and the exemption of a mother as follows (*Kiddushin* 29b):

> 'To teach him *Torah*.' How do we know it? Because it is written: 'And you shall teach them to your sons'.[4] And if his father did not teach him, he must teach himself, for it is written, 'and you shall study'.[5] How do we know that she has no duty [to teach her children]? Because it is written, 'and you shall teach', [which also reads] 'you shall study': whoever is commanded to study is commanded to teach; whoever is not commanded to study is not commanded to teach. And how do we know that she is not obliged to teach herself? Because it is written 'and you shall teach' – 'and you shall learn'. The one whom others are commanded to teach is commanded to teach to oneself; and the one whom others are not commanded to teach, is not commanded to teach oneself. How then do we know that others are not commanded to teach her? Because it is written: 'And you shall teach them to your sons' – but not your daughters.

This complicated piece of *Talmudic* argumentation reinforces a very simple principle. As Rachel Biale puts it:

> Men in every generation are within the cycle of learning and teaching. Women are always outside it … Only in regard to men do we have a biblical verse which commands others to teach them: 'And you shall teach them to your sons'. There is no commandment to teach the law to our daughters. Women do not have to be taught, and therefore do not have to teach themselves and do not have to teach others. They remain outside the bond of teaching which connects father to son in every generation.[6]

And of course the male bond of teaching which connects the generations is not simply a biological bond – which brings us back to the passage from tractate *B'rachot* (17a): the fathers who teach their sons, and the sons who learn from their fathers, leave the home – the

---

4 Deuteronomy 1.19.
5 Deut. 5.1.
6 Rachel Biale, *Women and Jewish Law*, Schocken Books, New York 1984, pp. 32-3.

sphere of the wives and mothers – and go off to the synagogue and to the study house to participate in the cycle of learning with other fathers and sons. And so the *Torah* is 'received' by males and 'transmitted' to males from generation to generation.

It is in this context that we encounter B'ruria in the pages of rabbinic literature: B'ruria, the only woman included, as a scholar in her own right, in the record of male scholarly discourse; B'ruria, the daughter of Rabbi Chananya ben Teradion, a third generation *tanna* (teacher), who together with his more famous colleague Rabbi Akiva was put to death by the Romans following the unsuccessful 'Bar Kochba' revolt of 135 CE; B'ruria, the wife of Rabbi Meir, a disciple of Rabbi Akiva, whose collection of *halachah*, legal decisions, formed the basis of the *Mishnah*;[7] B'ruria, the daughter and wife of men who had a place in the network of relationships through which Jewish teaching was developed and transmitted. Did B'ruria have a place too? Rabbinic literature designates B'ruria as the daughter and wife of scholars, but makes no mention of her teachers and pupils. So how did she learn? And how is it that her teachings were recorded? Rachel Adler suggests that B'ruria was a 'replacement for a worthless son' who neither learned nor taught well, and who came to a bad end.[8] That's how she managed to get herself included: B'ruria 'stood in' for her brother.

Evidence for this explanation can be found in one of the earliest texts in which B'ruria's teaching is recorded – in the *Tosefta*, the collection of *tannaitic* teachings which were not included in the *Mishnah*.[9] In the tractate *Kelim Bava Kama*, in a paragraph dealing with the questions concerning at which point an oven becomes ritually impure (4.17), we learn that the answer of the 'daughter' of Chananya ben Teradion is 'better' than the answer of his 'son':

---

7 See David Goodblatt, 'The B'ruria Traditions' in William Scott Green, ed., *Persons and Institutions in Early Rabbinic Judaism*, Scholars Press, Missoula, Montana 1977, 207-35, for an account of B'ruria's 'family connections'. See *Sifre* Deuteronomy 307 for the responses of Chananya ben Teradion's wife and daughter to his execution.

8 Rachel Adler, 'The Virgin in the Brothel and other Anomalies. Character and Context in the Legend of B'ruria' *Tikkun* 3.6, 1989, 28-32, 102-5.

9 These two references are both cited by Roslyn Lacks, *Women and Judaism, Myth, History and Struggle*, (Doubleday, New York 1980), 129n.

When they put these words before Rabbi Y'hudah bar Bava, he said: 'His daughter speaks better than his son'.

Y'hudah bar Bava was a colleague of Rabbi Akiva, and shared his fate, and that of Chananya ben Teradion, when the Romans quashed the 'Bar Kochba' revolt. But more importantly, he played a crucial role in ensuring the maintenance of the chain of Jewish learning at this time, by ordaining Rabbi Meir and Meir's colleagues, in secret, before his execution – which is what makes his comment in the passage from the *Tosefta* I have quoted quite significant. It is as if Y'hudah bar Bava, who took it upon himself to ensure the continuation of rabbinic leadership, also assumed the task of determining which of Chananya ben Teradion's children, his son, or his daughter, was worthy to succeed him.

Of course, the issue would never have come up if B'ruria's brother had not been such a bad sort. In the *Talmud*, tractate *S'machot*, which focuses on the laws of death and mourning, we read (49b):

It is related of the son of Rabbi Chananya ben Teradion that he took to evil ways and robbers seized and killed him. After three days his swollen body was found; they placed him in a coffin, set him on a bier, took him into the city and paid him a eulogy out of respect for his father and mother.

The text goes on to quote the verses from the Book of Proverbs, with which the father and mother of the no-good son expressed their disappointment, ending with B'ruria's testimony:

'Bread of falsehood is sweet to a man; but afterwards his mouth shall be filled with gravel.' [10]

According to a parallel account of B'ruria's brother's death in *Eichah Rabbah*, a collection of *midrashim* on the Book of Lamentations [11] – the son of Chananya ben Teradion 'became associated with a band of robbers whose secret he disclosed, so they killed him and filled his mouth with dust and gravel'. Since this *midrash* is commenting on the verse, 'He has broken my teeth with gravel', [12] it is not surprising

---

10 Comment on Proverbs 20.17.
11 III:6. *Eichah Rabbah* was compiled around the same time as the *Talmud* (400-500 CE).
12 Lamentations 3.16.

that it tells us that the no-good son had his mouth filled with the gritty stuff, and of course, B'ruria's quotation from Proverbs fits well in this context. But what is more important from the perspective of understanding B'ruria's status in rabbinic literature as a 'substitute' for her worthless brother is that because his mouth was filled with 'dust and gravel' – because he had nothing worthwhile to contribute to the scholarly discourse – she assumed the 'right' to speak words of wisdom in his place.

Having explored how the texts seem to provide a rationale for B'ruria's exceptional status, we now have to examine the implications of her singular position. B'ruria may have engaged in scholarship in his place, but she certainly did not take up his 'place' in the study house, and become involved in the collegial relationships which went with it. This becomes evident when we explore her teachings. While the teachings of the rabbis are usually presented in the rabbinic texts as part of a debate or an exchange between two or more scholars, B'ruria's scholarly options are either presented on their own, albeit in a context in which other opinions are also recorded, or as a dialogue with her husband Rabbi Meir.

In the *Tosefta*, there is one other text in which her view is recorded. In a section concerned with the question of which 'vessels' are susceptible to ritual impurity, there is a discussion about a door bolt:

A door bolt: Rabbi Tarfon [says it is susceptible to] unclean-ness, while the sages declared it clean; and B'ruria said: '[Detach it and] drag it from this door and hang it on another [door] on *Shabbat'*. When they put [these] words before Rabbi Y'hudah, he said: 'B'ruria spoke well'.[13]

Rabbi Tarfon, a third generation *tanna* of B'ruria's father's generation, takes the view that a door bolt is unclean; but this is not the view that was accepted by the majority of the scholars. The sages say it is 'clean' and this consequently became the *halachah*. B'ruria's opinion is in accord with that of the sages, but more than this, she provides an explanation for their view: B'ruria does not consider the door bolt to be a complete vessel, therefore it cannot be carried on *Shabbat*; it can be 'dragged along', but not carried and hung on another door on *Shabbat*; therefore it is not susceptible to the laws

---

13 *Kelim Bava Metziah* 1.6.

of purity (which only affect complete vessels). Rabbi Y'hudah (bar Bava), who commended B'ruria's opinion in preference to those of her brother in the other *Tosefta* passage, again adds his authority to her words. On this occasion, not because she has spoken 'better', but because she has provided a rationale for the majority view which has been transmitted, and perhaps is therefore the crucial link of teaching between the generation of scholars slaughtered by the Romans and the generation of Rabbi Meir and his colleagues, ordained by Rabbi Y'hudah before his own death at Roman hands.

But if this looks like startling evidence of B'ruria's place in the chain of tradition, look again. B'ruria's teaching is recorded in the *Tosefta*. A parallel passage in the *Mishnah* makes no mention of her – indeed, her teaching in given in the name of another scholar two generations earlier, Rabbi Y'hoshua ben Chananya.[14] And of course, B'ruria has disappeared from the debate.

What are we to make of this? Did the editors of the *Mishnah* simply find an older source for B'ruria's view – the 'original' source perhaps? Because Rabbi Y'hoshua is a second generation *tanna*, and Rabbi Tarfon belonged to the third generation, Rabbi Y'hoshua's view carried greater authority. Is this also significant? Rabbi Y'hoshua was a teacher of Rabbi Akiva, who in turn was a teacher of Rabbi Meir – B'ruria's husband. Does the *Mishnah* text tell us something about how B'ruria 'acquired' her teaching without having an official place in the chain of transmission? Did she learn her teaching from Rabbi Meir? But perhaps an even more radical interpretation is in order. Perhaps B'ruria's explanation of the majority view of the sages as we find it in the *Tosefta* passage was her view. Perhaps the attribution to Rabbi Y'hoshua is an attempt to strike this anomaly off the record, and find a more appropriate 'spokesman' for the sages? We don't know.

Rabbi Meir probably provided B'ruria with her source of contact with the teachings of the *tanna'im*. He was perhaps her 'unofficial' teacher. But if this was the case, it is interesting that the two examples recorded of their dialogue with one another, it is B'ruria who does the teaching. We read in tractate *B'rachot* (10a):

There were some 'highwaymen' in the neighbourhood of Rabbi

---

14 *Mishnah Kelim* 11.4.

Meir who caused him a great deal of trouble. Rabbi Meir accordingly prayed that they should die. His wife B'ruria said to him: 'How do you make out [that such a prayer should be permitted]? Because it is written, let "sins" cease? Is it written "sinners"? It is written "sins".[15] Further, look at the end of the verse: "and let the wicked men be no more". Since the sins will cease, there will be no more wicked men! Rather pray for them that they should repent, and they will be wicked no more.' He did pray for them, and they repented.

B'ruria adopts a line of interpretation much more in keeping with the prevailing rabbinic notion of 'sin' and 'repentance', of sinners 'turning' away from their wrong-doing, than it is evident in the response of her husband. But what is more important, Rabbi Meir accepts her teaching and changes his attitude.

It is important to note that this passage, in common with the other passages from the *Talmud* that record B'ruria's teaching, was edited several generations after the time when B'ruria lived, indeed over three hundred years later. This is significant, because it tells us about the preservation of her scholarship by the *amora'im*, the interpreters of the teachings of the *tanna'im*. Somehow, B'ruria's words were passed down, although she herself was not part of the chain of transmission.

B'ruria's discourse with her husband in *B'rachot* 10a is followed by another passage, which makes us particularly aware of this curious paradox, for two reasons. First, in marked contrast to the dialogue with Rabbi Meir, B'ruria is presented as a scholar on her own, answering a question put to her by an 'outsider' to rabbinic discourse; second, the account of the encounter between B'ruria and the 'outsider' is followed by a similar encounter between Rabbi Abahu, a third generation Palestinian *amora*, and another 'outsider'. B'ruria has no colleagues with whom she can debate, and at the same time, her teaching is edited together with that of a well-known *amora* who taught more than 150 years after her death. This is how the text presents B'ruria's teaching:

---

15 In Hebrew, the consonants of the words 'sins' and 'sinners' are the same; the vowels determine how the words may be read.

A 'heretic' said to B'ruria: 'It is written: "Sing, O barren one, you that did not bear".[16] Because she did not bear is she to sing? [B'ruria] replied to him: 'You fool! Look at the end of the verse, where it is written: "for the children of the desolate shall be more than the children of the married wife, says the Eternal." But what then is the meaning of "O barren that did not bear"? Sing O community of Israel, who resembles a barren woman, for not having borne children like you for G'henna.'

The questioner is addressing the problem of a verse in Isaiah which suggests that the barren woman should 'sing'. How can this be? B'ruria resolves the problem by reading the end of the verse, which she seems to interpret to mean that, in the future, 'the children of the desolate', that is the vanquished Jews, will be more than their Roman oppressors. In this context, she explains why the 'barren' sing: while the 'hell' of persecution persists, the community of Israel may well rejoice in the fact that it has not produced offspring to be slaughtered.

As in her dialogue with Rabbi Meir, B'ruria's exegetical approach, her method of interpreting scripture, involves reading 'the end of the verse'. Anne Goldfeld suggests that since looking at the end of the verse 'became an exegetical rule current among later sages of the *Talmud*, [t]he sages, therefore, must have looked with favour upon [B'ruria's] skills and methodology'.[17] Does this account for why B'ruria's teachings were preserved by the *amora'im*? Is it possible that, although she wasn't a teacher in the sense of having disciples of her own, whom she 'taught', B'ruria, nevertheless, did function as a 'teacher' for subsequent generations of scholars?

Again and again, we come back to the problem of how we make sense of B'ruria's relationship with the scholars of her generation. There is little doubt that she had no named 'teachers' and no named 'pupils', but surely she must have entered into discourse with some scholars apart from her husband? A short text in tractate *Eruvin* (53b-54a) provides us with ambiguous information which heightens our curiosity. We read:

---

16 Isaiah 53.1.
17 Anne Goldfeld, *Women as Sources of Torah in the Rabbinic Tradition*, (Schocken Books, New York 1976), 264.

B'ruria once discovered a student who was learning in an under-tone. Rebuking him, she exclaimed: 'Is it not written, "ordered in all things and sure".[18] If it is "ordered" in your 248 limbs it will be "sure", otherwise it will not be "sure".'

Who is this (anonymous) student? Was he a student of B'ruria? Where did she 'discover' him? Surely, not in the study house? Perhaps, in her home? Was he a student of Rabbi Meir? We don't know. Nevertheless, the text does make it clear that even if the student was not B'ruria's in an official sense, she did take up the role of 'teacher' towards him. By a clever interpretation of King David's last words, she teaches him that his learning will only become sure if he articulates clearly, using his 'limbs' – that is, his organs of speech.

A discernible pattern emerges from all the *Talmudic* passages in which B'ruria's teachings are recorded. She is clearly teaching in a direct sense, and the texts make no bones about the 'authority' of the teacher. She instructs Rabbi Meir in the appropriate attitude to take towards those who sin. She lets the heretic know how the text of scripture should be interpreted. She tells the student how to learn. And in all these different contexts, she makes use of her skill in scrip-tural exegesis, revealing her profound knowledge of biblical texts and her subtle understanding of language.

While in the *Tosefta* passages, the authority of B'ruria's teaching derives from the commendation of her words by Rabbi Y'hudah bar Bava, in the later passages included in the *G'mara*, B'ruria's author-ity seems to be quite simply self-evident – which says something about the attitude of the *amora'im* towards her. A specific reference to this attitude is made in tractate *Pesachim* (62b). We read:

Rabbi Simlai came before Rabbi Yochanan [and] requested him: 'Let the Master teach me the Book of Genealogies' ... 'Let us learn it in three months,' [Rabbi Simlai] proposed. [Thereupon Rabbi Yochanan] took a clod and threw it at him, saying: 'If B'ruria, wife of Rabbi Meir [and] daughter of Rabbi Chananya ben Teradion, who studied three hundred laws from three hundred teachers in [one] day, could nevertheless not fulfil her obligation in three years, how do you propose [to do it] in three months!'

18 II Samuel 23.5.

Rabbi Simlai was a first-generation *amora*, who came from Lydda [Lod] in southern Palestine, and went to study in the famous academy of Nehardea in Babylonia. Rabbi Yochanan gives force to his disdain of Rabbi Simlai by holding up the unparalleled scholarly example of B'ruria in a way which begs many questions. Is he suggesting that B'ruria had, if not 300, then at least, several 'teachers'? Or is he, perhaps, referring to all the scholars up to and including B'ruria's time as her 'teachers'? Furthermore, is he intimating that when B'ruria studied '300 laws a day', she was attempting 'to fulfil her obligation' to study the commandments? Rabbi Yochanan makes use of the technical expression designated by the rabbis to express the legal obligation to fulfil commandments – *chiyyuv*. And yet, as we saw earlier, the rabbis exempted women from the obligation of study. Interestingly, the Soncino translation of the *Talmud* attempts to get round the 'problem' of Rabbi Yochanan's reference to B'ruria's 'obligation' by suggesting that we read 'study it adequately' in place of 'fulfil her obligation'. But the 'problem' remains. Did the rabbis of B'ruria's generation and thereafter treat her as an exception to the rule exempting women from study? And how are we to read Rabbi Yohanan's flamboyant reference to B'ruria's scholarly ability? Is he holding her up as an exemplary scholar, or as a *woman*, who was an exemplary scholar?

B'ruria may have been an exception to the rule exempting women from study. She may have taken the obligation upon herself, and her scholarly ability may have earned her the right to do so in the eyes of sages, but that did not mean that she had a place in the study house and that she was able to study with, debate with, the male scholars of her time. The evidence for this comes not only from the fact that she had no teachers and no pupils – note that Rabbi Yochanan refers to B'ruria as 'the wife of Rabbi Meir', 'the daughter of Rabbi Chananiah ben Teradion', but from B'ruria's own wry comment, recorded in tractate *Erurvin* 53b. We read:

> Rabbi Yosei the Galilean was once on a journey when he met B'ruria. 'By what road,' he asked her, 'do we go to Lydda?' 'Foolish Galilean,' she replied, 'did not the sages say this: "Engage not in much talk with women". You should have asked: "By which to Lydda"?'

Clearly, B'ruria is parodying the sages' negative attitude towards too 'much' talk between men and women, which we find recorded in *Pirkey Avot* (5.1) as follows:

> ... the sages have said: 'Anyone who talks much to a woman causes evil to himself, and desists from words of *Torah*, and his end is that he inherits G'hinnom.'

When B'ruria speaks the words of the sages back at this 'sage', she is laughing at him. We can only guess at the freight of anger that lay behind her words. Because of what 'the sages' said, B'ruria was barred from entering into discourse with the scholars of her generation, lest she might lead them astray and keep them from their studies. Because of what the sages said, she studied at home. Of course, she was 'lucky'. Her husband, Rabbi Meir, was happy to study with her; she stumbled over the occasional 'student' whom she could instruct; and an important scholar of her father's generation, Y'hudah bar Bava, commended her words. But if her comment to Yosei the Galilean is anything to go by, she was all too aware of her position as a woman in a male-dominated world.

B'ruria was an exceptional woman, certainly, but still a woman, occupying a woman's place. This is perhaps most poignantly obvious in the reference to B'ruria most frequently quoted, which is included in the *midrash* on the Book of Proverbs.[19] We read (31.1):

> When two of their sons died on *Shabbat*, B'ruria did not inform Meir of their children's death upon his return from the Academy in order not to grieve him on *Shabbat*! Only after the *havdalah* prayer[20] did she broach the matter, saying, 'Some time ago a certain man came and left something in my trust, now he has called for it. Shall I return it to him or not?' Naturally, Meir replied the affirmative, whereupon B'ruria showed him their dead children. When Meir began to weep, she asked: 'Did you not tell

---

19 The *Midrash* on Proverbs was compiled sometime between the middle of the 7th and the beginning of the 10th centuries.

20 *Havdalah* is the ritual, which makes a 'distinction' (from the Hebrew root *Beit Dalet Lamed* to 'distinguish') between the Sabbath and the ordinary days of the week. The Sabbath, a day of joy, should not be a time of grief – and indeed, traditional mourning rites are suspended on the Sabbath. And so, B'ruria waited until after the Sabbath had ended before making her husband aware of the death of their two sons.

me that we must give back what is given on trust? "The Eternal gave, and the Eternal has taken away."'

The *midrash* relates that while Rabbi Meir was at the academy studying with his colleagues, B'ruria waited for him at home. While she waited, their two young sons died, and she gathered all of her resources together to face the tragedy, and to help her husband face it. Here she is the mother, the wife, the biblical interpreter and scholar all in one – on the home ground. This is the only text that mentions the physical context in which B'ruria studied and taught, and it serves to remind us that, although B'ruria may have been a lone exception to the rule that exempted women from study (*Kiddushin* 29b), the custom which ensured that 'a woman's place' was in the home, 'waiting' for her husband (*B'rachot* 17a), applied to her as much as it did to all the other wives and mothers.

I could end it here, with the image of B'ruria as the daughter of.../wife of.../mother of .../home-bound teacher and scholar ... and make a few pertinent comments about the isolation of a lone intellectual woman in a world in which the roles and spheres of men and women were so clearly delineated and separate, but the 'story' of B'ruria doesn't end here. It closes instead with B'ruria's downfall – with a tale of sex scandal put about in mediaeval times and stated 'authoritatively' by Rashi, the great 11th century Biblical and *Talmudic* commentator.

The occasion for the story is the mysterious account of Rabbi Meir's disappearance recorded in the tractate *Avodah Zarah* (18a-b), which begins with B'ruria asking her husband to try and get her sister out of a brothel. What was her sister doing in a brothel? A passage in tractate *S'machot* (47b) relates that 'the Romans sentenced Chananya ben Teradion to be burnt, and his wife to be executed, and consigned his daughter to a brothel'. In the passage in *Avodah Zarah*, B'ruria – who perhaps escaped persecution because she no longer lived with her family – is determined to free her sister.

So Rabbi Meir sets out on his mission. Disguised as a 'customer', he finds his sister-in-law, and decides to test her virtue. Claiming that she is menstruating, she refuses his attentions, and he buys her freedom from her warder. But then the government learn of what Rabbi Meir has done, and they try to find him. One day they catch sight of him, chase after him, and he takes refuge in a brothel –

presumably not the one in which his sister-in-law was held captive. The story is all a bit far-fetched, and, not surprisingly, the text supplies numerous explanations of Rabbi Meir's second visit to the brothel. The account then closes with Rabbi Meir's flight to Babylon, annotated by the following cryptic comments:

> Some say it was because of that incident that he ran to Babylon. Others say it was because of the incident about B'ruria.

So what was 'the incident about B'ruria'? That was the question which exercised the scandal-mongers, and provided an opportunity to defame the memory of this exceptional woman. The story in *Avodah Zarah* is one attempt to provide one explanation for Rabbi Meir's disappearance; the mediaeval commentators, attempting to flesh out 'the incident about B'ruria', offered another. Rashi, who himself had two scholarly daughters and should have known better, wrote:

> At one time [B'ruria] scoffed concerning what the sages said [about] 'women [being] light-headed.'[21] And [Meir] said to her: 'The end of your life might yet testify to their words.' Then he commanded one of his students to test her, to seduce her. And [the student] urged her many days until she yielded. And when she realised [what had happened], she killed herself, and Rabbi Meir fled from the disgrace.

What is this? Did Rabbi Yosei the Galilean, insulted by B'ruria's mockery of him, gossip about the way in which she had ridiculed the sages' words? Or perhaps, B'ruria did indeed 'scoff' about the sages' attitudes to women in the presence of her husband. But can we believe that he would respond as the story says he did – even if he didn't extend his respect for her to include other women – notably her sister? The story completely betrays their relationship, with a message which is clear and unequivocal: B'ruria was 'only a woman' – and Meir was just like any other contemptuous husband, after all.

To make sense of the vicious tale, we have to understand what B'ruria represented to male students of rabbinic literature. Faced with the reality of B'ruria, the brilliant scholar, those who inherited her along with their sacred texts had two choices: they could either

---

21 *Kiddushin* 80b.

revise their views of women or they could find a way of proving that B'ruria was really a 'woman' in the 'accepted' sense of the word. Obviously, the latter approach could be accommodated more easily, so the 'tale-bearers' went about their wicked work, and even Rashi was eager to peddle their story.

But what did the tale really accomplish in the end? An 'uppity' woman is put in her place. An intimate relationship is broken. But more than this, as Rachel Adler points out,[22] the story even 'profanes' the 'bond between teacher and student' – which in my reading of the whole saga of B'ruria is the 'profanity' which provides the final irony. The bond between teacher and student was a male bond. It was not a bond that B'ruria could experience, however much she 'taught' and 'studied'. To prove this, the only real teacher/student she ever had, her husband, Meir, had to profane his relationship with her, and also his bond with his student.

And so the tale 'works'. It works because it 'corrects' a problematic anomaly, and so deals with the threat which B'ruria posed for men who didn't know her, who didn't know how circumscribed her life actually was, for whom she stalked the pages of the sacred rabbinic texts like a trespasser, an unwelcome intruder on their exclusive inheritance.

We will never know why Rabbi Meir fled to Babylon. We will never know what 'the incident about B'ruria' was all about. Perhaps it all started with Rabbi Yosei's wounded pride on the road to Lydda .... What we do know is that Rashi's lascivious footnote of a tale only serves to heighten the message of the true story of B'ruria as it emerges from the pages of rabbinic literature. B'ruria was alone, shut out of the network of male scholarly relationships. She was also cut off from relationships with other women who did not share her scholarly endeavours. And she did not even have the women of her family around her for support. Her mother was dead, her sister, condemned to a female fate that could have been hers too, was in a brothel.

Rachel Adler points out that because B'ruria lacked the 'authority' which participation in 'the web of rabbinic relationships' would have given her, 'whatever her gifts and capacities, they funnel, ultimately,

---

22 Adler, 'The Virgin in the Brothel' (see note 8), p.104.

into a void'.[23] This is true, but it is only half the story. B'ruria's gifts 'funnel into a void', not only because she was excluded from the men-only chain of transmission, but because she was not part of a scholarly community of women, creating their own chain of transmission.

Of course, such a 'community' could not have existed at this time; B'ruria was, quite literally, alone.[24] But that precisely is the principal message of the story of B'ruria. As long as the tradition rests solely in the hands of men, a woman on her own cannot claim it, shape it, make it as much 'hers' as it is 'theirs', and then pass it on to the next generation. Although numerous 'sayings' of our mother B'ruria are scattered inside the pages of rabbinic literature, they do not belong to Jewish women because she was not in a position to bequeath them to us. We have no inheritance as women.

But for all that, Jewish women today do have something, something which B'ruria lacked: *we have one another.* Since the 1970s, Jewish women, as a community, have been laying claim to the tradition. We have been talking with one another, sharing our insights and experiences, and making sense on our own terms of the tradition which has excluded us. It is impossible to say what exactly will emerge from our endeavours, but one thing is certain: we carry a heavy burden of responsibility. We cannot do anything about the fact that despite our efforts to excavate and re-examine our 'mothers' – from the Bible onwards – their 'sayings' are largely unavailable to us, but we can do something to ensure that the sayings of the *daughters* are passed on and form an inheritance for future generations.

Our work today is *that* crucial, it is *that* difficult. At the beginning of the 1980s, I engaged in research into the early feminist movement in Britain. In the course of that research, I read my way through the eighty-plus feminist journals which were produced by women while the movement raged from the mid-19th century through to 1930. The early feminist movement disappeared. It disappeared so

---

23 Ibid., p. 32.

24 Were there other women scholars besides B'ruria? As indicated at note 1, other women are included in the pages of the *Talmud.* However, B'ruria is alone in her independent scholarly opinions – and, in any case, both Imma Shalom and Yalta, for example, lived at different times, so could not be colleagues for her. Perhaps B'ruria is an amalgam of several women; perhaps the sages were only able to tolerate one exceptional woman on 'their records'.

completely that in the mid-1960s women 'invented' it – again. In an article I wrote in 1982,[25] I attempted to make sense of this disappearance, realising that unless women of today maintain a reference point which exists outside the male framework, our own understanding of our experience in a patriarchal world, our efforts to transform our lives could also disappear.

When I first investigated B'ruria, and wrote this paper in 1989, Jewish women had only recently begun to interrogate Judaism. Fortunately, since that time, Jewish women have been engaged in studying and teaching, and creating contexts to learn and study together. But there is still so much more that needs to be done. We need to make sure that men, as well as women, benefit from the scholarship and teaching of Jewish women. Maintaining our own understanding of our experience, also involves taking responsibility for sharing it, for writing it and for transmitting it from generation to generation. If we are to develop our understandings as Jewish women today and bequeath our work to those who will both preserve it and re-shape it for themselves after us, we have to create the material conditions – the meeting places, the study houses – in which this vital process can take place. As Jewish women today pay tribute to B'ruria, and ensure that her story is told and her legacy transmitted, may we also celebrate our achievements and acknowledge that, unlike B'ruria, we are in a position to engage in such a project.

---

25 'Female Performers on a Male Stage. The First Women's Liberation Movement and the Authority of Men, 1890-1939'. In Scarlet Friedman and Elizabeth Sarah, eds., *On the Problem of Men*, (The Women's Press, London, 1982), pp. 135-56.

CHAPTER FOUR

Fräulein Rabbiner Regina Jonas and the Mysterious Disappearance of the First Woman Rabbi

Introduction: 'Finding' the 'lost' woman rabbi

Since Sally Priesand became the first woman to receive *s'michah*, rabbinic ordination, from the Hebrew Union College in 1972, hundreds of women have been ordained as rabbis in the United States, Britain and continental Europe[1] and have been contributing to a transformation of Jewish life and thought in many parts of the Jewish world.

For twenty years following Sally Priesand's ordination, women rabbis made sense of themselves largely in the context of the Women's Liberation Movement which re-emerged in the late 1960s and led to profound changes in the lives and expectations of women throughout the globe. In other words, we saw ourselves as a new phenomenon.

---

1 See http://www.loyno.edu/~wessing/docs/KeyDatesJudaism.html for a time-line of the key dates in the development of women in the rabbinate in the USA to 1993. The largest progressive Jewish denomination in the USA is Reform Judaism. RJ rabbis and cantors train at Hebrew Union College. The statistics website for HUC at http://huc.edu/about/statistics.shtml states that 'The College-Institute has ordained 2899 rabbis, including 552 women rabbis as of 2008.' See also: 'The History of Women in the Rabbinate: A Case of Communal Amnesia', the lecture given by Rabbi Sybil Sheridan at the first gathering of Bet Debora – European Conference of Women, Rabbis, Cantor and Scholars, in Berlin in 1999, held at the newly re-opened Oranienburger Strasse Synagogue, which had been shut down by the Nazis. In 2006, I undertook research into the current position regarding women's ordination for a paper entitled, 'Women Rabbis: A New Kind of Rabbinic Leadership?', which I presented in 2006 at the rabbinic conference to mark the 50th anniversary of the Leo Baeck College (LBC) – the only college ordaining rabbis in Europe after the *Sho'ah* until the foundation of the Abraham Geiger College (AGC) in 1999. I found the following concerning women rabbis in the main progressive Jewish denominations in the United States: Sandy Eisenberg

And then, in the early 1990s, we heard about a German woman rabbi called Regina Jonas, who worked as a pastor, preacher and teacher in the Berlin Jewish community, and then in the Terezin/Theresienstadt ghetto, and who died in Auschwitz in 1944.[2]

Sasso became the first female rabbi in Reconstructionist Judaism in 1974 (one of 110 by 2006); and Amy Eilberg became the first female rabbi in Conservative Judaism in 1985 (one of 177 by 2006). I also found that as of July 2006, 30 women had been ordained by the Leo Baeck College since it was established in 1956 – out of a total of 158. Of these, French-born Pauline Bebe, ordained in 1990, became the first woman rabbi in France, working in Paris, Hungarian-born, Rabbi Katalin Keleman, ordained in 1998 became the first woman rabbi in Hungary, working in Budapest, and Russian-born, Nelly Kogan, ordained in 1999 became the first woman rabbi in Belarus, working in Minsk, and thereafter in other parts of the FSU. In addition to these developments, sixty years after Rabbi Regina Jonas began working as a rabbi in Berlin, Bea Wyler, who had begun her studies at LBC and completed them at JTS (Jewish Theological Seminary), became the first woman rabbi in post-war Germany in 1995, working in Oldenburg. More recently, in November 2010, AGC ordained the first woman rabbi to study in Germany since Rabbi Regina Jonas in 1935: Alina Treiger, 31, who was born in Ukraine but moved to Berlin in 2001. As the first woman rabbi in Germany since Rabbi Regina Jonas, the milestone received widespread coverage in the press.

2 In focussing on the first woman rabbi, it's important to be aware of other women, who occupied positions of religious leadership, who were not ordained. My 2006 paper, cited above, included the following information: Long before Regina Jonas was born, Lily Montagu became one of the religious leaders of the emerging movement of Liberal Judaism in Britain. She officiated at *Shabbat* services, delivered sermons and conducted life-cycle ceremonies (See Jacobi, Margaret, 'Lily Montagu' in Sheridan, Sybil, ed., *Hear Our Voice. Women Rabbis Tell Their Stories*. SCM Press, London, 1994). A few years later, on the other side of the Atlantic, there were two other non-ordained women who fulfilled rabbinic responsibilities. In 1938, Tehilla Lichtenstein became the first woman to serve her congregation as rabbi after the death of her husband, Rabbi Morris Lichtenstein. Tehilla Lichtenstein also served as Leader of the Society for Jewish Science from 1938 until her death in 1973. Likewise, from 1951-54, Paula Ackerman, served as rabbi to a congregation in Meridian, Mississippi, after the death of her husband, Rabbi William Ackerman (See http: //www.loyno.edu/wessing/docs/ KeyDatesJudaism.html). It was as early as 1893 that a young woman called Rachel Frank, began attending classes at Hebrew Union College HUC), and introduced the notion of women rabbis to an American rabbinic institution. However, she did not complete her studies – and neither did another woman who attended the seminary at the same time, Lena Aronsohn (See: *Lesbian Rabbis. The First Generation* edited by Rebecca T. Alpert, Sue Levi Elwell, and Shirley Idelson [Rutgers University Press, New Brunswick, New Jersey, and

And we wondered, what contribution might she have made to Judaism if she had survived? What difference would her survival have made to the development of women in the Rabbinate? If Hitler had not come to power shortly after Regina Jonas completed her studies ... if German Jewry had not become preoccupied with simple survival ... if European Jewry had not been consumed by the fire of Nazism... what would have become of Regina Jones and the other twenty-six women who studied with her at the *Hochschule für die Wissenschaft des Judentums* (the 'High School for the Science of Judaism') in Berlin?[3]

But these questions, vital though they are, are not the questions with which I began my investigation. There is no reference to Regina Jonas in the *Encyclopaedia Judaica*. There is no reference to Regina Jonas in H.G. Adler's monumental work, *Theresienstadt, 1941-1945,*

London, 2001], p.13). Meanwhile, around the same time that Lily Montagu was teaching and preaching in England, Henrietta Szold became a special student at the Jewish Theological Seminary (JTS) in 1903, but was admitted on the understanding that she would not seek ordination (ibid.). In 1921, the issue of ordaining a woman rabbi was first raised formally after Martha Neumark, a student at the HUC in the second year of studies, and daughter of an HUC professor, asked permission to lead High Holy Day services. Her request was granted and the college President convened a faculty committee to consider the issue of women's ordination. The HUC faculty and the Central Conference of American Rabbis (CCAR) concluded that there was no reason not to ordain women, but the HUC Board of Governors agreed in 1923 to maintain the policy of ordaining only men as rabbis (See Meyer, Michael, *Response to Modernity: A History of the Reform Movement in Judaism* (OUP, New York and Oxford, 1988), p.379). For a history of women religious leaders, both, pre- and post-ordination, see also: Baskin, Judith R., 'Women Who Would Be Rabbis: A History of Women's Ordination, 1889-1985 (review)'. *American Jewish History,* Volume 88, Number 1, March, pp. 171-174 (John Hopkins University Press, 2000).

3 See Annual Report of the *Hochschule* for 1932 cited both in 'The *Hochschule für die Wissenschaft des Judentums* in the Period of Nazi Rule. Personal Recollections' by Richard Fuchs (*Leo Baeck Institute Year Book*, XII, 1967, p.7) and in 'Frl. Rabbiner Regina Jonas. Eine religiose Feministin vor ihrer Zeit' by Katharina von Kellenbach (*Schlangenbrut* Nr.38, 1992, pp.35-39). Fuchs points out (p.7) that there was a rise in the student population at the *Hochschule* after the First World War. In 1921, there were 63 regular students and 45 external students. In the summer of 1932, the total number rose to 155, including 27 women.

published in 1960.[4] Ditto the testimony gathered by the Council of Jewish communities in the Czech Lands, entitled *Terezin* published in 1965. Ditto Richard Fuchs' article on 'The *Hochschule für die Wissenschaft des Judentums* in the Nazi Period' published in 1967.[5] Similarly, in his article included in *Living Judaism* in Spring 1967, in which he argues for the ordination of women, Aryeh Dorfler, Lecturer in Rabbinics at the Leo Baeck College at the time, made no mention of the precedent set by Regina Jonas.[6]

Interestingly, in the account of 'The Last Days of the *Hochschule*' by Alexander Guttman published by Hebrew Union College in 1972 – the year that the first woman, Sally Priesand, was ordained by that institution – Guttman refers to the dissension regarding Regina Jonas. And yet, in *Response to Modernity. A History of the Reform Movement in Judaism*, published in 1988, Michael Meyer makes only passing reference to Regina Jonas in his discussion of the controversy about women's ordination at the Hebrew Union College.[7] Even more perplexing, the specialist study, *Women of Theresienstadt: Voices from a Concentration Camp* by Ruth Schwertfeger, published in 1989,[8] does not include the voice of Regina Jonas – a spectacular omission. Regina Jonas lost her life in the *Sho'ah*, and, it seems that the memory of her life and work also vanished practically without trace.

Why? Of course, there was the problem of written evidence. While Regina Jonas is included in institutional records of the *Hochschule*,

---

4 *Theresienstadt. 1941-1945. Das Antlitz einer Zwangsgemeinschaft, Geschichte Soziologie Psychologie.* Mohr, Tübingen, 1955. English edition published in 1960 by H.G. Adler – who was deported from Prague to Theresienstadt in February 1942 together with his wife and her family.

5 In the *Leo Baeck Institute Year Book* (XII) of 1967.

6 My thanks to Rabbis Jonathan Magonet and John Rayner, z"l, for drawing my attention to the articles by Fuchs and Dorfler, respectively.

7 Michael Meyer, *Response to Modernity. A History of the Reform Movement in Judaism.* (Oxford University Press, 1988). He writes: 'When [women's ordination] was raised again (note: the first time was in 1922 with the case of Martha Neumark) among Sisterhood leaders in 1958, even they were initially divided. By then, however, one woman, Regina Jonas, had received private ordination upon completing her studies at the Liberal seminary in Berlin, and for a brief time had served as a rabbi before perishing in the Holocaust.' (p.379).

8 Ruth Schwertfeger, *Women of Theresienstadt. Voices from a Concentration Camp,* Berg, 1989.

the *Judische Gemeinde* (Jewish Community) of Berlin, Theresienstadt
(Terezin) and *Yad Va-Shem* – and there is lively discussion of the
special case of Regina Jonas in the Jewish newspaper of the time,
Israelitisches Familienblatt – until the Berlin Wall came down, Regina
Jonas' letters and papers – including her rabbinic thesis – rested
undisturbed in the *Bundesarchiv* (State Archives) in Coswig, 100 kilo-
metres east of Berlin, for over four decades.

But the political realities of Germany after 1945 do not explain
why the official records were not investigated earlier. And then there
is the question of the leading Jewish figures who knew Regina Jonas
and survived the *Sho'ah* – like her teacher at the *Hochschule*, Leo
Baeck, and Viktor Frankl with whom she worked in Terezin. As far as
we know, they did not breathe a word about her.[9] Why was this? A
surviving fellow *Hochschule* student – who became a senior Progressive rabbi in Britain – told me, when I made enquiries, that she
simply had not interested him; she was not his 'type'![10]

But at the time at least, there were others who were far less indifferent and dismissive. During her early years at the *Hochschule*
(1926-1929), Regina Jonas corresponded with two of her teachers
there – Eduard Baneth and Ismar Elbogen – and their letters to her
are preserved in the archives.[11] Indeed, there is clear evidence from
this correspondence that these distinguished scholars recognised the
difficulties she faced as a woman. As early as 1927, Elbogen wrote to
Regina Jonas at *Purim* urging her not to be pessimistic of her chances
of getting work. He added that the community should not pay her
less than the going rate.[12] Perhaps Ismar Elbogen and Eduard Baneth
would have remained stout supporters of their colleague following

---

9 Leo Baeck's biographer, Albert Friedlander, z"l, does not recall any reference
   made by Leo Baeck to Regina Jonas (private conversation, 20.6.94) and his
   biography, *Leo Baeck, Teacher of Theresienstadt*, Holt, Rinehart, Winston, New
   York, 1968 certainly makes no reference to her. As for Viktor Frankl, he
   discussed his experience of the camps in his books *From Death Camp to Exis-
   tentialism*, later revised and included in a larger work, *Man's Search for
   Meaning. An Introduction to Legotherapy*, (Hodder and Stroughton, London,
   1962). However, although he worked with Regina Jonas in Theresienstadt,
   this text, at least, does not mention her.
10 Rabbi Curtis Cassell, z"l. Private conversation 14.6.94.
11 75D JO 1 is the *Bundesarchiv* reference no. for the letters addressed to Regina
    Jonas.
12 ibid.

her ordination. But Eduard Baneth, a renowned Talmudist who originally conducted the rabbinic examination of Regina Jonas, died in
1930, during the course of it[13] and Ismar Elbogen, the famous liturgist, emigrated to New York in 1938 where he joined Hebrew Union
College and died in 1943.[14] So these two scholars did not live to
relate their experiences of Regina Jonas.

And what of Leo Baeck, who survived the *Sho'ah* and lived in
London for eleven years until his death in 1956? His letters to
Regina Jonas span the period from 1934 to 1940, and reveal that he
was not just a teacher, he was a friend. Indeed, this is also true of
Leo Baeck's wife, Natalie, who also corresponded with Regina Jonas.
What is more, Leo Baeck and Regina Jonas were in Terezin at the
same time – although Regina Jonas was deported to the ghetto in
November 1942, and dispatched to Auschwitz two years later, and
Leo Baeck was incarcerated there from 1943 until its liberation in
1945.

So why didn't Leo Baeck keep the memory of his student alive
and pass it on to the next generation? One can only speculate – and
in all fairness to the memory of Leo Baeck himself, speculation is
dangerous. Perhaps he did mention her. But if he did, nothing he
said seems to have been recorded[15] Perhaps, too, Ellen Littman, a
fellow student of Regina Jonas, who taught Bible at Leo Baeck
College in the early years, also mentioned Regina Jonas to her
students. But if she did, the knowledge that a woman student at the
Hochschule had received *s'michah*, does not seem to have excited the
curiosity of the first post-war generation of European progressive
rabbis.

And yet, by contrast, for one woman who was taught by Regina
Jonas as a girl for a brief period (between the years 1934 and 1937)
at a non-Jewish school in Berlin, where she was a visiting teacher,
'Dr Jonas', as she was known there, left a 'lasting impression'.[16] When
the news of Regina Jonas' ordination certificate and photograph was
published in December 1993 in *Inform*, the newsletter of the Reform
Synagogues of Great Britain, a delighted Inge Kallman of Southport

13 See 'Tribute to Rabbi Regina Jonas of Berlin' by Hans Hirschberg in *Leo Baeck
College News*, 1993, p.46.
14 Fuchs, 1967, p.23.
15 See note 9.
16 Inge Kallman, letter to Jonathan Magonet, 4.1.94.

quickly wrote to the Leo Baeck College and the Principal, Rabbi Dr Jonathan Magonet, kindly passed her letter on to me.[17] In her next letter,[18] she recalled that at twelve years of age, she was encouraged by 'Dr Jonas' to attend her first *Oneg Shabbat*. And she went on to say that it was also at the instigation of Regina Jonas that she attended an *Erev Shabbat* service that her teacher conducted at an old people's home near the Jewish Hospital in Berlin. It was here that she remembers seeing Regina Jonas in her rabbinical robes for the first time. In addition to these more formal settings, this former pupil also remembers 'one occasion when the few Jewish children still remaining at the school were invited to her flat for biscuits and coffee, a flat she shared with her mother.'

Why did it take so long for these memories to surface? Inge Kallman writes: 'Whenever I asked previously, it seems that although her existence was known, there was no evidence.'[19] No substantial written evidence, clearly. But if those who had known Regina Jonas, who taught her, studied with her, worked with her, had made an effort to transmit their experience of her to others, we would have had the evidence of oral testimony, and it would not have been necessary to rediscover Regina Jonas almost fifty years after her death in the archives where she herself deposited her letters and papers.[20]

Regina Jonas may have expected to retrieve her own work from the archives after the war – or perhaps, she did not think she would survive and hoped that future generations would rediscover her contribution to Jewish life. But she died in Auschwitz and now it is our responsibility to commit ourselves to the task of retrieval.

When I began my investigations in 1993, a German Christian feminist, Katharina von Kellenbach, was the only scholar to have begun a concerted study of Regina Jonas.[21] Since that time, Elisa

17 ibid.
18 Inge Kallman, letter to Elizabeth Sarah, 27.4.94
19 Inge Kallman, letter to Jonathan Magonet, 4.1.94
20 See Hans Hirshberg, pp.46-7.
21 I remain indebted to Katharina von Kellenbach's article published in the journal *Schlagenbrut* in 1992 (Nr.38), translated for me by Maren Freudenberg, and to the short tribute by Hans Hirschberg published in *Leo Baeck College News* in 1993, for much of the information about the life and work of Regina Jonas contained in this paper.

Klapchek has written a study of Rabbi Jonas in German,[22] now translated into English, which has generated more interest.

I conducted my own very modest piece of research in November 1993, when I visited the archives at Coswig – which have since been transferred to Potsdam. Although I was only given access to a few letters, they helped to illuminate aspects of Regina Jonas' experience as a student and rabbi and her relationships with her scholars/teachers. Fortunately, after going to see Dr Hermann Simon, Director of the Zentrum Judaicum Foundation at the Oranienburger Strasse Synagogue in East Berlin, he agreed to let me have the microfilm containing all the archive material – including Regina Jonas' rabbinic dissertation on the ordination of women – which I finally received in March 1994.[23] Following my initial research, I was very proud to be invited to give the first public lecture, devoted to the life and work of Fräulein Rabbiner Regina Jonas in October 1994, fifty years after her death.

In an important sense Rabbi Regina Jonas is no longer 'news'. However, given her mysterious disappearance for almost half a century, and despite her 'discovery' in recent years, few people, even now, know about her. So I offer this brief study as an introduction to her life and work, and as a cautionary tale, reminding us of how easy it is for women to be hidden from history.[24]

---

22 In the years since my humble efforts, important work in the retrieval of Regina Jonas' legacy has been undertaken: Most significantly, Elisa Klapheck, who grew up in Germany, and was ordained in 2004, under the auspices of the Aleph Rabbinical Programme in the United States, has written a biography, which includes Rabbi Jonas' 1930 rabbinic thesis, "Can Women Serve as Rabbis?" and has been translated into English by New York-born, Toby Axelrod. See: Klapheck, Elisa, ed. *Fräulein Rabbiner Jonas—The Story of the First Woman Rabbi* (San Francisco: 2004), [*Fräulein Rabbiner Jonas—Kann die Frau das rabbinische Amt bekleiden?* (Teetz: 2000)]; Axelrod, Toby, 2009: "My years with Regina Jonas" in: *Bridges. A Jewish Feminist Journal*, Autumn 2009, Vol. 14, No.2, pp.27-31. Also see: Herweg, Rachel Monika. "Regina Jonas (1902–1944)." in *Meinetwegen ist die Welt erschaffen, Das intellektuelle Vermächtnis des deutschsprachigen Judentums. 58 Porträts*, edited by Hans Erler, Ernst Ludwig Ehrlich and Ludger Heid (Frankfurt, New York: 1997). For a summary account of Regina Jonas, see the article by Elisa Klapheck in the Jewish Women's Archive: jwa.org/encyclopedia/article/jonas-regina

23 I deposited the microfilm in the Library of the Leo Baeck College.

24 The socialist feminist historian, Sheila Rowbotham, coined this phrase in her ground-breaking book, *Hidden from History: Three Hundred Years of*

From Teacher to Rabbi

Regina Jonas was born on 3rd August 1902 in Berlin. At the age of twenty-one she began working as a teacher of religion in the Ortho-dox Jewish School in Berlin, where her brother, Abraham, also taught. She spent the next twenty-one years until her death inten-sively engaged in Jewish learning and teaching.

However, Regina Jonas was not content with being a teacher. She attended the *Hochschule* from 1924 to 1930 attaining the qualifica-tion, 'Academic Teacher of Religion'.[25] Did she plan to become a rabbi or did her studies at the *Hoschschule* lead her in that direction? What we do know is that towards the end of her studies, she clearly sought ordination. She devoted her thesis to an exploration of the *Talmudic* sources regarding Women's Ordination and waited to receive *s'michah*.

But it was not to be – at least not under *Hochschule* auspices. Although Regina Jonas had the support of the majority of her teach-ers, the *Talmud* Professor, Dr Chanoth Albeick, declined to put his name to a rabbinic diploma. The controversy raged but was unre-solved[26] and despite the fact that Leo Baeck was her teacher for many years, he did not ordain her. Hans Hirschberg argues that: '[a] possi-ble explanation might be that Baeck presided over the General Association of Rabbis in Germany which also included Orthodox and Conservative Rabbis. The ordination of a woman as Rabbi', he writes, 'may have led to unwanted arguments, likewise in Berlin, where Leo Baeck had to work with non-liberal colleagues in unified congregation (*Einheitsgemeinde*)'.[27]

Women's Oppression and the Fight Against It, published by Pluto Press in 1973. The radical feminist lesbian poet, Adrienne Rich, spoke of women being, 'gaslighted for centuries' – see her essay, *Women and Honor: Some Notes on Lying*, which originated as a talk at the Hartwick Women Writer's Workshop, 1975, and was then published as a pamphlet by Motheroot Press, (Pitts-burgh,1977), and re-printed in *Heresies: A Feminist Magazine of Art and Politics*, vol. 1, no. 1, 1979, and included in her book, *On Lies, Secrets, and Silence: Selected Prose 1966-1978* (W.W. Norton & Company, New York, 1979).

25 Hirschberg, 1993, p.46.

26 Some of the controversy found public expression in the journal *Israelitisches Familienblatt*, quotations from which are included in Katharina von Kellen-back's article (see note 21).

27 Hirschberg, pp.46-7.

But the issue of ordination – or rather the lack of it – did not end there. At the request of the Union of Liberal Rabbis in Germany on 27th December 1935 she received *s'michah* from Rabbiner Max Dienemann, a liberal-minded rabbi who worked in Offenbach, who having examined her declared her 'qualified to occupy the office of Rabbi'.[28] Interestingly, Leo Baeck wrote to her just four days later on 31st December, congratulating her on her performance in her examination.[29] And it was Leo Baeck again, who, over six years later on 6 February 1942, signed a certificate confirming her *s'michah*.[30]

It is this certificate alone – presented by Dr Hermann Simon, to Leo Baeck College on 3rd October 1993, together with a photograph of Regina Jonas in her rabbinical robes – that provides the incontrovertible evidence of her ordination, and sets her apart as the first woman whose status as a rabbi received formal acknowledgement. Interestingly, Inge Kallman recalls her teacher saying that 'apart from a woman rabbi in America, she was the first woman rabbi'.[31] Who was *that* woman rabbi? Perhaps Regina Jonas was referring to Martha Neumark, the daughter of a professor at the Hebrew Union College, who provoked an outcry when she requested ordination in 1922. Michael Meyer discusses the controversy briefly in *Response to Modernity*.[32] Apparently, while the HUC faculty were unanimous in their support of Martha Neumark, a majority of the College's Board of Governors decided against changing the policy of ordination for males only. So, Martha Neumark did not receive *s'michah*. But if Regina Jonas was alluding to Martha Neumark when she spoke of 'a woman rabbi in America' then it seems that Fräulein Rabbiner Regina Jonas, at least, considered her a colleague.

Working as a Rabbi

What kind of woman was Regina Jonas? And what kind of a rabbi did the first woman to officially assume that role, turn out to be? The evidence explored so far is sparse but it reveals a picture of a determined individual, a dedicated teacher and pastor. Here are some of the pieces in the puzzle:

---

28 ibid.
29 Archive: 75D JO1
30 Hirschberg, p.47.
31 Inge Kallman, letter to Jonathan Magonet, 4.1.94
32 Meyer p.379. See note 7.

The first piece is a picture: a photograph. Her face is strong: piercing eyes, firm chin, resolute mouth; her stance is defiant. She looks like a force to be reckoned with.

Regina Jonas was a bold individual. There are clear signs that she would not allow the absence of 'official' recognition to stand in her way. And no doubt the fact that the dispute spilled out into the wider Jewish community, turning her into a public figure, helped to embolden her still more. Shortly after she completed her examination at the *Hochschule*, the Jewish Journal, *Israelitisches Familienblatt*, published an article entitled 'It strikes us' on June 4th 1931, in which the author expressed his ambivalent reaction – and perhaps that of many others – to the anomalous position of Regina Jonas.

He wrote:

> One is rightfully permitted to be proud of her. One is rightfully permitted to see this as a good sign of the times when a young woman out of her own inclination and zeal grasps hold of the Jewish teaching profession .... But nevertheless it strikes us that in this certificate which the *Hochschule* for the Science of Judaism has bestowed, it was not stated that it is only a teaching and not a preaching Diploma ... As long as it is not the regular norm that women ministers are appointed and as long as ... many small communities ... give people with Academic Religion certificates, rabbinic functions, it must be said that this Diploma when bestowed on a woman should not include the qualification to preach which normally a certificate like this includes. Otherwise it could happen that other Academic and Seminary-educated women religion teachers could climb the pulpit and claim to be qualified by their educational institutions to do so.

Perhaps if Germany's Jewish community had not been overtaken by external events, some of the other female students at the *Hochschule* may have risen to this challenge. In any case, Regina Jonas pursued the case for women rabbis. She gave a lecture at the *Judischer Frauenbund* in Berlin with the title, 'Can Women Become Rabbis?' which was reported in the same journal (*Israelitisches Familienblatt*) on 5th November 1931, beginning with an historical sketch of the origin of rabbinic ordination. She explained:[33]

---

33 See von Kellenbach, 'Frl. Rabbiner Regina Jonas', p.36.

In earlier times, there existed no exams for rabbis. Leaders of the community were learned people who were authorised by other learned people to practice the rabbinical function. They themselves had the right to name as rabbis, men who seemed to them to be worthy.

Regina Jonas knew that there were rabbis who considered her to be worthy – and members of the Berlin community with which she worked, too. Perhaps that is what made her so tenacious. And yet there continued to be many detractors[34] and the ambiguity which surrounded her role persisted even after she received s'michah. A survivor recalls:[35]

> In Berlin there lived at this time in the thirties the first woman rabbi, Fräulein Rabbiner Regina Jonas. She watched carefully that one said 'Fräulein Rabbiner' to her because a 'Frau Rabbiner' was the wife of a rabbi … She came into the hospital and old age home very often, and there she wanted to function as a rabbi. Generally, this worked in the old age home. In the hospital, she came into the synagogue, wearing a purple robe – not black – she sat herself downstairs next to a man on the rabbi's seat. She wanted to give her lecture or sermon during the prayers, but always when this doctor was there and prayed with the people, he said to her, 'you can do what you want, but for the prayers you go upstairs to the women, and afterwards you can come downstairs.'

Fräulein Rabbiner Regina Jonas worked with the old and with the young primarily as a pastor and teacher. However, she found that despite resistance from people, once the violence and deportations began, she increasingly assumed an overt pulpit presence. Hans Hirschberg writes:[36]

> After Kristallnacht in November 1938, she preached in various synagogues in Berlin, after replacing rabbis who were thrown into concentration camps or had emigrated.

---

34 Von Kellenbach quotes opponents of Regina Jonas.
35 See von Kellenbach, 'Frl. Rabbiner Regina Jonas' p.38. Despite Regina Jonas' express wish to be addressed as 'Fräulein Rabbiner' there is evidence that she continued to be addressed as 'Frau Rabbiner'. See, for example, a letter from the central office of the *Judische Gemeinde* (Jewish Community) of Berlin, of 11.9.40, concerning her work at the old people's home (75 D JO1).
36 Hirschberg, p.47.

Ironically, the increasing brutality of the Nazi regime created new rabbinic opportunities for Regina Jonas. But, of course, she did not escape persecution. She was ordered into forced labour in a factory. Despite this she continued to minister to people and to preach. According to Hirschberg:[37]

> Contemporaries praised her extraordinary personality and oratorical gifts. Where and whenever she preached to those who were to perform forced labour, they filled the place to capacity and those who did not manage to get in, stood in the doorways as far as the street.

On 3rd November 1942, Regina Jonas completed a declaration form listing her property – including her books – which was officially confiscated 'for the benefit of the German Reich' two days later. On 6th November, she was deported to Theresienstadt.[38] But her rabbinic work did not end with deportation. In the ghetto, she continued functioning as a rabbi, working together with the well-known psychologist, Viktor Frankl. Her particular task was to meet transports at the railway station and help people deal with their initial shock and disorientation.[39]

Curiously, Viktor Frankl, while he wrote extensively about what he learned from his experience in the camps after the war, did not mention his work with Regina Jonas.[40] However, when approached by Katharina von Kellenbach in 1991 and asked directly about her, Frankl described Regina Jonas as 'loaded with energy and a very impressive personality'. He also called her 'a blessed preacher and speaker'[41] – a reference to the fact that, in addition to her pastoral work, Regina Jonas also gave sermons and lectures. The amazingly full cultural life of Terezin is well-documented, and she contributed to the programme of activities. A hand-written list of her lectures, entitled, 'Lectures of the one and only woman rabbi, Regina Jonas' has survived in the Terezin archives.[42] Of the twenty-three different titles, five concern the position, meaning and history of Jewish

---

37 ibid. p.47.
38 von Kellenbach, p.38.
39 ibid.
40 See note 9.
41 von Kellenbach, p.38.
42 ibid., pp.38-39.

women, five deal with *Talmudic* topics, two with biblical themes, three with pastoral issues, and nine offer general introductions to the basic contents of Jewish beliefs, ethics and the festivals.

Like Viktor Frankl and her teacher, Leo Baeck, who both survived Terezin, Regina Jonas was clearly an inspiration to all those who knew her. A glimmer of her spiritual strength is apparent in the one sermon delivered in the ghetto to have survived – which includes these words of hope.[43]

> Our Jewish people is sent from God into history as 'blessed', 'from God blessed' which means, wherever one steps in every life situation, bestow blessing, goodness and faithfulness – humility before God's selflessness, whose devotion-full love for His creatures maintains the world. To establish these pillars of the world was and is Israel's task. Men and women, and women and men have undertaken this duty with the same Jewish faithfulness. This ideal also serves our testing Thereseinstadt work. We are God's servants and as such we are moving from earthly to eternal spheres. May all our work which we have tried to perform as God's servants, be a blessing for Israel's future and humanity.

After two years of tireless work on behalf of her fellow prisoners in the ghetto, Fräulein Rabbiner Regina Jonas was dispatched to Auschwitz. There is some dispute about the date. Katharina von Kellenbach, citing the Transport List held in the archives at *Yad Va-Shem* on which Regina Jonas is included as No.722/44 says that the date was 9th October 1944. Hans Hirschberg states that the date was 12th December 1944. The *Yad Va-Shem* reference itself seems to be dated 20th December.[45] In a later article, von Kellenbach stated that the date was 12th October.[46] What is certain is that Regina Jonas did not live to see the New Year of 1945 and liberation in the spring.[47]

---

43 ibid., p.39.

44 Von Kellenbach, p.38; footnote 22, p.39.

45 ibid.

46 "God Does Not Oppress Any Human Being". The Life and Thought of Rabbi Regina Jonas' by Katharina von Kellenbach. *Leo Baeck Year Book*, No.39, 1994.

47 There is no doubt that the last transports to Auschwitz took place in October. Perhaps Regina Jonas was killed in December. As it happens, there is no firm evidence concerning her death.

Although, since the time that I conducted my research, there have been further studies, much of the mystery that surrounds Fräulein Rabbiner Regina Jonas remains. It is clear that she was a gifted, courageous individual and a committed rabbi. The circumstances of her time meant that she was, in her own words, 'the one and only woman rabbi'. We cannot know how many other women may have become rabbis after her if the *Sho'ah* had not happened. We cannot know if Regina Jonas would have made a special contribution to Jewish life if she had been one of *many*, and European Jewry had not been rounded up and slaughtered. The chain was broken. But today, women rabbis, who now make up half of the progressive rabbinate, are creating a new chain, and as we do so, we are proud to restore a missing link with our past:

Fräulein Rabbiner Regina Jonas – *zichronah livrachah* – may her memory be a source of blessing for all our lives. Amen.

PART TWO

Making Trouble: The Struggle for Equality and Inclusion

As I make clear in 'My Journey', my rabbinate has been rooted in, and shaped by, my commitment to challenging the patriarchal nature of the Jewish heritage, and working for gender equality and the inclusion of lesbian and gay individuals and couples in Jewish communal life. The chapters in Part Two reflect these major concerns.

Chapter 5, Gender Trouble and the Transformation of Judaism,[1] provides an overview of the Jewish Feminist agenda of the past forty years, and explores the extent to which Jewish life has become transformed during that time.

In contrast to the broad sweep of Chapter 5, Chapter 6, Beyond the Divine Autocrat: Speaking of God Today, focuses specifically on the issue of how we speak and think about God after a century of slaughter, and in the context, both, of the contemporary world, and the issues raised by Jewish Feminism.[2]

Motivated by my personal experience of exclusion and my determination that lesbian Jews should no longer live on the margins of Jewish life, Chapter 7, Judaism and Lesbianism: A Tale of Life on the Margins of the Text, is a study of the textual sources[3]. My exploration demonstrates, that contrary to popular belief, the first rabbis were aware of lesbianism, and that the marginalisation of lesbian experience was both particular, and part of the broader phenomenon of the marginalisation of women.

As the account of my experience as a lesbian rabbinic student and rabbi set out in 'My Journey' reveals, the single most important issue that has impacted on my rabbinate has been my determination to secure same-sex marriage. With revisions to reflect changes in the law in recent years, regarding lesbian and gay partnerships, my arti-

---

1 This chapter is a revised version of my article of the same name, which was published as the Manna Essay in MANNA 103, Spring 2009.

2 With some revisions to bring the context up-to-date, the text for this chapter was written in 1995, for the Jewish keynote lecture I gave at the conference of the International Council of Christians and Jews, held in Budapest that year. It was subsequently published as the Manna Essay in MANNA, No. 52, Summer 1996 – and later published in Spanish with the title, 'Hablar de Dios Hoy', in *El Olivo* XXI, 47, 1997.

3 This chapter is an updated version of an article included in a special issue of *The Jewish Quarterly* in 1993 (Vol. 40, No. 3, Autumn), and then in *Jewish Explorations of Sexuality* edited by Jonathan Magonet (Berghaan Books, 1995).

cle published in 2000, arguing for same-sex marriage[4], appears here as Chapter 8, 'Marriage by Any Other Name': Lesbian and Gay Civil Partnership.

Even before this piece was published in 2000 – and before the storm created by my sermon on *Yom Kippur* eve in September 1996 – I put the case for same-sex marriage in my article, 'Towards an Inclusive Jewish Sexual Ethic', which was published in 1996[5]. Again, with some revision to bring it up to date, Towards an Inclusive Jewish Sexual Ethic, forms Chapter 9. I have put it last, although it was published earlier, because in setting out the parameters of a new sexual ethic that is applicable to all Jews, regardless of their sexuality, it moves beyond the themes of Jewish lesbian and gay experience, specifically, to encompass contemporary Jewish life in general – and so, forms a bridge with Part Three of the book, The Struggle with Trouble.

In 1984, I was one of a group of Jewish feminists who created a new Jewish feminist magazine, *Shifra*, which was launched in December of that year, just three months after I had embarked on the rabbinic programme at Leo Baeck College. To set the scene for this section of the book, I am including the article I wrote for the first issue of *Shifra*, which explored the emergence of my Jewish consciousness, in the context of my lesbian feminist identity, and why I had become religiously engaged and decided to study for the rabbinate.

---

4 While I suffered the consequences of being a pioneer on this issue at a time when many, even the Progressive Jewish world, were not ready for it, I was very grateful that my article, 'Marriage By Any Other Name: Lesbian and Gay Commitment Ceremonies', which I began working on in 1996, was included in the second anthology of the writings of women rabbis, *Taking Up the Timbrel: The Challenge of Creating Rituals for Jewish Women Today*, edited by rabbis Sylvia Rothschild and Sybil Sheridan (SCM Press, London, 2000).

5 In *Renewing the Vision. Rabbis Speak Out on Modern Jewish Issues* edited by Jonathan A. Romain, one of the leading rabbis of the Reform Movement (SCM Press, London, 1996). That article was based on the sermon I gave at the 13th conference of the International Congress of Lesbian and Gay Jews in London, 30th April – 3rd May 1993. The double *Torah* portion on the *Shabbat* during the conference, *Acharey Mot-K'doshim*, Leviticus 18 to 20, which contains, both, the Holiness code - the key ethical injunctions - and the sexual prohibitions, was the perfect vehicle for the presentation of a new, inclusive approach to sexual ethics.

Knowing No Bounds – Or, What's a Nice Jewish Lesbian Doing Holding the Sefer Torah?[6]

I could write about being a lesbian and a Jew – in both a cultural and a religious sense – in a number of ways. And I have tried many of them out (in my head) for as long as I first began to acknowledge that my Jewishness did not fit neatly into a slot marked 'culture'. In fact, I haven't stopped trying to articulate all the different parts of me ever since I first began to recognise that there were different parts that needed articulating.

In the beginning...

I was born Jewish and I have always lived with the Jewish year regulated by the Jewish festivals and their special flavours and aromas and object lessons – with *Seders*, with Friday nights, with *Yiddish* and Hebrew songs, with stories, with political debates, with Eastern European Jewish chopped liver and chicken soup and lemon tea, and (when we could afford it) Viennese Jewish *goulash* and *schnitzel* and *kaffee-mit-schlagobers* – but until three years ago I lived my Jewishness outside feminism and despite it.

My mother, the ninth child and seventh daughter of parents who fled the Russian Pale of Jewish settlement in the wake of pogroms in the early 1900s and found refuge with thousands of other Jews in Whitechapel, East London, rejects Orthodoxy, yet loves *Yiddishkeit*, is a passionate socialist and a passionate Zionist – and a feminist too. My father, a Viennese Jew whose immediate family managed to escape Nazi Europe before all the exits were sealed (but not before his father had been beaten to a pulp in Dachau, protesting, 'but I am an Austrian...'), is fervently anti nationalist and individualist, a 'liberal' who is forever looking beyond the parameters of Jewish concerns, and yet cannot help being part of them.

And my parents are part of me. The battle between Eastern European and Central European Jewish life, between two 'murdered worlds'[7], fought out in the kitchen and around the dining table, in *Yiddish* and in German, with music and with silence, is part of me.

---

6 See 'My Journey', note 7.
7 In Sheila Shulman's untitled poem which begins with the words, 'Rosh Hashanah/came and went', two lines read: 'I hear the voices/of a murdered world' (Spinster 6, Winter 1983/84: 7-8).

And I am also a lesbian and a feminist who is choosing new Jewish parts as well as old ones, who is engaged in creating and preserving, who is claiming all the 'strong' women and all the 'weak' men, and who is drawing on the sustenance of *Torah* and a dynamic tradition of remembrance, celebration, humour and hope – as much as on the insights and analysis of feminism, past and present.

Getting down to basics...

In many ways, my eclectic approach is more Jewish than it is feminist. Jewish survival has always demanded myriad Jewish responses, while feminism, however radical its break with masculinist thinking, like other explanatory systems which attempt to isolate what is wrong with the world and what it is that needs to be changed, is not geared to acknowledging complexity and non-resolvable contradictions. A central assumption of feminism is that the identity 'woman' is a fundamental one; that everything an individual woman is can be reduced to one basic fact: she is a woman. It is this assumption that has led to another: the identity of all women in our essential womanhood – sisterhood: basically, we are all sisters because our shared womanhood underlies all other experiences – individual, cultural, economic – which separate us. The prototype feminist of the 1980s is not the prototype feminist of the late '60s and early '70s (more of that in a moment), but her basic feminist impulses remain: she is a woman who has experienced the click phenomenon, and with the truth revealed, has cast-off all the old bonds which tied her – to family, to class, to culture, to religion, to nation – to emerge a new woman, unfettered and eager to join hands with her sisters across the globe and create a new world.

Well, this had been the theory of it. In practice, some of us had to cast off more than others. The new woman, early '70s variety, could be white, middle class and culturally Christian, because that is the norm in the countries where modern feminism initially developed – and so, nobody noticed; she couldn't be black, working class, Jewish[8] – because that would mean her loyalties were subject to conflicting pulls, and anyway, we all know how much more patriar-

---

8 'Lists' of oppressions are problematic – and sometimes dismiss more than they acknowledge. This list isn't definitive – and the list of dominant assumptions isn't either.

chal these other cultures are... Yet, lots of 'other' women did try to become 'new' women too: rejecting, denying, repressing, forgetting, or simply camouflaging – with the rhetoric and new reflexes of sisterhood – 'old' rituals, habits, customs, fears and allegiances.

We tried – and then we stopped trying. I don't think it is possible to isolate a particular moment in time when the other feminists decided that we weren't going to keep our otherness discreet and apart from feminism any longer. I do know that by the time I began to think about being Jewish within the Women's Liberation Movement, sisterhood had already lost its rosy glow for me, the divisions – between heterosexual feminists and lesbian feminists, between different groups of lesbians, between different feminist styles and approaches – were bitter and anguished enough to indicate that sisters were capable of hurting one another and that some sisters were 'sisters' and some weren't. But it was only when I found myself caught up in these conflicts that I became aware of the extent to which the assumption prevailed that all feminists should share the same experience, and the extent to which, that same experience we were all supposed to share, excluded large parts of me and my experience.

The 'other' feminists have now begun to make our presence felt inside feminism – so much so, that in the last two or three years the terms of feminist discourse have actually changed slightly: are less one-dimensional and simplistic. Feminists now say words like 'diversity' with increasing frequency (and decreasing meaning?); feminists speak of 'multiple' oppressions; feminists are beginning to acknowledge (although this acknowledgement is often little more than token), that women do not share the same experience – that differences in sexuality, class, race, culture, religion, make for differences between women, as do the differences which are less systematic, but no less significant in a hierarchical society: the experience of mothering; physical and mental disablement; variations in body size, and many more. Feminists are beginning to recognise that 'sisterhood' is neither a simple, nor an automatic bond. And feminists are also beginning to acknowledge that if diversity exists between women, it certainly inheres within individual women; that it's not simply a question of accepting that there are black women and Jewish women and lesbians and mothers and women with disabilities – a single woman may have all these identities (and others as well).

The fit-ness obsession... and some fit-ing strategies...

Well, whatever the limitations of current feminist understandings, when I first began to bring my Jewishness within the orbit of my feminism and to think of myself not only as a lesbian and a Jew, but as a Jewish Lesbian, a feminist vocabulary which could accommodate me was not yet available, and so my overriding concern was to make my Jewishness fit and to ensure that my feminist profile remained intact. The first strategy I adopted was to use the language of my lesbian consciousness for my new-found consciousness as a Jewish lesbian. I could make being a lesbian and being Jewish fit because they were symmetrical experiences: coming out as a lesbian in a society dominated by institutionalised heterosexuality; coming out as a Jew in a society dominated by institutionalised Christianity.

The second strategy acknowledged that it was a bit more complicated than that (but only a bit). Being a lesbian and being Jewish were not symmetrical experiences; they were different. However, while different, they were equal (a familiar argument?) The fact that they were, both, equally important to me, and equally fundamental to my existence, urged me to give them equal value ... On the surface, this may seem like a sensible approach. The problem was, I spent a lot of time trying to prove that they were equal: quantifying them, measuring them up against one another-using indices of pain or joy or both ... oy yoy yoy ...

These fit-ing strategies have involved 'sorting things out', 'smoothing out contradictions'. When emphasising the symmetrical nature of my lesbian and Jewish experiences, I have had to select those aspects that are symmetrical (almost): coming out; the place of separatism as both means and ends in the survival strategies of Jews and lesbians. When granting equal status to my Jewishness and my lesbianism, I have attempted to evaluate things that could not be easily evaluated, to comprehend the incomprehensible: centuries of anti-Jewish persecution and the unique horror of the Holocaust; the burning of witches and 'faggots' in mediaeval Christian Europe and the exclusion of lesbians and gay men from the terms of the Law of Return: Israel may be a refuge for heterosexual Jews only.[9]

My attempts to make being a lesbian and being Jewish fit did not emerge in a linear fashion; I draw on both strategies from time to

9 See 'My Journey', note 5

time, depending on my state of mind, while trying to develop a third – a sort of anti-strategy to help me resist 'making sense' of my experience, while encouraging me to acknowledge as much of it as I can. This anti-strategy became necessary when I realised that the neat way in which I had managed to contain my Jewish experience wasn't working any more. Not only was I giving it more than equal space in my life – feeling overwhelmed by the imperative of Jewish survival after Auschwitz – it was changing... in many ways I had never predicted: I was 'getting' religion – or it was 'getting' me – or both. Needless to say, it is difficult to fit what you can no longer predict, so when the realm of the spiritual started to complicate matters, I stopped trying...

The Getting of ... Religion: Opiate or Antidote?

Once I got over the initial shock, it did not seem at all surprising that my Jewishness had a religious dimension. Being open to the Jewish heritage available to me; wishing to explore what Jewishness has meant to Jews historically – to women and men, to Sephardi and Ashkenazi communities; wanting to understand a little of how Jews have lived and endured, has meant confronting religion. Yes, many of the Jewish festivals have cultural and agricultural referents: liberation (*Chanukkah, Purim, Pesach*); the cycle of the seasons (*Pesach, Shavuot, Sukkot*) and these are very important. The Jewish people were, indeed, born in the liberation/Exodus from Egypt, and *Pesach*, the festival which commemorates the Exodus occurs in the spring, during the first month of the Jewish year – *Nisan* (the New Year – *Rosh Hashanah* – occurs during the seventh month: *Tishri*). But the birth of the Jews was not simply an act of revolt on the part of an oppressed people; it was a sign of Divine intervention; an acknowledgment of human limitations and an affirmation of faith in the One, unfathomable, God of Deliverance.

Like many good radicals intent on revolution, the thought of God (when I thought of God) used to strike me as both absurd and repugnant: to acknowledge that people were not capable of doing and creating anything we chose was tantamount to blasphemy (secular variety); to suggest that something might transcend human beings, seemed an admission of pre-ordained hierarchy (with humanity occupying the second rung); to believe in that non-provable something was completely irrational (a very grave crime indeed). Now, I am less certain – and more humble. I do not and cannot know what God is, if God exists. What does seem fairly clear, however, is that the idea of God may be an essential antidote to the arrogant pretentions of human beings. As committed 'revolutionaries', we (feminists and socialists) want to control our own lives, to empower ourselves, to overthrow (however non-violently) existing (oppressive) social arrangements – and all on the basis of the assumption that when we are no longer oppressed, oppression will cease; the world will be a better place. But how do the oppressed liberate themselves, without becoming dangerously arrogant and self-righteous in the process? (viz. developments in the Soviet Union, Israel, North Vietnam – the list goes on.) I don't know. And feminists who try to avoid the issue by viewing domination and violence as somehow inherently male (on the basis of either biological or historical-conditioning arguments) are doing feminism a disservice: power lies in the hands of those (any one/any group) in a position to exercise it.

Significantly, the *Torah* acknowledges the fact that the experience of oppression does not transform people into morally superior beings. The ex-slaves – still wandering in the Wilderness – were commanded to 'Love thy neighbour as thyself' and not to oppress the 'stranger' in their midst. But these commandments beg an important question: do ethical standards regulating conduct between people (and peoples) have to be regarded as Divinely-ordained for them to be recognised as Absolute and binding on everybody? It's a difficult question. As far as I am concerned, if there is such a thing as The Absolute, it certainly doesn't exist within the world. Human beings don't and can't know everything, and I'm much happier taking The Absolute out of human affairs. This does not mean I submit to passive fatalism: the fact that we can never grasp The Absolute Truth, Perfectionism, does not mean that we shouldn't strive continually to perfect the world, to re-shape and re-create it – this, after all, is what being a feminist is about: modern feminism at its best has always emphasised process, the means by which we liberate ourselves, rather than the end of liberation.

The role of Religion in the overthrow of 'Systems': some heretical thoughts
Both Marxism and feminism are concerned with changing the world

– with removing power and inequality, hierarchy and oppression – although these problems are defined differently within each framework. For both Marxists and feminists the impetus to change the world is provided by commitment to a system of ideas which explains what is wrong with the world and what it is that needs to be changed. But these systems of ideas are necessarily incomplete; any system by virtue of its coherence leaves out of account anything that cannot be resolved and made to fit. The crunch comes when, in the unity of theory and practice, which is at the basis of any connection between our ideas about the world and our will to change the world, our ideas prove to be too limited to encompass the complexity of social reality. What do we do when changing the world in accordance with our ideas becomes much more difficult than we expected? There seem to be a number of options: we can change our ideas slightly, modifying the system we subscribe to while still upholding it (a common Marxist approach); we can look to an entirely different system; or, if we've exhausted all the available systems, we can become pessimistic, deciding that change is impossible. Sooner or later, large numbers of 'revolutionaries' find themselves left with this 'option'.

But perhaps there is another alternative. Perhaps one way a continual commitment to changing the world can be maintained in the absence of workable 'solutions' and the entrenchment of the power we oppose – patriarchy, capitalism, imperialism, institutionalised racism – is if the impetus to create change is acknowledged as an ethical imperative which is not dependent on the efficacy of any particular system of ideas: opposing 'wrong' and creating 'good' is the purpose of our existence. Or, to put it more Jewishly: life is a commandment. And to live life to the full, we have to hope and dream and work and learn and struggle to perfect ourselves and the world. Of course, the notion of such an ethical imperative is not confined to religious thinking. Humanists, for example, believe not in a God, but in the 'inherent goodness of man' (sic). However, as with belief in God, this belief demands faith which is not contingent upon reality. In fact, religious people are often more realistic and pragmatic: religious Jews, for example, seeing human beings as limited, with a capacity for good and evil, regard belief in God and God's commandments as the ethical imperative, compelling people to strive for good. Somehow, the idea of God, more awesome than fallible humanity lays a stronger claim to my belief.

Knowing No Bounds...

These are some of my recent thoughts on religion and God ... and while I don't expect women to accept them (God forbid!), I do expect women – feminists – to respect them... because, like it or not, I'm a feminist too... And if this respect isn't possible within the terms of feminism as we know it, then perhaps we need a new feminism to do justice to all our lives and all our dreams – and that we includes white, gentile, middle class feminists as well as all the others ...

The only feminism worthy of its name is one that genuinely challenges patriarchy – patriarchy as a way of making sense of the world: of ordering, selecting, valuing and devaluing. And what we identify as patriarchy today was not a once-and-for-all event, born of a life/death struggle between two distinct forces/principles/modes of social organisation: patriarchy versus matriarchy; men versus women. Patriarchy did not happen, it has emerged. And as it has emerged, it has taken shape and gained definition. In the *Torah*, for example, we find multiple and contradictory truths and realities; the consummate patriarchal mode, which has become most explicit in the last two hundred years with the rise of science and accelerated historical development, knows of only one truth, one reality. And for all its theoretical sophistication, feminism, like socialism has been formed in a patriarchal universe in which truth is simple and reason supreme and progress inevitable – and good always triumphs over evil...

It is not inevitable that feminism fulfils its patriarchal legacy, but it is possible. After almost two decades of women's liberation, some feminists are now deciding just how far other feminists may take our Jewish/Black/Working Class identification – and still call ourselves feminists. And the message I am receiving is, that it is okay to be Jewish culturally – that is, within a liberation-culture framework – but not religiously; it is okay to make connections with Jewish women's traditions, as long as the traditions of Jewish men are rejected in the process. In other words, if I keep my Jewish identification strictly limited within existing feminist parameters, I can do no wrong. But as it happens, I'm making no promises...

As it happens, I am a lesbian and feminist who expresses her

Jewishness both culturally and religiously – an entity which doesn't exist in either Jewish or feminist terms, and yet here I am. It doesn't all 'fit', but it is me – not because I was born that way, and not because this is what some definition of correct political practice dictates, but because this is what I have chosen. I am a Jewish lesbian feminist who is choosing to explore what Jewishness – in all its dimensions – means and has meant to Jews – to women and men, to Sephardi and Ashkenazi communities. And in choosing to explore the meanings Jews are making and have made, I am also choosing to explore my own Jewish life and the meanings I might make – it is an exciting, daunting, bewildering, exhilarating process.

And I am choosing much more than I have been able to write here: language is limited; it cannot contain me. I will not and cannot predict what I will be thinking and saying tomorrow – although I'm sure that whatever it is, I'll do my best to be persuasive! The only certainty I have is that I'm learning all the time. And I hope I never succeed in suppressing, diminishing, ignoring anything I learn which is difficult or challenging or incongruous – but no doubt like anyone else making sense of things, I'll try...

CHAPTER FIVE

Gender Trouble and the Transformation of Judaism

Since the 1970s, Jewish women have been making trouble with Judaism. Why? To respond to this question, in good Jewish fashion, let us ponder four more: Why Jewish feminism? What is Jewish feminism trying to achieve? What difference has over three decades of Jewish feminism made to Jewish life and teaching? Is it possible for Jewish feminism to transform Judaism in such a way that Jewish daughters, together with Jewish sons, receive an equal inheritance?

Daughters in a world of sons

As you ponder, let me remind you of a biblical tale that is sometimes overlooked.

Who isn't familiar with the story of Joseph and his brothers?[1] Intriguingly, after Joseph's brothers have sold him to a travelling caravan of merchants, the *Torah* interrupts the Joseph narrative and turns to a story about Judah, one of Joseph's older brothers, and Jacob's fourth son.

We read in Genesis chapter 38 that after 'he went down' from his brothers, Judah 'took' the daughter of a Canaanite named Shu'ah, who bore him three sons, Er, On and Shelah. Later, Judah 'took' a wife for Er named Tamar. But Er's wickedness incited the Eternal to kill him. After this, On refused to produce a son with his sister-in-law in his dead brother's name, and so was also killed by God – for spilling his seed. Judah then promised Tamar that when Shelah grew up, she would be married to him.

But Judah did not keep his promise – and so Tamar was forced to take drastic action (:12ff). When Tamar learnt that her father-in-law was going up to Timnah to shear his sheep, she took off her widow's garments, disguised herself, and waited for him along the way. Mistaking his daughter-in-law for a prostitute, Judah approached her

---

1   Genesis, ch. 37.

and offered her a 'kid of the goats' in return for her services. Tamar responded by asking him to leave her a pledge until the kid arrived. Later, when Judah returned to look for the prostitute and bring her the kid, he could not find her and was told that a prostitute had not been there. Three months later, Judah was informed that his daughter-in-law had 'played the harlot' and was now pregnant. In response to this information, Judah called for her to be brought out and burnt. But then Tamar showed her father-in-law the items that he had left her as a pledge, and seeing them, he acknowledged that 'she is more righteous than I, because I did not give her to Shelah my son' (:26).

Yes, Tamar was 'more righteous' than Judah, who had casual sex just because he felt like it. Trapped in her widowhood, Tamar could not simply return to her father's house as if she were an unmarried girl. In the patriarchal world the *Torah* describes, a childless widow had only one option – to marry again, and bear a son. She was not an independent actor and, unlike Judah, she could not simply decide to go her own way. Yet, trapped by her situation and status as a childless widow, Tamar took the initiative – took charge of her own fate in the only context that was possible for her – by becoming a mother. And so, the tale that begins with Judah ends with Tamar giving birth to twin sons, Zerah and Peretz (:28-30).

The story of Joseph resumes again at Genesis chapter 39. But the purpose of this detour is not simply to highlight the role of a key brother in the Joseph narrative: Tamar's twin sons signify the next generation. Tamar went to the limits of her position as a dependent woman to take action for the sake of the future. But it is precisely in the act of doing this that the tale of Tamar underscores the nature of the patriarchal universe of the *Torah*, and so reminds the reader of the gender-score.

In this way, this interruption in the Joseph narrative is very similar to the story of Jacob's only daughter, Dinah, which interrupts the Jacob narrative[2]. Who was Dinah[3]? Leah's seventh child and Jacob's only daughter, she is largely overlooked amongst all those sons. What does the *Torah* tell us about Dinah? At the beginning of Genesis chapter 34, we read:

---

2 Genesis chapter 34.
3 Gen. 30:21.

134

> Now, Dinah the daughter of Leah, whom she had borne to Jacob, went out to see the daughters of the land.

In a clear echo of her father Jacob's journeys, Dinah 'went out' (*va-teitzei*) – she headed out on her own, purposefully – perhaps even eagerly[4]. Among the children of the family, Dinah alone 'went out' on her own journey. But she did not just step out of her own volition, 'she went out to see the daughters of the land'. Why? Who were 'the daughters of the land'? Why are 'the daughters of the land' mentioned? We do not find answers to these questions by reading what follows – or by investigating any other texts in the *Torah*. The *Torah* usually tells us about individual 'daughters', when relating something about particular male characters. Otherwise, 'daughters' do not get a mention – let alone a *collectivity* of daughters.

How ordinary it seems to a modern reader that Dinah 'went out to see the daughters of the land' – but how extraordinary in the context of this ancient text and the patriarchal society it reflects. And then, how disappointing that Dinah experienced the fate of so many daughters, who dare to go out on their own – in every age: she was raped (34:2):

> Then Shechem, the son of Hamor the Hivite, the prince of the land, saw her, and he took her, and he lay with her, and humbled her – va-*yy'anneha*.

Va-yy'anneha – based on the three-letter Hebrew 'root', *Ayin Nun Hey*, this word in the intensive (*pi'el*) form we find it in this verse means to 'humble' or 'afflict'; in relation to a man 'afflicting' a woman, 'humbling' is a euphemism for rape. But do we need to be told that 'he humbled her'? After all, the words, '… saw her, and he took her, and he lay with her' already tell us everything. If we turn again to the story involving Dinah's brother, Judah, we learn that after 'Judah saw a daughter of a certain Canaanite… and he took her and came into her' (38:2), the unnamed woman simply bore Judah's sons (38:3-5). There is nothing unusual about a 'daughter' being seen and 'taken' by a man – indeed that is how 'marriage' was practiced in ancient times before it was ritualised as a social institution. The difference in the case of Dinah is that in addition to having a

---

4   See Genesis 28:10: 'Jacob went out – *va-yeitzei* - from B'eir Sheva.'

significant father, she also had *brothers*.

And so it was that after Shechem fell in love with 'the young woman' and wanted to marry her (34:3-4), her brothers entered into negotiations with Shechem's father, Hamor, concerning an 'alliance', which was conditional upon all the men of Shechem being circumcised (34:14-17). But that was not the end of the matter: three days after their circumcisions, when the men of Shechem were 'in pain', 'two of the sons of Jacob, Shimon and Levi, Dinah's brothers, took each one his sword, and came upon the city unawares, and slew all the males' (34:25).

Years later, at the end of his life, in Jacob's final address to each of his sons, he condemned Shimon and Levi for their violence (49:5-6). He had come 'in peace' to the city of Shechem (33:18), and they had destroyed any hope of this (34:30). So, the text is clear that Shimon and Levi did wrong – and the narrative may even be read as a polemic against brothers engaging in 'honour killing'. But as soon as the reader accepts this resolution – she or he is in danger of colluding in a double betrayal: Dinah 'went out to see the daughters of the land'. Instead of finding them, Shechem 'saw her, then took her and lay with her, and humbled her.' (34:2). From there on the text centres not on *her* experience – having stepped out, Dinah is then completely passive and silent throughout the rest of the narrative - but on how the male members of her family set about dealing with the offence against *them*.

So, what are we to make of the story of Dinah? Is it a cautionary tale, perhaps? Ironically, the story of Dinah, that ends in a revenge fest, as her brothers murder the men of Shechem's city in retaliation for Shechem's 'outrage against Israel' (34:7), begins with Dinah going out 'to see the daughters of the land' (34:1): The only daughter in search of other daughters – who in the landscape of the *Torah* are only rarely to be seen.

The tales of Dinah and Tamar interrupt the flow to remind us to notice how women serve whatever *Torah* tale they play a part in, but are never served by it. Why am I reminding you of them when they reflect a world long since past? I have chosen to begin this exploration of Jewish feminism with Tamar and Dinah for three reasons:

The first reason: There are still parts of the world today, where the only life-path available to daughters is to leave the house of their father, marry, and produce sons for their father-in-law's family. There are also still parts of the world, where women suspected of having sex outside marriage are killed by their families, and there are still parts of the world today, where the brothers of an unmarried sister, who has lost her virginity to a man that has not been chosen for her by her father, will avenge her lost honour by wreaking violence on the offending man and his family – and all too often, on their sister as well.

The second reason: One of the most important contributions Jewish feminists have made to Jewish teaching in recent years has been to read the *Torah* from the perspective of Jewish women. In doing this, Jewish feminists have not only highlighted the patriarchal stance of the *Torah*, they have also drawn attention to the few female characters included in the *Torah*'s narratives and to their various contributions to the Jewish inheritance.

The third reason: Since the annual re-reading of *Torah*, week after week, remains a central rite of Jewish life, we are continually returned to the roots of our tradition in a patriarchal world. And so, we are challenged by at least another four questions that go beyond the four with which I began. Is it possible to create an egalitarian Jewish present and future despite a patriarchal past, which continues to reassert itself? Given the role of Rabbinic Judaism in reinforcing the gender divisions we find in the *Torah* by creating a framework for Jewish life, in which women and men occupy utterly separate and unequal roles, what needs to be changed in order for Jewish women today to participate fully and equally, alongside Jewish men? Given the continuing attachment of the vast majority of orthodox Jews to rabbinic *halachah* and centuries of tradition, is it possible to make these changes in a meaningful way mainly only within the confines of Progressive Judaism? In so far as it is possible for Jewish feminism to transform Judaism into an egalitarian inheritance, to what extent would that egalitarian inheritance still be recognisable as Judaism?

'The house of Jacob' and 'the children of Israel'

These questions go to the heart of the Jewish feminist project. To address them, we need to acknowledge that, in reading the *Torah* each week, we are not only endlessly repeating the tales of our beginnings, we are also reminding ourselves that the *Torah* is the source of Jewish teaching. So let us return to the *Torah* to ask another question – one raised by the Revelation narrative. When the ex-slaves were gathered at Mount Sinai, seven weeks after their departure from Egypt, did the women enter the covenant with the Eternal One, or were they simply onlookers?

Just prior to the account of Revelation, we read in Exodus chapter 19 (:10-11): 'The Eternal One said to Moses: "Go to the people, and sanctify them today and tomorrow, and let them wash their garments, / and be ready for the third day; for on the third day the Eternal One will come down in the sight of *all the people* upon Mount Sinai."' But then, when Moses is repeating this instruction, he only addresses the men (19:15): 'Then he said to the people; "be ready for the third day; *do not come near a woman."'*

So, did God address everyone – or only the males? A few verses earlier, just after the people have arrived at Sinai, the first encounter there between the Eternal One and Moses, opens with this proclamation (19:3): 'Thus shall you say to the house of Jacob and declare to the children of Israel'. Interpreting what looks like repetition, we find this comment in the *midrash*, in *M'chilta d' Rabbi Yishma'el*: 'The house of Jacob refers to the women; the children of Israel to the men'.[5] This rabbinic comment suggests *inclusion* – but if we examine the comment more closely, we see that it also suggests *segregation*. Rabbinic teaching, rooted in the sages' interpretations of the *Torah*, makes it clear that while men are responsible for the public realm of Jewish life, women are confined to the home, where, exempt from prayer and study, their main obligations centre on lighting the *Shabbat* and festival candles, dividing the *challah* dough, and maintaining the laws of family purity – *taharat ha-mishpachah*.[6] Women are included, but their role within Jewish life, defined by men, is privatised and limited. In other words, the rabbis were responsible for constructing a *halachic* framework in which the male 'children of Israel' occupied the public stage, while the females who constituted 'the house of Jacob' were confined to the domestic arena.

In chapter 3, I investigated the exceptional woman scholar, B'ruria, and her anomalous situation in the landscape of second century male rabbinic discourse. In exempting women from study, and limiting their obligations to the domestic arena, the rabbis also

---

5 *M'chilta d' Rabbi Yishma'el, Ba-Chodesh* II.
6 See, for example, *Talmud Bavli, Kiddushin* 33b-35a.

ensured that women were not equipped to challenge the patriarchal order. Let us imagine that women had also participated in the academies of Yavneh, Sura and Pumbedita, and shared in the discussions of the laws that became the foundation of the *halachah*: what would they have brought to the debates? Had the rabbinic sages been women as well as men, would the record of their deliberations have included a tractate called, 'Women' (*Nashim*)? How different would the *Talmud* look – and *halachah* as a system, predicated on gender division, and the subordination of women – if women had been included and had participated with the men as equal partners?

The feminist transformation of Judaism

Of course, these are absurd questions. We cannot change the patriarchal past of Judaism, and we still live in a male dominated society. But during the last three decades something has begun to change. For the first time since the sages deliberated in their academies over two thousand years ago, Jewishly-educated women – many of them rabbis – writing, and engaging with one another consciously as Jewish women, have begun to study the *Torah* and the corpus of rabbinic literature. In doing so, they have not only challenged the gender divide, but also the gender of God. Despite Moses' mysterious encounter with the nameless, elusive, ineffable One,[7] God is presented in both the *Torah*, and subsequent rabbinic teaching, predominantly as male. As long as He speaks, He commands, mirroring the power of men in the world, women must, by definition, be the subordinate gender.

And so, alongside feminist interpretations of the *Torah* and rabbinic texts, feminists have challenged the patriarchal God by re-interpreting the Eternal One – in myriad ways. At one end of the spectrum there are those who address the Eternal One in feminine terms – drawing on the *kabbalistic* notion of the *Sh'chinah*, the immanent, feminine aspect of the Divine. At the other end of the spectrum are those who, taking their cue from the feminist liturgist, Marcia Falk, who speaks of the Eternal One in impersonal terms as *Eyn Chayyim*, 'the Source of Life'. What all feminist approaches to the Eternal share in common is the awareness of the power of language

---

7 See Exodus 3:14 – and my reflections on this passage in Ch. 6 Beyond the Divine Autocrat.

and imagery about the Divine to shape and reinforce gender relations. When God ceases to be regarded as *Adonai Tz'va'ot*, 'the Lord of Hosts' and *melech malchey ha-m'lachim*, 'the king above the king of kings', the power of warrior lords and of kings and emperors and dictators of various kinds is no longer legitimated 'on high'.[8]

So, what has been the impact of Jewish feminism on Judaism over the past three decades? An anthology published in the United States, entitled, *New Jewish Feminism. Probing the past, Forging the Future*, edited by Rabbi Elyse Goldstein,[9] demonstrates the immense scope of Jewish feminist creativity that has taken place in the second largest Jewish community in the world today – encompassing theology, liturgy, ritual, study, the synagogue, gender, sexuality, age and leadership. Many of the book's forty contributors are female rabbis; which, in itself, says a lot about the impact of Jewish feminism on Judaism. The majority of the book focuses on transformations within Progressive Judaism, although changes within Conservative and Orthodox Judaism are also discussed. Apart from the section on Israel, *New Jewish Feminism* reflects the American Jewish context. Nevertheless, the major issues it raises about the nature of the Jewish feminist project, and its implications for Judaism, are relevant for Jewish life elsewhere – not least in Britain.

Women as leaders

As in the United States, the leadership of women rabbis in Britain has been crucial. The first woman rabbi in Britain, Jackie Tabick, was ordained in 1975 before Jewish Feminism arrived on the scene. By the early 1990s, there were not only now more than a dozen women rabbis, but, following the initiative of Rabbi Marcia Plumb, the women rabbis came together to set up *The Half-Empty Bookcase*, a network encompassing study days, annual gatherings and a quarterly newsletter, and committed to developing educational resources reflecting the perspectives of Jewish women.

In addition to this, the women rabbis also contributed to a ground-breaking anthology, *Hear Our Voice*, edited by Rabbi Sybil Sheridan, which, dedicated to the memory of the first woman rabbi,

---

8 See Chapter 6 for a fuller treatment.
9 Jewish Lights Publishing, (Woodstock, Vermont, 2009).

Regina Jonas (1902-1944), ordained in Germany in 1935, was the first work of Jewish feminist scholarship to come out of the British context.[10] A further anthology of the writings of the women rabbis, *Taking Up the Timbrel*, edited by Rabbis Sylvia Rothschild and Sybil Sheridan,[11] presented the work that the British female rabbinate was doing in the area of new ritual and liturgy.

In the meantime, directly as a result of the work of women rabbis, in 1995 the Liberal and Reform movements published their first inclusive language prayer-books, *Siddur Lev Chadash* (Liberal) and the Pilgrim Festivals *Machzor* (Reform)[12] – although only *Siddur Lev Chadash*, created primarily for daily and Sabbath use, has, thus far, had a significant impact on congregational life. More recently, in 2008, the Movement for Reform Judaism has also published an inclusive language *siddur* for *Shabbat* and daily use, which will also, hopefully, play a positive role in promoting gender equality in Reform synagogues.

The development of inclusive liturgy is a significant achievement. However, as yet, with the exception of Rabbi Alexandra Wright, Senior Rabbi of the Liberal Jewish Synagogue and, more recently, in 2011, Dame Julia Neuberger, Senior Rabbi of West London Synagogue, Rabbi Deborah Kahn-Harris, Prinicipal of Leo Baeck College and Rabbi Laura Janner-Klausner as the Movement Rabbi for MRJ, most of the three dozen women rabbis working in Britain serve medium to small congregations, with more than half of them working on part-time contracts. No doubt, one of the reasons why some women rabbis work part-time is to ensure that they are available for childcare. But this only applies to some and in any case, as a rationale for part-time working, it begs the question about those male rabbis, who have children, but, nevertheless, work full-time.

For the first time in the history of the Jewish people, women, ordained as rabbis – who now constitute half the progressive rabbinate in Britain – have the potential to transform Jewish life and teaching. In order to play this role, women rabbis need a level playing field with men in the employment arena. But that's not all.

---

10 SCM Press, 1994.

11 SCM Press, 2000.

12 Union of Liberal and Progressive Synagogues, London; Reform Synagogues of Great Britain, London. Since 1995, each movement has been renamed: Liberal Judaism, and the Movement for Reform Judaism, respectively.

Individuals and communities need to begin to recognise the authority of the female rabbinate and have the vision to see women rabbis
as offering a much-needed new leadership of Progressive Judaism –
which means being prepared to acknowledge the need for change.

Jewish women on the move

The importance of women assuming leadership roles, especially as
rabbis, cannot be over-estimated. But, of course, women's leadership
is only half the story – albeit crucial. What does it mean for Jewish
women as a collectivity, to move from the margins to the centre;
from the private to the public arena of Jewish life?

The first Jewish feminist conference in Britain was held in London
in January 1982. There followed subsequent gatherings in Oxford
and Leeds. Strikingly, these conferences brought together Jewish
women from within the Jewish community, as well as Jewish
women, who were not affiliated; many of whom subsequently chose
– like me – to become involved in communal Jewish life. By the mid-
1980s it became clear that the impetus to transform the gender
divide was beginning to emerge across the Jewish spectrum, as
groups of women began to gather together for study and celebration
– often forming *Rosh Chodesh* (New Moon) groups, which met
monthly to celebrate the new moon in creative ways and to study
together. At this time, a group of progressive feminists got together
under the auspices of the Reform Synagogues of Great Britain to
examine the issue of 'Women and *Tallit*' (prayer shawl).[13] It was also
around this time that orthodox women began to hold women's services with *Torah* readings and women's *Purim M'gillah*[14] readings at
the modern orthodox centre, Yakar, in north London, as well as in
women's homes.

---

13 The RSGB 'Women and *Tallit*' Working Party, set up in 1986, consisted of:
Rabbi Barbara Borts, Dee Eimer, Karen Goldman, Dorothea Magonet and
myself. The booklet, *Women and Tallit: Jewish Women and the Ritual of Prayer*
was published by RSGB in 1987. A second edition of the booklet was
published in 1997, edited by Dee Eimer and myself.

14 *Purim M'gillah - Purim* Scroll. Also known as *M'gillat Esther* – the Scroll of
Esther. Five of the books in the *K'tuvim*, the 'Writings', the third section of the
TaNaKH, the Hebrew Bible, are also produced as scrolls for liturgical
purposes and are connected to five of the Jewish festivals and commemorations.

And so in Britain, too, Jewish women as a collectivity have begun to transgress the divide between 'the house of Jacob' and 'the children of Israel'. But this has not been a simple matter of battering down the door to the men's club of Jewish life. One of the major issues raised in *New Jewish Feminism* revolves around the relative merits of 'imitative' and 'inventive' Jewish rituals.[15] As Elyse Goldstein demonstrates, Jewish feminists are engaged, both, in adapting rituals defined by Jewish men and adopting them as Jewish women – the *tallit* is a good example – and in inventing new female rituals, previously excluded from Jewish practice. Both those associated with the regular rhythms of women's lives, like menstruation and menopause, and in response to disruptive and traumatic experiences, like miscarriage, infertility, rape and mastectomy.

In other words, Jewish feminists are both laying claim to spaces, roles and practices that rabbinic tradition has assigned to men, and expanding the arena of Jewish life to include and reflect women's particular perspectives and experiences. But both strategies have their limitations. Goldstein writes: '... imitative rituals ... say nothing of us as women. They do not mark the unique moments that happen only to women ... They express Judaism in ways that still are male ways of envisaging the universe, male ceremonies invented and designed by men. They are still largely male answers to the question, how shall I mark this moment?'[16] On the other hand, in the process of inventing new rituals, Jewish feminists are challenged '... to probe into the meaning of authenticity... What makes an inventive ritual authentic?'[17] Goldstein identifies that it takes time and practice – and also: 'These practices need to be collected, published, promulgated by the lay and professional arms of our movement'.[18] In other words, for an inventive ritual to become authentically Jewish it must both become incorporated into regular Jewish practice and be authorised by recognised authorities. One of the implications of this transformation is that what was inventive becomes habitual. The new ritual reflecting spontaneity and *kavvanah* – particular intention – becomes *keva* – fixed and normative.[19] Is this inevitable? Is it possi-

---

15 Goldstein, 2009, pp.81-89.
16 ibid. p.85.
17 ibid. p.88.
18 ibid. p.89.
19 Lori Hope Levkovitz and Rona Shapiro, in Goldstein, 2009, pp.78-80.

ble to maintain a spirit of creative inventiveness alongside the quest to authenticate new rituals? In what ways do progressive approaches to Judaism, which empower the individual to make informed choices, help to promote an on-going dynamic spirit of creativity?

Lots of questions – and more questions than answers. Since the 1970s, Jewish feminists have been engaged in transforming Jewish teaching and the key institutions of Judaism: both the synagogue and the home. Consequently, Jewish feminism has the potential to transform the lives, not only, of Jewish daughters, but also, of Jewish sons. What would the synagogue and the home look and feel like if women and men played full and equal parts in both domains? What difference would it make to the life of the Jewish people as a whole if Jewish teaching was transformed in such a way that it reflected the perspectives and experiences of Jewish women as well as those of Jewish men? There are huge differences between the contexts of Jewish life: between Britain and the United States; between Britain and mainland Europe; between the diaspora and Israel; between the progressive and orthodox Jewish worlds. Nevertheless the same issues and questions challenge all those who are committed to transforming Judaism into an inclusive, egalitarian inheritance.

CHAPTER SIX

Beyond the Divine Autocrat: Speaking of God Today

An opening tale

Once upon a time in a remote, barren, never-never land, *achar ha-midbar*, 'behind the wilderness',[1] a lone shepherd met with God. It was a strange, miraculous, elusive meeting which he later transmuted into images and words – he *saw* a burning bush that was not consumed by the flames, he *heard* a voice calling him out of the midst of the bush, the voice commanded him to approach and urged him to return to his people and liberate them from slavery.

The man felt the commanding power of his encounter with God but he did not think he could convey what happened, second-hand, to the slaves. And in the absence of the experience, he was sure that the people would demand concrete pieces of information, like 'who sent you to us?' and 'what name did the voice go by?' So, in the midst of his overwhelming meeting with God, the man attempted to extract these details. But as soon as he tried to capture the experience, he could grasp nothing more than an indistinct breathy, non-consonantal whisper-of-a-sound: *'ehyeh asher ehyeh'. 'Ehyeh asher ehyeh'* had sent him?[2] What would that mean to the slaves?

Ehyeh – the breath of God dissipated into the thin air and the man was left alone with his experience. All he could do now was to express the encounter, imperfectly, in the form of a story. He would tell a tale of a 'burning bush' and a 'voice' called 'I am' and 'I will be' and hope that his listeners would discern the ineffable truth that lay behind it.

---

1 Exodus 3:1.
2 ibid:14. The translation is 'I am that I am', or, 'I will be who I will be'. *Ehyeh*, from the Hebrew root, *Hei Yud Hei*, is the imperfect first person singular of the verb to be, which corresponds to the future/present-future tense.

Speaking of God

The tale told in Exodus chapter 3 has a powerful message for us. 'Speaking of God' is not possible – has never been possible, at any time and in any place. The literary critic, Gabriel Josipovici, points out that:[3]

> The phrase, *ehyeh asher ehyeh* … is as near as we can get in language to pure breath, non-articulation, non-division. In uttering, God both defines himself as pure potential and repudiates the kind of definition Moses – and we – are looking for. But he also indicates by his palindromic utterance, with its repeated 'h' and 'sh' sounds, that his is the breath that lies beneath all utterance and all action, a living breath which does not move forward yet does not remain static, upholding both speech and the world.

It is impossible to speak of God but in every time and in every place, human beings have done just that – speaking of God in the context of the world they inhabited. Long ago, when people were rooted in one place and daily life was dominated by the cycle of the seasons and survival depended entirely on fecundity, God was a woman, a mother, *Chochmah*, the 'wisdom' underlying all existence.[4] Later, when the Hebrew people were struggling in the midst of others to establish their own distinct identity in their own land, God was a tribal warrior-king, YHVH,[5] leading the people out of bondage, destroying both the enemies of His people and the gods they worshipped. At a later time still, when, after successive conquests by their enemies, the Temple in Jerusalem was laid waste once and for all and the people of Israel faced slavery or homelessness, God was *Sh'chinah*, a Presence which went into exile with Her people and suffered with them.[6]

---

3 In *The Book of God. A Response to the Bible.* (Yale University Press, Yale and London, 1988), p.74.
4 See 'The Goddess in Judaism – an Historical Perspective' by Asphodel Long in Alix Pirani, ed.,*The Absent Mother, Restoring the Goddess to Judaism and Christianity.* (HarperCollins, London, 1991); *in a Chariot Drawn by Lions, The Search for the Female in Deity* by Asphodel Long (The Crossing Press, Freedom, CA, 1993).
5 See Chapter 1 – note 9.
6 The *Sh'chinah* goes into exile with Israel and will return with them at the End of Days (*Talmud B'rachot* 6a). 'Wheresoever they were exiled, the *Sh'chinah*

Of course, it is not quite as simple as this. As Judith Plaskow, the feminist theologian, reminds us[7] at no time has there been one single image of God. The point is, however, that God is both ineffable, beyond our grasp and also the eternal mirror, reflecting the realities of every 'today' from time immemorial.

Speaking of God Today

So, what of *our* 'today'?

Today is a day after a century of genocide from the fields of Arnhem to the villages of Rwanda. And in the midst of a century of bloodshed: systematic technology-aided slaughter; the triumph of de-humanised human intellect and will over humanity and God – the bridge of death that links Auschwitz and Hiroshima.

Today is a day after the first decade of a new century, marked by new/old wars and unresolved conflicts, by suicide bombings and state terrorism.

Today is a day when scientific advances allow millions to be annihilated in a single moment and which can also bestow the gift of extended life and health for millions of others. And scientific development has reached the realm of the unknown – and perhaps, the unknowable. The revelation of certain truths about the Universe has disappeared into black holes and an endless series of unanswered questions.

Today is also a day when the speed of technological development builds obsolescence into every new invention; a day when speed is becoming the ultimate value, and having friends in cyberspace is more important than inviting friends into your home.

Today is a day when I can be in London and Budapest and Bombay – all in one day. I can encounter a host of different societies, cultures, religious systems. Indeed, I don't actually have to travel to do this: multicultural Britain is inhabited by a plethora of differing communities espousing differing 'truths' – Judaism, Christianity, Islam, Hinduism, Buddhism, Sikhism, Paganism – each one, itself, an umbrella for a multiplicity of expressions and meanings.

---

went with them.' (*Talmud M'gillah* 29a). The Divine was to dwell among the *exiled* children of Israel even in their impurity (*Talmud Yoma* 56b; *M'gillah* 29a).

7 In *Standing Again at Sinai.* (Harper Collins, San Francisco, 1990), pp.161ff..

Today is also a day when a global culture of consumerism has become the dominant religion of the West, and even life and love are consumer items; when half the world consumes incessantly, insatiably, while the other half of the world starves.

Today is a day when our exploitation of the planet and its resources is approaching danger levels, and we face the possibility of catastrophe unless we reduce our ever expanding 'wants', and focus on our human needs.

Today is also a day when the world remains divided between the rich and the poor, and yet the hierarchical divisions which have characterised human societies for millennia are being challenged and dismantled in response to the insistent demands of the oppressed. The rule of white over black, of man over woman, of the state over the people, of humanity over the earth is giving way to equality, self-determination and a holistic approach to existence on this planet.

Today is a day when millions of people the world over, remain absolutely certain that their particular religion represents the only truth – and a minority are even prepared to kill themselves and others in the name of God – and when millions of other people are equally certain that God does not exist.

Today is also a day when each individual is finding her own unique voice and exploring his own dreams; when, whatever their allegiances and the personal circumstances of their lives, and however they identify themselves, she or he is resisting established communal definitions and controls in order to forge new connections and participate in creating open, inclusive, pluralistic communities. So, how shall we speak of God today?

Shall we speak of 'Almighty God', the redeeming God of justice and mercy, after the *Sho'ah* and nuclear devastation, and in the face of continuing genocide, oppression and poverty?

Shall we worship the ingenious products of our minds and hands, or rediscover God in the reaches of the heavens and on the earth we inhabit?

Shall we continue to lay claim to singular truths in the context of religious diversity?

Shall we perpetuate a hierarchical notion of God as Lord and King reigning over us, even when His human counterparts on earth have ceased to rule?

Shall we resist or embrace the spiritual creativity of individuals both within and outside religious institutions?

Of course, each individual will ask different questions and find different answers – so, *how* shall we speak of God today? And another, related question: *who* shall do the speaking? The changes we witnessed in the 20th century and which continue today not only demand that the world religions speak of God in new ways, they challenge all those who have not had a voice – the working classes, peasant peoples, black peoples, women, those who are lesbian, gay, bisexual or transgender – *to speak*. And indeed, this is what has been happening. Paradoxically, the past one hundred years have seen both the most extreme manifestations of male domination and the emergence of women as a collectivity across the globe, offering, through the world view of feminism, alternative ways of living and of experiencing relationships – between women and women, between women and men, between men and men, between races, peoples, communities, between humanity and other species, between humanity and God.

Jews Speaking of God Today

Speaking of God today means transforming our religious languages both to reflect the new realities in which we live and to include the voices of all those who wish to speak.

Jewish liturgy relishes in oft-repeated formulaic phrases such as *Baruch Attah, Adonai Eloheinu, Melech ha-olam* – 'Blessed are You, Lord our God, King of the Universe'. These six words are an integral, regular feature of both daily services and the prayer of the individual. Most observant Jews know them by heart but do they stop to examine what they mean? As it happens, the word which is translated as 'Lord' – *Adonai* – is a substitute for the name of God – YHVH – which may not be uttered. YHVH – the consonants which convey God's *being* are present, in a verbal form, in the breath-of-a-word, *Ehyeh*.[8] But when the Sages fashioned this formula for the recitation of blessings two thousand years ago, they did so in the spirit of the biblical tradition in which God was *Adon*, Lord and *Melech*, King. And they went further. As the people of Israel were driven into exile and scattered across many lands, the Sages extended the realm of God's rule beyond one land and one people to encom-

---

8 See Chapter 1 – note 9.

pass the whole world. Indeed, in the *Aleynu* prayer originally composed for inclusion in the liturgy for *Rosh Ha-shanah*, the New Year, the Sages spelt out the dimensions of the phrase *Melech ha-olam*, 'King of the Universe'. In this text, included in all three daily services to this day, God is spoken of as *Melech Malchei ha-M'lachim*, 'the King above the King of Kings', whose glory dwells in the heavens above and the presence of His power reaches into furthest space.

Today, in response to feminist challenges to he-man language,[9] progressive forms of Judaism no longer address God as the Lord and King of the Universe. And yet, faithful Jews, and those with little faith, continue to recite God's qualities as Lord and King of the Universe. Somehow, these images have survived conquests and enslavements and exiles and pogroms for centuries – and even the *Sho'ah*. Meanwhile, for many other Jews, who see themselves as secular, God's omnipotence was finally annihilated along with the six million, eclipsed by a greater power and it is not possible to pretend otherwise. The God who redeemed His people out of Egypt did not save them from the pits and the gas chambers. There have been many Jewish theological responses to the *Sho'ah*. Of these, only the approach of Eliezer Berkovits seriously attempts, in my view, to preserve the image of God's enduring omnipotence. For Berkovits because God is *erech apayim*, 'long suffering' towards evildoers, giving them an opportunity to repent, it is inevitable that while God waits patiently for the return of the wicked, the righteous will suffer.[10] At the other extreme, there are those, like Richard Rubinstein, for whom, God 'died' in the death camps.[11] While Martin Buber, true to the spirit of the relationship between the 'I' and the 'Eternal Thou', suggests simply that God was 'silent'.[12]

Whatever theory one adopts and there are many, many more, it is hard to escape the feeling, that Almighty God was overshadowed by the smoking chimneys of the crematoria – and some might say that

---

9 Dale Spender's book, *Man-Made Language* (Routledge & Kegan Paul, London, 1980), based on her Ph.D. thesis, was the first feminist work to systematically examine patriarchal language.

10 In *Faith After the Holocaust*. (Ktav, New York, 1973), pp.101ff.

11 See *After Auschwitz: Radical Theology and Contemporary Judaism*. (Bobbs-Merrill, New York, 1966).

12 See *Eclipse of God: Studies in the Relation between Religion and Philosophy*. (Victor Gollancz, London, 1953).

God has been diminished ever since. And yet, numberless Jews still continue to find God after the *Sh'oah* – both in their own life experiences and in the wonder of existence. Abraham Joshua Heschel's ecstatic declaration of 'radical amazement' in the presence of Creation resonates deeply with many.[13] For many people, the natural world provokes a response of deep astonishment. And if anything, scientific discoveries in the past fifty years have only served to heighten a profound sense of awe.

However, while radical amazement helps to restore the notion of God's *transcendence*, it has been the confrontation with God's apparent powerlessness and inaction during the *Sho'ah*, which has enabled Jews to begin to find new ways of meeting God. If God is not All Powerful and if human beings have a seemingly limitless capacity to dominate and destroy, then it is our responsibility to commit our energies to the task of creating relationships of mutual respect and equality between people and peoples. The Sages believed that each person is born with an inclination for good – *yeitzer tov* – and an inclination for evil – *yeitzer ra* – it is up to each individual to act to ensure that the good predominates. Paradoxically, the God who seemed to be 'absent' because He did not deliver us with 'a mighty hand and an outstretched arm', becomes an abiding *presence* with us and within us when we acknowledge that we are God's hands. God is the good we do. God is the strength and endurance we can muster. God is the source of our life, the foundation of our being. In this context, traditional liturgical expressions like, *Tzur Yisrael*, 'Rock of Israel', *Eitz Chayyim*, 'Tree of Life', *Elohim Chai*, 'Living God', *Oseh Shalom*, 'Maker of Peace', *Av Ha-Rachamim* 'Source of Mercies', *Yoseid Aretz*, 'the One who makes the Earth firm', all serve to convey a sense of God as *Sh'chinah*, 'the One who dwells' with us.

New Jewish liturgy draws on these images and has also used classical biblical and rabbinic expressions to fashion new names for God, like *M'kor Ha-B'rachah*, 'Fountain of Blessing' and *Eyn Ha-Chayyim*, 'Wellspring of Life'. However, new Jewish ways of speaking to God are not simply responses to the dethronement of God during the *Sho'ah*, they are also attempts to express the values which have

---

13 See *God in Search of Man: A Philosophy of Judaism*. (Farrar, Straus and Giroux, New York, 1980), pp.66-7.

come to the fore in recent global socio-political, economic and ecological changes. Some of these values, like peace, justice and compassion, have deep roots in biblical tradition. Others like equality, democracy and pluralism, have evolved over the past two hundred years, gathering pace in the last few decades. As Judith Plaskow argues, 'religious symbols do not simply tell us about God; they are not simply models of a community's sense of ultimate reality. They also shape the world in which we live functioning as models for human behaviour and the social order.[14] In a world in which equality, democracy and pluralism become the order of the day, the images of God as Lord and King are clearly no longer appropriate. In their place we find new images, which 'picture divine power not as something above and over us but in and around'.[15]

The American feminist liturgist, Marcia Falk, not only incorporates the non-hierarchical image of God as *Ein Ha-Chayyim*, 'Wellspring of Life', into her blessings but the formulations she has developed completely transform both the image of God conveyed and the way in which the relationship between God and people, God and the world, is expressed. In place of the passive word, *Baruch*, 'Blessed', she says *N'vareich*, 'Let us bless' and so empowers those invoking the blessing, including everyone, male and female in this gender-neutral term. In addition, as we see in her version of the blessing for wine on festivals, the text continues in a way that extends the blessing beyond a ritual transformation of a moment, into an acknowledgement of both God's continuing creativity and the active, creative part played by us, in making the traditions we have inherited live in our lives:[16]

> *N'vareich et-Ein ha-Chayyim matzmichat p'ri ha-gafen, v'nishzor et sarigei chayyeinu b'massoret ha-am.*
> Let us bless the Wellspring of Life that nurtures fruit on the vine as we weave the branches of our lives into tradition.

Marcia Falk's blessing acknowledges both the egalitarian values

---

14 Plaskow,1990, p.126.
15 Ibid., p.140.
16 See 'Beyond Naming: Reflections on Composing the Book of Blessings' in *The Reconstructionist*, Vol.59, No.1, Spring: New Thinking on Naming and Imaging God, 1994, p.68.

implicit in new forms of community and the rich texture of diversity which they encompass. As we bless 'the Wellspring of Life', each individual participates in weaving his or her life into the communal experience. And this simple blessing accomplishes even more than this, it conveys a sense of ultimate wholeness, of the oneness of existence, which God, 'the Wellspring of Life' represents. And further – the non-anthropomorphic metaphor is not accidental. Marcia Falk explains:[17]

[A]s long as we image divinity as a person, whether female or male, we tend to forget that human beings are not the sole, not even the 'primary' life-bearing creatures on the planet. We allow our intelligence and our unique linguistic capabilities to deceive us into believing that we are 'godlier' than the rest of creation. And in so doing, we neglect the real responsibility attendant upon the gift of human consciousness – to care for the earth in ways that respect all human and non-human life upon it.

So we have in one simple blessing an evocation of equality, inclusivity, diversity and wholeness.

The pursuit of wholeness embraces the whole earth. The *kabbalistic* concept of *tikkun olam*, 'repair of the world', calls each Jew to the task of uniting the sparks of divinity which are embedded in every element of God's Creation. As Marcia Falk's liturgical work demonstrates, 'images of God as fountain, source, well-spring or ground of being, remind us that God loves and befriends us as the One who brings forth all being and sustains all existence.'[18] The images of God as lover and friend are powerful ones provoking us to read *Shir Ha-Shirim*, 'The Song of Songs', once again, in metaphorical terms. While clearly a text about human love as modern scholars have claimed – indeed, as Rabbi Sybil Sheridan demonstrates, probably the work of a woman in love[19] – the insistence of Rabbi Akiva, the 2nd century sage, that the book describes the love of God and God's

---

17 See 'Notes on Composing New Blessings. Towards a Feminist Reconstruction of Prayer' in *Weaving the Visions: New Patterns in Feminist Spirituality*, edited by Judith Plaskow and Carol Christ. (Harper Collins, New York, 1989), p.132.
18 Plaskow, 1990, p.165.
19 See 'The Song of Solomon's Wife' in *Hear Our Voice:Women Rabbis Tell Their Stories*, edited by Sybil Sheridan. (SCM Press, London, 1994).

people, strikes an even more compelling contemporary note. As Judith Plaskow argues:[20]

> The images of God as a lover, friend, companion, co-creator – are more appropriate metaphors for the God of the covenant than traditional images of Lord and King. Defining God's power not as domination but as empowerment, they evoke a God who is with us instead of over us, a partner in dialogue who ever and again summons us to responsible action.

'Responsible action' – there's the rub. What good are all these fine, new or reclaimed images and names for God, if they remain words on the page and do not inspire us to act? If new religious language expresses a new sense of our covenantal relationship with God, then we must be active partners with God in 'renewing the work of Creation day by day' (*Yotzeir* prayer in the daily morning service). If inclusive, egalitarian liturgy has emerged largely in response to the emergence of equality, democracy and pluralism, then those who *pray* must also *work* to ensure that these new concepts and values become living realities throughout the world. *But how?* The key to answering this question lies in the creation of participatory communities which live the values they speak. But the generation of new forms of community presupposes the emergence of individuals committed to the task of *tikkun olam*, 'repair of the world', which itself assumes that individuals have the opportunity to realise their full spiritual and human potential. Given that half the world's individuals seem to spend all their free time spending money and consuming, and the other half are totally preoccupied with keeping themselves alive, there does not seem much hope that more than a handful of individuals will have the space or the inclination to realise themselves. On the other hand, perhaps, free of the distractions accumulated with the accumulation of wealth, those who *have* less, may be more able to *be* with themselves and with others.

And then, even people caught on a treadmill find that its endless course is halted by a breakdown from time to time. It is in the crises which interrupt our lives – death, illness, divorce, loss of home or work – that individuals through their pain, anguish and dislocation, may discover, however slowly and fitfully, opportunities for personal

20 Plaskow, p.64.

growth and spiritual renewal and for making new connections with others. I know this has been true for me, and, working as a congregational rabbi, I have seen other people walk through 'the valley of the shadow of death' (Psalm 23) and emerge into new life. This is not to say that shock and disorientation and grief are necessary for spiritual growth. There is no doubt that opportunities for spiritual growth are available at other times, perhaps all the time, if we open ourselves to the possibility. The story of Jacob, waking from his dream-filled sleep after his first night away from home, reminds us that it is possible to wake up at any moment and recognise that the Eternal, the Ineffable 'is in this place', although we may not have realised it a moment earlier.[21] Nevertheless, it is when our lives break apart that we are often most likely to crash into the rock of our existence and discover the values we hold most dear. *Personal crisis is a spiritual opportunity.*

Speaking of God – a closing tale and a conclusion

Another wilderness tale: Long, long ago – long before Moses heard the breath of God whispering in the wilderness – a female servant from Egypt who lived with her Hebrew mistress and master in the land of Canaan, fled into the wilderness in a state of utter despair and met with God. Because this story is not well-known, let us now listen to the handmaid's tale:[22]

My life as a servant was uneventful but as each year passed and my mistress failed to conceive, the atmosphere grew increasingly tense. Eventually, after ten long years, she suggested to her husband that he should cohabit with me so she might obtain a child through me. Needless to say, I was not consulted. So, my master came in to me and I conceived. But the tension got worse. I could not help feeling that I wanted my child and to tell you the truth, I looked down on my mistress a little. She became very envious and treated me harshly. When I could not bear it any more, I fled into the wilderness. But then, I found myself by a fountain and when I thought I was completely alone, a messenger of God found me there and spoke to me. The messenger insisted that I

---

21 See Genesis 28:16: "When Jacob awoke from his sleep he said: 'Surely the Eternal One is in this place, and I did not know it.'"
22 See Gen. 16: 1-13

return and submit to my mistress's harsh treatment. In return for my acquiescence, my descendants would 'multiply' and the child I was bearing would be called 'Yishmael', 'God will hear', because God had heard my affliction. My son would become a 'wild man'. He would not submit to anyone's hand, he would fight back and dwell among his people. It was hard for me to hear the message, to accept the burden with the blessing. But I heard that God was with me and in that moment I called aloud, 'Attah El ro'i', 'You, God, see me' and knew that I was speaking God's name.

There are many familiar elements to this tale of domestic rivalry and abuse and some very remarkable ones. Not only did the Egyptian servant-woman experience God in the wilderness, communing with her in her distress, giving her hope for the future but the power of the encounter impelled her to name it, to name God, *Attah El ro'i* – 'You, God, see me'. As Jane Litman points out, 'Hagar is the only person in the Hebrew Bible to name God.'[23]

Like Moses centuries later, Hagar found herself in the wilderness and met the Eternal. But unlike Moses, the changeling–prince turned fugitive, who had been saved from the plight of his fellow Hebrews as a baby, Hagar knew what it was to be subjected to the will of another, she had tasted bitterness and despair. Moses was quietly tending his father-in-law's flock when he led them astray into the wilderness, but Hagar fled into the wilderness, wild with desperation. When she met the Eternal and God recognised her pain and spoke to her hopes and her fears, she did not have to ask for God's name, she uttered the name which her experience evoked in her – 'You, God, see me'.

In many ways, Hagar's experience prefigured that of the Hebrews in Egypt – in reverse: she, an Egyptian servant in Canaan, fled from her Hebrew mistress. But unlike the Hebrews, who were ambivalent about leaving their house of bondage and had to be 'driven out'[24] by the Egyptians into a barren wilderness, Hagar, emboldened by the new life growing within her, propelled herself out of servitude and so found the waters of renewal she needed.

---

23 See 'Postmodernism, Jewish Theology and Naming God' in *The Reconstructionist*, Vol.59, No.1, Spring 1994, p.78.
24 Exodus 12:39.

But tragically, ironically, having led herself out of bondage, she also had to make the hard decision to go back for the sake of her child and the future of their people. Hagar's liberation was short-lived.

Hagar is not one of the Bible's celebrated heroes: an alien; a servant; a lone woman; other, dependent, utterly marginal. Yet out of her distress, she heard God's voice and she found the words to express her experience. And so she becomes a model for each and every one of us – particularly for all those who have not had the courage to speak yet or whose voices have not been heard. Hagar's tale is a source of inspiration, reminding us not only that the power-less have the power within them to name God but also that each individual has that possibility. The task of speaking of God is not the responsibility of the religious institutions alone. This message is particularly pertinent today when the 'autonomy' of the individual has become one of the core values in many societies. Of course, acknowledging the potential of individuals to evoke God in their lives is a risky business, threatening religious hegemony. On the other hand, without the living religious experiences of *individuals*, the danger is that the spirit of the religious *institutions* will wither and die.

When Moses met God in the wilderness, God eluded his grasp but he did not miss the message of the encounter: Although he felt terrified and unequal to the task, he had to return to Egypt and lead the slaves out of bondage. The purpose of speaking to God is not to delude ourselves into thinking that we can prove the existence of God, or finally capture the essence of God with our limited human language. The purpose of speaking to God is to acknowledge that the Eternal *is* and *will continue to be*, in and around us, *speaking* to us, with us and through our lives – urging us to act.

CHAPTER SEVEN

Judaism and Lesbianism:
A Tale of Life on the Margins of the Text

In the process of my own personal struggle for equality and inclusion as a lesbian within the mainstream Jewish community, it has been important for me to engage with and interrogate the Jewish source texts concerning lesbianism. So, what has Judaism got to say about lesbianism? Few people asked that question fifty years ago. Today, after forty years of feminism, and lesbian and gay liberation, Jewish lesbians are coming out as Jews, and troubling their inheritance. This is one reason why it is necessary to insert the conjunction 'and' and explore the relationship between the body of received tradition, 'Judaism' and lesbianism. The other reason emerges from the relationship between Jewish teaching on lesbianism and Jewish teaching on women. On the one hand, Jewish law views lesbianism as a sub-category of 'homosexuality'. On the other hand, the treatment of lesbianism within Jewish law is an extension of the treatment of women. And so a general study of homosexuality and Judaism is not sufficient: it is essential to consider what Jewish teaching has to say *specifically* about lesbianism.

Interestingly, sexual intimacy between women was not mentioned at all in Jewish texts until 1,500 years ago. When we turn to the first source of Jewish teaching, the *Torah*, the five books of Moses, redacted either as early as the 10th century or as late as the 5th century BCE, we find that the sections which outline prohibited sexual unions, Leviticus chapters 18 and 20, do not include a single word about lesbianism. Leviticus 18:22, addressing the individual male, states clearly: 'You shall not lie with a male as with a woman. It is an abhorrence' (*to'eivah*). And Leviticus 20:13 adds: 'And a man who lies with a male as with a woman, both of them have committed an abhorrence: they shall surely be put to death; their blood shall be upon them.' The context of each verse is a lengthy statement detailing prohibited sexual unions. The operating rationale is the separation of Israel from the peoples around them, and their consecration to God. And it is here, right at the beginning of the story of homosexuality and Judaism, that we find a clue to the assumptions underlying Jewish teaching on lesbianism which emerged centuries later. Women are included in the texts of Leviticus 18 and 20, of course, but with the exception of the case of bestiality[1], women are the *objects*, not the *subjects*, of different types of sexual union, and there is no mention at all of women *in relation to one another*

The first fleeting allusion to sexual contact between women is made by the rabbinic sages in *Sifra*,[2] a work of *halachic midrash*, that is, rabbinic exegesis of legal biblical material, which comments on the Book of Leviticus, and was edited no earlier than the end of the 4th century CE.[3] Here, referring to the 'laws' of Egypt and Canaan which the Israelites are prohibited from following,[4] the text cites as an example that, 'A man would marry (*nosei*) a man, and a woman a woman' – a clear reference not only to same-sex intimate *acts*, but also to on-going *relationships* between same-sex partners.

The next brief comments are found in the Babylonian *Talmud* – edited about one hundred years later in two different tractates, *Shabbat* and *Y'vamot*. *Shabbat* 65a/b refers to the father of Samuel (Samuel being the pre-eminent authority among Babylonian Jewry in the middle of the 3rd century) not permitting his daughters 'to sleep together'. The text offers two explanations for his position. One view links it to a teaching of Rav Huna (a disciple of Samuel's principal colleague, and sparring partner Rav): 'For R. Huna said: "Women that play around (*ha-m'sol'lot*)[5] with one another are unfit (*p'sulot*) for the priesthood [i.e. to marry a High Priest]."' The majority of the sages, however, reached a different conclusion: 'No: it was in order that they should not become accustomed to an alien body (*gufa nuchra'ah*).'

Y'vamot 76a makes it clear *why* the law does not follow Rav Huna. After quoting his teaching the text adds:

> And even according to Rav Eleazar, who stated that an unmarried man who cohabited with an unmarried women with no matri-

---

1 Leviticus 18:23.
2 *Sifra Acharey Mot* 9:8.
3 Around the time when the Jerusalem *Talmud* the *Y'rushalmi* was completed.
4 Lev. 18:3.
5 I have chosen a common English euphemism for sex, 'play around', to translate the rabbinic euphemism *ha-m'sol'lot*.

monial intention rendered her therefore a prostitute (*zona*), this disqualification ensues only in the case of a man, but when [the case] is that of a woman [playing around with another woman] the action was regarded as mere obscenity.

Rav Huna's teaching is rejected because, unlike heterosexual cohabitation, sexual intimacy between women does not render the individual women concerned 'unfit'. It is *p'ritzuta*, 'obscentity', not *z'nut*, 'unchasitity' or 'harlotry'. And if the women's behaviour does not render them 'unfit', they are not thereby debarred from marrying a High Priest (who must only marry a virgin – that is, a woman who it 'fit'). Interestingly, the expression 'play(ing) around', *ha-m'sol'lot*, is a rabbinic euphemism for sexual behaviour (sometimes translated as 'making sport' or 'committing lewdness') and is only used of women who engage in intimate acts with each other or with their 'little sons'.[6] While the term is very dismissive (in its simple form, the root, *Samech Lamed Lamed*, means to 'swing', to 'be light'), it is not at all ambiguous.

After the completion of the Babylonian *Talmud* at the beginning of the 6th century, there were no further textual references to lesbian behaviour until Moses ben Maimon clarified the *halachic* position in his code, the *Mishneh Torah* he wrote:[7]

For women to play around with one another is forbidden and belongs to 'the practices of the Egyptians' concerning which we have been warned, 'You shall not copy the practices of the land of Egypt' ... But though such conduct is forbidden, it is not punishable by lashing since there is no specific prohibition against it and in any case no sexual intercourse takes place at all. Consequently, such women are not forbidden to the priesthood, on

---

6 The expression *ha-m'sol'lot* is used in the *Tosefta* (collection of *Tannaitic* teachings parallel to the *Mishnah*) and in both the Jerusalem and the Babylonian Talmuds, as a euphemism for women who engage in proscribed sexual acts – the examples being 'a woman that plays around with her son' (*Tosefta Sota 5:7 Sanhedrin 69b; Y'rushalmi Gittin VIII, 49c*) and 'women who play around with one another' (*Shabbat 65a; Y'vamot 75a*). Note that Maimonides uses the same expression: '*Nashim ha-m'sol'lot zo b'zo asur*' - 'For women to play around with one another is forbidden' (*Mishneh Torah, Hilchot Issurey Bi'ah 21:8*).

7 Moses ben Maimon (1135-1204) – also known as Maimonides or Rambam *Hilchot Issurey Bi'ah* 21:8.

account of unchastity; nor is a woman prohibited to her husband because of it, since this does not constitute unchastity. But it is appropriate to flog such women since they have done a forbidden thing. A man should be particularly strict with his wife in this matter, and should prevent women known to indulge in such practices from visiting her, and her from going to visit them.

Maimonides' formulation of the *halachah* (Jewish law) was upheld by Jacob ben Asher in his *Arba'ah Turim* a century later[8], and by Joseph Caro, whose *Shulchan Aruch*[9], published in 1563, became the authoritative guide to *halachah* throughout the Jewish world – a status it still occupies within Orthodox Jewry today. The *Shulchan Aruch* was the 'final word' on the subject for four hundred years.

Torah is silent on the subject of lesbian behaviour; subsequent Jewish teaching has had very little to say. But it is clear, sexual acts between women came to be regarded as 'forbidden' (*asur*). And the reasons for the prohibition are quite apparent in the different key texts. I shall now analyse those reasons.

First, the *source* of the prohibition is drawn from the *Torah*. While the *Torah* omits any explicit reference to female sexual unions, the 'practices' and the 'laws' of Egypt and Canaan – which are not detailed in *Torah* – may be understood, according to the rabbis and to the *halachah*, to include sexual relations between women[10] even if women who 'played around with one another' were guilty of 'obscenity' only and not of 'unchastity'.[11]

Second, the *purpose* of the prohibition seems to be to ensure that 'they should not become accustomed to an alien body' (*gufa nuchra'ah*).[12] In my view, the argument here makes most sense if put in the context of the line of reasoning articulated throughout the Book of Leviticus.[13] Just as the people of Israel must separate themselves from the *alien* nations surrounding them (their *neighbours* with whom they might otherwise *identify*) in order to be 'holy' to God, so

---

8 Jacob ben Asher, c.1270-1340. *Even ha-Ezer* 24
9 Joseph Caro, 1488-1575. The section in Caro's *Shulchan Aruch* is also called *Even ha-Ezer* 24.
10 *Sifra: Acharey Mot* 9:8, *Mishneh Torah: Hilchot Issurey Bi'ah* 21:8.
11 *Y'vamot 76a.*
12 *Shabbat* 65b.
13 See especially, Leviticus 18:3-5, 24-30; 20:22-26.

individual females must separate themselves from *alien* bodies – other *females* with whom they might otherwise identify – in order to become attached to individual males.

While the prohibition on lesbianism articulated in *Sifra*, the *Talmud* and the later codes is primarily justified in terms of the same rationale used in Leviticus for outlawing sex between men, it is clear that lesbian behaviour is not regarded in the same way as male homosexual behaviour. A crucial reason for the difference stems from the rabbinic interpretation of the first commandment of the *Torah*: 'Be fruitful and multiply and fill the earth'.[14] On the face of it, this command is given equally, to 'male' and 'female'.[15] But after the eating of the fruit of the forbidden tree,[16] the *Torah* does not continue in this even-handed manner. With the exception of Lot's daughters,[17] and Judah's daughter-in-law, Tamar[18] – none of whom may be regarded as 'daughters of Israel' – sexual initiative is a male preserve in the *Torah*. And so 'fruitfulness' became the responsibility of men too. Indeed, Genesis 28:1-10 relates God's lethal punishment of Onan, Judah's second son, for 'spilling' his seed on the ground rather than impregnating Tamar, his dead brother Er's childless wife.[19]

In the main, the narratives of the *Torah* make it clear that men are the central actors in every sphere of life – sexual, social, economic,

---

14 Genesis 1:28.

15 Gen.1:27.

16 Gen. ch.3.

17 Gen. 19:30-39 relates how Lot and his two daughters dwelt in a cave after the destruction of Sodom and Gomorrah. Because they believed their father to be the last man left on earth, the daughters got him drunk and had sex with him, in order to ensure the birth of heirs. The firstborn bore a son and called him Moab – the father of the Moabites – the younger daughter bore a son and called him Ben-ammi, the father of the Ammonites.

18 Gen. 38:12-30 relates how Tamar, the widow of Judah's first-born, Er, pretended to be a prostitute in order to get her father-in-law, Judah, to sleep with her when he failed to marry her to his third son, Shelah, as he promised. With the second son, Onan, having been killed by God for spilling his seed, Judah represented Tamar's only hope for a child. If one goes beyond the *Torah* to the text of the Bible as a whole, one finds other examples of women taking a sexual initiative –e.g. Ruth, the Moabite, a descendant of Lot's eldest daughter, when she 'uncovers' Boaz's feet at the threshing floor during the night (Ruth 3:6-15).

19 See Chapter 5 for a brief treatment of the Tamar narrative.

political.[20] And this picture is reinforced by the law – first set out in the *Torah* and later developed through the *Mishnah*, the *Talmud* and the medieval codes. With the exception of widows and divorcees (with a *past* attachment to a man), single women and married women do not have an independent existence, but are rather defined in relation to their fathers and husbands, respectively, who have authority over them.[21]

Herein lies the reason why sexual intimacy between men is explicitly mentioned in the *Torah* – and condemned – while no reference is made to sexual intimacy between women. Women are not seen to *lie together* because, unlike men, they do not officially *relate together* in any other area of life.

And yet, as the text from *Sifra* indicates, by the end of the 4th century, the rabbis were aware that among the nations of Egypt and Canaan, at least, 'A man would marry a man and a woman a woman'.[22] And the references in the *G'mara*, the commentary on the *Mishnah*, suggest that the sages of Babylon were wary of young girls 'sleeping together' and knew of Jewish women who 'played around with one another'.[23] It seems that, while, in theory, women were completely subject to the authority of men, in practice women may have had a little more freedom of action.

But even though legal texts from *Sifra* onwards acknowledge both the *possibility* and the *reality* of sexual intimacy between women, the tone of the pronouncements is very different from the savage rejection of sexual acts between men first articulated in Leviticus. The clue to this difference in tone may be found in the passage in Maimonides' *Mishneh Torah* cited earlier: 'But though such conduct is forbidden, it is not punishable by lashing since there is no specific prohibition against it and *in any case no sexual intercourse as such takes place at all*'.[24] When a man 'lies with a male *as with a woman*',[25] sexual

---

20 Of course, there are strong women in the *Torah*, in particular, Sarah, Rebecca and Miriam. See Ch. 2 for an exploration of Miriam.

21 See Exodus 21, Numbers 5 and 6, and Deuteronomy 21:10 ff for the key sources in *Torah* outlining the dependent position of women, which form the basis for later rabbinic teaching.

22 *Sifra Acharey Mot* 9:8.

23 *Shabbat* 65a/b and *Y'vamot* 76a.

24 *Mishneh Torah: Hilchot Issurey Bi'ah* 21:8.

25 Leviticus 18:22.

intercourse takes place, and *both* men may be deemed to have 'spilled' their seed. As we read in Leviticus, sexual acts should only take place between a man and a woman who is not 'near-kin'.[26] In this way the procreative purpose may be ensured. Not only are women free of the responsibility of ensuring procreation, but two women cannot lie together as a man does with a woman: sexual intercourse in the sense of penile penetration and ejaculation of semen does not take place. This is why, in the *Talmudic* discussion we find in Y'vamot 76a, sexual intimacy between women is 'obscenity', p'ritzuta, and not 'unchasity', z'nut.

However, as we have already seen, although intimate contact between women is not sexual intercourse, it is 'obscenity', it is 'forbidden' (*asur*), and it must be prevented. The *Talmud* reveals that Samuel's father 'did not permit his daughters ... to sleep together';[27] Maimonides urges husbands to keep their wives away from women known to engage in lesbian behaviour. Indeed, Maimonides, in particular, seems to suggest that not only was 'obscenity' between women a recognised phenomenon, but women who customarily engaged in intimate relations with other women were also known in the community. What is more, while Jewish teaching on same-sex intimacy focuses on individual acts, not relationships – *Torah* does not consider for one moment that men who lie with one another might be engaged in a long-term liaison – two rabbinic comments hint at other possibilities. As we have seen, *Sifra*[28] speaks of the 'laws' of Egypt and Canaan, whereby 'A man would *marry* a man, and a woman, a woman'; the *Talmud* suggests that young women might sleep together on a regular basis and so become 'accustomed to an alien body'.[29]

While Jewish teaching on male homosexuality and lesbianism has not changed in the last four hundred years since codification of the laws was officially completed, the late 20th century, and the first decade of the twenty-first, has seen a massive transformation, both, in the roles of women and men, and in personal lifestyles and domestic arrangements. In this climate, lesbians, in common with women in general, have been claiming the right to define their own

26 ibid. 18:6.
27 *Shabbat* 65a
28 *Acharey Mot* 9:8.
29 *Shabbat* 65b.

lives. In these circumstances, lesbians, like their gay brothers, have been 'coming out' and asserting their desire not only to engage in same-sex intimate acts, but to live as lesbians and establish lesbian relationships. Some of these lesbians are Jews, not only by birth, but by choice and conviction (whether 'cultural' or 'religious', or both). Indeed, like other Jewish women, lesbians today are taking an increasingly active part in Jewish communal life – including becoming rabbis and cantors.

And it has been this phenomenon, of lesbians – and gay men – becoming involved in leadership roles within the progressive Jewish community, that has been the principal catalyst for change. And so, the evidence of new approaches began to emerge in the last decade of the 20th century. In the early 1990s, the progressive movements in both Britain and the United States began to tackle the legal prohibition against same-sex intimacy[30] and, as we shall see in the next chapter, since that time, Liberal Judaism in Britain has taken the lead in the progressive Jewish world, regarding the inclusion and equal treatment of lesbian and gay Jews.

So what kind of tale will Judaism tell about lesbianism – and male homosexuality – in the coming years, as lesbians and gay men, move from the margins of Jewish life to the centre? And how will Judaism respond when bisexual Jews and transgender Jews begin to lay claim to Judaism, and to full participation in Jewish life? Hopefully, lesbian and gay rabbis will be involved in the development of new Jewish teaching to ensure that the practice of inclusion and equality is also extended to these Jews, too. Judging by how much has changed since I took my first steps as a lesbian into the Jewish community in the early 1980s, I have no doubt that the next decades will see a profound transformation in Jewish teaching and practice

---

30 In 1990, the leaflet, *Where We Stand on Homosexuality*, was published by the Union of Liberal and Progressive Synagogues. In that same year the *Report of the Ad Hoc Committee on Homosexuality and the Rabbinate* was adopted by the Central Conference of American Rabbis, on 25th June 1990; in 1992 the Reconstructionist Rabbinical Association in the United States produced, *Homosexuality and Judaism: The Reconstructionist Position; The Report of the Reconstructionist Commission on Homosexuality*, Federation of Reconstructionist Congregations and *Chavurot*; and that same year, the Reconstructionist Press published, *Homosexuality and Judaism: A Reconstructionists Workshop Series*, ed. Rabbi Robert Gluck.

concerning equality and inclusion to encompass bisexual and transgender Jews – which may even, before the dawn of the 22nd century, begin to impact on the orthodox Jewish world as well.[31]

---

31 For the beginnings of an orthodox approach to inclusion of gay and lesbian Jews, see Steven Greenberg's book, *Wrestling with God and Men. Homosexuality in the Jewish Tradition*. (The University of Wisconsin Press, 2004).

CHAPTER EIGHT

Marriage by any Other Name: Lesbian and Gay Partnership

The politics of language: what we call 'it'

Before the advent of civil partnership in Britain, in December 2005, lesbian and gay couples, who wanted to make a public declaration of their commitment to one another, would have a commitment ceremony, which had no legal implications or rights associated with it.[1] Civil partnership has made a huge difference. Lesbian and gay couples now have the right to inherit from one another, to be each other's next of kin, and are treated as a unit for pension purposes. But civil partnership is not civil marriage. If it were the same phenomenon, there would be no need for a separate term.

There are small legal differences between civil marriage and civil

---

1   The broad range of publications in the United States between 1989 and 1998, gives a strong sense of the mood that was emerging at the end of the 20th century. For examples of those focussing on lesbian and gay partnerships and ceremonies, see: Balka, Christie and Andy Rose, *Twice Blessed: On being Lesbian, Gay and Jewish.* (Beacon Press, 1989); Berner, Leila Gal and Renee Gal Primack, 'Lesbian Commitment Ceremonies', in Debra Orenstein (ed.), *Life Cycles: Jewish Women on Life Passages and Personal Milestones.* (Jewish Lights Publishing, 1994); Butler, Becky, *Ceremonies of the Heart: Celebrating Lesbian Unions,* (Seal Press, 1990); Elwell, Sue Levi, 'Honor the Holiness of Lesbian and Gay Marriages', *Reform Judaism,* Winter, 1998; Gilbert, Beth, 'Gays and Lesbians under the Chuppah', *Reform Judaism,* Summer, 1996; Johnson, Susan E., *Long Term Lesbian Couples.* (Naiad Press, 1990); Johnson, Susan E., *For Love and Life, Intimate Portraits of Lesbian Couples.* (Naiad Press, 1995); Martinac, Paula, *The Lesbian and Gay Book of Love and Marriage* (Broadway Books, 1998); Sherman, Suzanne, *Lesbian and Gay Marriages* (Temple University Press, 1992); Smith, Moon and Susan Saxe, 'A Commitment Celebration' in Elizabeth Resnick Levine (ed.) *A Ceremonies Sampler, New Rites, Celebrations and Observances of Jewish Women.* (Woman's Institute for Continuing Jewish Education, San Diego, CA, 1991).

partnership[2], but the main issue in the public discourse seems to revolve around whether or not the term 'marriage' is appropriate for same-sex couples.

This issue also surfaced in the discussions within Liberal Judaism. After the Liberal Judaism Rabbinic Conference set up a Rabbinic working party on same-sex commitment ceremonies and the inclusion of lesbian and gay Jews in 2000,[3] it became clear in the process of consulting with the Rabbinic Conference and the Council of Liberal Judaism that the consensus at that time was not in favour of using the language of 'marriage'. Consequently, the new Liberal Judaism policy on same-sex commitment ceremonies and the inclusion of lesbian and gay Jews agreed in 2002, did not describe such ceremonies as 'marriage' – although, by way of a compromise, the Hebrew term for marriage, *Kiddushin*, was used. And so it was that when Liberal Judaism published an anthology of liturgies in December 2005 to coincide with the Civil Partnership Act coming into force, the booklet was entitled, *B'rit Ahavah – Covenant of Love – Seder Kiddushin – Service of Commitment for Same-Sex Couples*[4].

However, things have moved on. As the climate of public opinion has changed with the advent of civil partnership, and the consequent increasing acceptance of lesbian and gay relationships, so reluctance to use the word 'marriage' has declined. It is in this climate that the equal marriage campaign has gathered pace. The goal of the campaign is the provision of equal choice: a change in the law that will enable all couples, whether they are lesbian, gay or heterosexual to have the choice of entering into, either, civil marriage or civil partnership.[5]

In February 2011, in response to the Equal Love Campaign, the Rabbinic Conference agreed and adopted a 'Statement on Equality

---

2 See: www.civilpartnershipinfo.co.uk/ for the Civil Partnership guide for lesbian and gay couples in the UK.

3 The Working Party, which was chaired by Rabbi Danny Rich, included the following members of the Rabbinic Conference: Rabbis Margaret Jacobi, Elizabeth Tikvah Sarah, Mark Solomon and Moshe Yehudai-Rimmer. In 2005, Rabbis Shulamit Ambalu and James Baaden also became involved.

4 Edited by Rabbi Mark Solomon. Liberal Judaism, London, 2005.

5 Known as the 'Equal Love Campaign' and led by Peter Tatchell: 'The legal bid to overturn the twin bans on same-sex civil marriages and opposite-sex civil partnerships in the United Kingdom.' – see http://equallove.org.uk

of Access to Marriage and Civil Partnerships'.[6] More recently, efforts to change the law have intensified, and Liberal rabbis and members have participated in a range of activities, including the first international LGBT Human Rights summit in Cardiff.[7] However, while a

---

6   The Liberal Judaism Rabbinic Conference 'Statement on Equality of Access to Marriage and Civil Partnerships', agreed and adopted on 15th February 2011,reads:
'Liberal Judaism's Rabbinic Conference supports the right of all couples, of any gender and sexual orientation, who are in a committed and exclusive relationship, to enter into a legally binding civil partnership or marriage. We will lobby for the necessary changes in UK law to bring about this much-needed equality, which will allow any couple to have civil marriage or civil partnership.
'We will also lobby for the right to conduct the legal as well as religious aspects of either marriage or civil partnership for all couples whom we understand to be Jewish.
'Liberal Judaism embraces the equality of the sexes and upholds the religious principle that all human beings are created in the image of God. We see kiddushin (Jewish marriage) today as a mutual covenant entered into by two people who share the desire to form an exclusive commitment and to build a home based on Jewish principles. We will give guidance and support that acknowledges, affirms and is appropriate to each person's gender and sexual orientation.'
As far as other progressive denominations are concerned: In March 2000 the Central Council of American Rabbis of the Union of Reform Judaism in the USA issued a new resolution stating 'We do hereby resolve, that the relationship of a Jewish, same gender couple is worthy of affirmation through appropriate Jewish ritual, and further resolve, that we recognise the diversity of opinions within our ranks on this issue. We support the decision of those who choose to officiate at rituals of union for same-sex couples, and we support the decision of those who do not.' To promote inclusion of LGBT members and clergy, the Reform movement established the Institute for Judaism and Sexual Orientation at Hebrew Union College. The other progressive movement in the USA, the Reconstructionist Rabbinical Association, encourages its members to officiate at same-sex marriages/commitment ceremonies, and in 2007, the RRA elected as president, lesbian Rabbi Toba Spitzer, the first openly gay or lesbian leader of a rabbinic association.
7   The first international LGBT Human Rights Summit, held in Cardiff, commenced on 31st of August 2011. At an event at the Scottish Youth Parliament offices on 28th of September 2011, bringing together representatives from the Unitarians, Quakers, Metropolitan Community Church, Pagan Federation, and Buddhist Communities. Rabbi Mark Solomon, of the Edinburgh Liberal Jewish Community, spoke on behalf of Liberal Judaism. See LJ Today, November/December 2011.

number of minority religious groupings, including Liberal Judaism and the Quakers, support equal marriage,[8] at this point, the Church of England and the Catholic Church and other major religious institutions remain opposed. Rather than explore the reasons why most of the Christian denominations and Islam – to mention the religions in Britain, with the largest numbers of adherents – cannot countenance lesbian and gay marriage, I would like to demonstrate why it seems to me that whatever the terms used to describe the public commitment that lesbian and gay couples make with one another, it is marriage by any other name.

Let me begin by raising a few questions. The terms Civil Partnership and Civil Marriage have fixed legal meanings, but apart from the formal, legal differences, in what ways does a Civil Partnership ceremony differ from a Civil Marriage ceremony? Do the differences revolve around the sexuality and gender of those concerned, or are they about matters of content – or both? What are the political and the religious implications of labelling the contracts that lesbian and gay couples are entering into as civil partnership ceremonies rather than marriage?

It is self-evident (to me, at least) that the bonds which some lesbian and gay couples are choosing to make with one and another are both like and unlike the bonds which heterosexual couples make with one another. On the one hand, in both cases, couples are making a public declaration of a covenant between them. On the other hand, although civil partnership has given legal recognition to lesbian and gay couples' relationships, as yet, only in the case of heterosexual couples is this covenant recognised by the state as 'marriage', and regarded by the traditions of all the major religions as divinely ordained.

Whatever difference differing sexualities may make to the experience and understanding of sharing a covenant on the part of the couples themselves, the distinction currently being made in the arena of public discourse between heterosexual marriage and lesbian and gay civil partnership reflects the historic presumption that only heterosexual unions are valid. Perhaps the most important aspect of the phenomenon of lesbian and gay commitment ceremonies is that, after millennia, lesbian and gay couples are challenging this presumption.

---

8 See note 7.

What is marriage?

Heterosexual marriage is an historical institution. It has changed over time. The label may have remained constant since days of old, but marriage is not the same phenomenon today that it once was. In addition, the meaning and the content of marriage varies according to its particular religious, cultural, ethnic, geographical, economic, political settings. The evidence from the Hebrew Bible suggests that Jewish marriage began in the form of the acquisition of a young virgin by a man from her father.[9] As the early rabbinic sages examined the legal texts of the Bible over two thousand years ago, they brought these together with the theological perspective of the biblical Creation narratives and the romantic-love lyricism of the biblical book, The Song of Songs, in their task of creating the rules and rituals of Jewish marriage.[10] These rules and rituals remain largely in force throughout the Jewish world to this day with some 'progressive' adjustments – in the face of massive social transformations.

So, Jewish marriage retains an element of acquisition of the bride by the groom, known as *kinyan,* an element of reciprocal covenantal love, and an underlying theology of God's dual purpose in creating humanity in two forms, male and female: the imperative of reproduction on the one hand, as related in Genesis 1.27-28, and the need for companionship on the other, as related in Genesis 2.18-25.

Originally two ceremonies separated in time – one involving betrothal (*Erusin* – also known as *Kiddushin*) and one, the marriage itself (*Nissu'in*) – the wedding ritual is conducted in two parts within one ceremony. In the first part, the dimension of acquisition is expressed by the groom placing a ring on the bride's index finger and saying the words of a legal formula of betrothal: 'You are betrothed to me by this ring according to the law of Moses and Israel'. And the notion of marriage as an economic arrangement is underlined in the words of the traditional contract document, the *k'tubbah,* signed by two witnesses before the ceremony, which sets out the husband's financial obligations towards his wife. In the second part of the ceremony, the theme of covenant is expressed, together with the Divine purpose underlying heterosexual union, in the recitation of Seven Blessings, the *Sheva B'rachot,* which celebrate

---

9 See Deuteronomy 22:13-28.
10 See the Babylonian *Talmud,* tractate *Kiddushin,* edited c.500 CE.

the groom and the bride.

As the understanding of marriage as a loving partnership became predominant in Western societies during the second half of the 20th century, progressive Jewish movements altered the traditional ritual and procedures of marriage ceremonies to reflect this. The formula of betrothal is reciprocal, supporting couples in their wish to exchange rings, and the *k'tubbah* has become a document which expresses the couple's promises to love and support one another. In making these changes Progressive Judaism has succeeded in completely undercutting the original aspect of *kinyan*, acquisition of the bride by the groom, while preserving the outward forms.

The best-known symbol of a Jewish wedding, the *chuppah*, 'canopy', under which the bride and groom stand, provides the most dramatic expression of the change in the meaning of Jewish marriage from biblical times to the present day. Originally, there was no cere-mony attached to the acquisition of a bride by a groom – he would simply take her into his home and have sex with her. The 'memory' of this form of marriage is present in the *chuppah*, and the canopy has, also, accumulated other meanings so that today, it also repre-sents the quality of the home that the couples hope to create together.

Re-defining *Kiddushin*

So, marriage, in general, and Jewish marriage, in particular, has evolved and changed. But is it possible to redefine *Kiddushin*, Jewish marriage, to encompass lesbian and gay couples? The traditional Jewish rationale for *Kiddushin* as the exclusive prerogative of hetero-sexual couples is rooted in the understanding that humanity was made in two forms, male and female, in order that these two forms might re-unite for the purposes of reproduction and companion-ship. This bi-polar reading focussing on the anatomical distinction between the sexes as delineated in the first Creation story, where the words male (*zachar*) and female (*n'keivah*) are used,[11] ignores the implications of the fact that both male and female are created as two aspects of a singular human being (*Adam*) 'in the image of God',[12] and that in the second creation story the similarity between the two

---

11 Genesis 1:27
12 ibid.

sexes are underlined with the use of the words woman, *ishah*, and man, *ish*, both of which derive from the root, *Alef, Nun, Shin*, to be *human*.[13]

The Jewish concept of holiness, *k'dushah*, is bound up with the notion of making separations, and this is reflected in the betrothal ritual (*Erusin – Kiddushin*), in which the bride is set apart from the groom. However, the marriage service as a whole is quite paradoxical. While the bride is consecrated to the groom in the first section of the ceremony in which the *difference* between them is emphasised, they are joined together in the *singular* image of humanity (*Adam*) in Eden in the *Sheva B'rachot*, which are recited in the second section of the ceremony.

Humanity is one. Humanity is also differentiated. While the Creation narratives posit differentiation simply in bi-polar terms, it is becoming increasingly evident that the differences within humanity are much more complex. Same-sex couples may share the same gender, but many express that gender differently, and indeed, are different from one another in a host of ways. Heterosexual couples may be divided by the outward 'signs' of gender, but share a similar disposition and way of being in the world. A ceremony that acknowledges the ways in which the individuals concerned are different from one another ritualises their consecration to one another, and celebrates their union, is equally relevant for all couples. A ceremony that includes these elements is *Kiddushin*.

Aping heterosexual marriage?

Every year, fewer and fewer marriages take place. However, a sizeable proportion of heterosexual people are choosing to get married, and increasing numbers of lesbian and gay couples would like to exercise a similar choice. In a society in which cohabitation is no longer considered 'living in sin' and the life-style choices for adults are many and varied, why do many people still want to get married? There are as many answers to this question as there are couples getting married.

Marriage is a changing phenomenon, and while many ritual elements appear to be the same, their meanings have changed. However, marriage was and has remained to this day, in all but a few

---

13 Genesis 2:23. See Chapter 1.

pioneering nations,[14] an institution for regulating heterosexual part-nerships. So what has it got to do with lesbian and gay people? From a Jewish perspective, the institution of marriage emerged in a context in which there was no concept of same-sex relationships. As my treatment of Judaism and lesbianism in the previous chapter reveals, the *Torah's* condemnation of two men 'lying' with one another set out in Leviticus 18, verse 22, and 20, verse 13, centres on a prohibi-tion against sex between men – and there is no mention of two women lying together, because throughout the biblical treatment of sex, with the exception of bestiality, it is men alone who act and initi-ate. The focus of the Bible's concern is with prohibiting sexual acts associated with the practices of other peoples – specifically, those of Canaan and Egypt.[15]

And yet, as we have seen, when the rabbis commented on the verses in Leviticus 18 and 20, they not only brought the notion of sex between women into the picture, but they explained that the people Israel were prohibited from following the 'laws' of Egypt and Canaan because in those societies 'a man would marry (*nosei*) a man and a woman would marry a woman'.[16]

The ongoing reality of same-sex relationships and marriages constitutes the 'underside' of the chronicle of humanity, a largely unwritten history. It was only in the last three decades of the 20th century that lesbian and gay life became more visible – in the West-ern world at least. And as same-sex relationships have emerged from the shadows, so increasing numbers of lesbian and gay couples today are choosing to lay claim to the public recognition of their commit-ment to one another and are choosing to celebrate their

---

14 Since 2001, ten countries have enacted legislation enabling lesbian and gay couples to marry: Argentina, Belgium, Canada, Iceland, the Netherlands, Norway, Portugal, Spain, South Africa and Sweden. Same-sex marriages are also performed and recognised in Mexico City and parts of the United States. Some places that do not perform same-sex marriages recognise same-sex marriages performed elsewhere: Israel, the Caribbean countries of the King-dom of the Netherlands, parts of the United States and all states of Mexico. See: http://en.wikipedia.org/wiki/Same-sex_marriage

15 See Leviticus 18:3.

16 See *Sifra Acharey Mot* 9:8. For a discussion of Jewish law on homosexuality in general, see 'The Jewish Homosexual and the Halachic Tradition' by Rodney Mariner, in *Jewish Explorations of Sexuality* edited by Jonathan Magonet. Berghahn Books, 1995.

relationships and 'marry' one another.[17] Whatever term a couple may decide to call the bond they are forging between themselves, if we were not talking about same-gender relationships, the obvious label to use would be 'marriage'. Heterosexuals know this and so do lesbian and gay people. That is why there is considerable opposition to it – on both sides. For heterosexual critics, marriage is their exclusive prerogative, an eternal sign of the special status of heterosexual relationships. For lesbian and gay critics, it is precisely because marriage is a heterosexual institution that lesbian and gay people should have nothing to do with it and should continue to live differently.

The critics on both sides share the fear that lesbian and gay marriage will erode the difference between heterosexuality and homosexuality and promote the notion that 'we are all the same'. This fear echoes that expressed by the opponents of women's liberation in the 1970s, that if women and men ceased to play different roles, we would all become androgynous. The evidence of the past forty years indicates, both, that the struggle for equality continues, and that when women and men are ostensibly doing the same things, they don't end up being the same. The biological/psychological/sociological reality of what is to be born and to be socialised as a female or male persists and women and men continue to express their differing experience of life when they are engaged in the same tasks.

We are all the same – we are all different. When lesbian and gay couples get 'married', they don't stop being lesbian and gay men. Lesbians and gay men are re-defining marriage for themselves, making it in their own image. And when they do this, they are actually part of a much broader phenomenon. One of the consequences of the transformation of gender roles during the last quarter of the 20th century was that heterosexual marriages began to change. In fact, in a sense, the differences between heterosexual marriages today and those which pre-date feminism are as great as the differences which differentiate heterosexual from lesbian and gay partnerships. Indeed, the differences have become so immense that one could argue that

---

17 See the Office for National Statistics website, for information concerning the number of civil partnerships conducted since December 2005: http://www.ons.gov.uk/ons/taxonomy/index.html?nscl=Civil+Partnerships

many heterosexual marriages today no longer fit neatly into the concept of marriage promulgated by religious institutions and the state.

What is more, marriage is not only changing, it is becoming much less prevalent. In a climate in which fewer and fewer heterosexuals are getting married, the notion of marriage as a choice defined by those who choose it, rather than as an inevitable state of existence for all heterosexual adults, is becoming more and more significant. And it is in this climate that we have witnessed the emergence of lesbian and gay marriage. Given the progress that has been made during the past forty years, I am in no doubt that it will not be too long before there is a change in British law to ensure that civil marriage and civil partnership are available to all couples.

Nevertheless, while the majority of the mainstream religious institutions, both in this country and throughout the world, continue to discriminate against lesbian and gay people, and given the evidence of continuing discrimination in many countries, and active persecution in several others,[18] we cannot afford to be complacent. Indeed, as lesbian, gay, bisexual and transgender people begin to achieve equality and inclusion in some countries, and continue to be persecuted in other parts of the world, the time has come for the struggle against homophobia, biphobia and transphobia to go global.[19]

18 While the death penalty is still in force in just five countries, including, Sudan, Iran and Saudi Arabia, lesbian and gay people continue to be punished with imprisonment in 72 countries, according to the report published by the International Lesbian, Gay, Bisexual, Trans and Intersex Association – see:
http://ilga.org/historic/Statehomophobia/ILGA_map_2009_A4.pdf
19 The International Lesbian, Gay, Bisexual, Trans and Intersex Association is engaged in campaigning for LGBTI rights across the world. Amnesty International is also now working in this area.

CHAPTER NINE

Towards an Inclusive Jewish Sexual Ethic

Sex Lessons in the *Torah*

It is significant that little is said directly about sex in the Genesis narratives, concerning the creation of humanity, except for the assumption that it is *heterosexual, monogamous* and geared to *reproduction*. Elsewhere in the *Torah*, however, in both narrative and legal texts, we find a number of teachings about sex which, together with Genesis 1 and 2, have become the basis of Jewish sexual ethics.

The most extended treatment of sex is contained in Leviticus 18 and 20, where the focus is on prohibited sexual acts – those between family members; a man and his neighbour's wife;[1] a man and a menstruating woman;[2] two men; a man or woman and an animal. In all these cases, with the exception of bestiality, where initiation of the act by both sexes is conceived, the individual male is the *subject*; the individual female is the *object*. And this perspective is reinforced in all the other references to sex in other legal texts in the *Torah*: a bride must be a virgin;[3] a father is prohibited from making his daughter a prostitute;[4] sex out of wedlock is not punished as long as the woman is an un-betrothed virgin and the man who lies with her, marries her.[5]

Interestingly, however, in two key *narrative* passages dealing with exceptions to the taboo surrounding incest, the active role is taken by women. Following the destructions of Sodom and Gomorrah, and the transformation of Lot's wife into a pillar of salt,[6] Lot's two daughters, left alone with their father, get him drunk on successive nights and lie with him to ensure they have offspring[7]. In another

---

1 See also Exodus 20:13.
2 See also Leviticus15:19ff.
3 Deuteronomy 22:20.
4 Lev. 19:29.
5 Ex. 22:15-16; Deut. 22:28-29.
6 Genesis 19:26.
7 ibid. 19:30-39.

case where the future is at stake, as we have seen in Chapter 5, Judah's daughter-in-law, Tamar, childless because Onan has spilled his seed rather than produce a child in the name of his dead brother, Er (Tamar's first husband), conceals her true identity with the garments of a prostitute and entices her father-in-law to lie with her so that she may conceive.[8]

These two exceptions highlight the hierarchy of values implicit in the system of sex laws outlined in the *Torah*: ultimately, the imperative of reproduction is so important it may even overrule incest taboos. What is more, *ethical* conduct as such is a secondary consideration. The primary principle underlying the rules of sexual behaviour is the maintenance of *social order* and the preservation of the *separateness* of the people of Israel. The laws regulating sexual acts in Leviticus 18 and 20 are set in the context of the book's concern with *k'dushah* – with *setting apart*: the offerings to be made on the altar from the remainder of property, the priests from the people, and the people from the other nations. As the preamble to the sex rules in Leviticus 18 indicates, ethical issues are less relevant to the laws regulating sexual conduct than the need to ensure that the people do not follow the ways of Canaan or Egypt, but rather walk in the way of God.[9]

But one rule in Leviticus 18, by contrast, does seem to emerge from a predominantly ethical concern. At verse 18 we read:

And you shall not take a woman to her sister, to be a rival to her, to uncover her nakedness, beside the other in her lifetime.

While there are no laws against bigamy in the *Torah*, and indeed bigamy was only out-ruled for Ashkenazi communities in the late 10th century by the ban of Rabbeinu Gershom ben Judah,[10] and

---

8 Genesis 38.

9 Leviticus 18: 2b-3.

10 Gershom ben Judah, (c. 960 -1040?), best known as Rabbeinu Gershom, 'Our teacher Gershom', was a famous Talmudist and Halachist within the Ashkenazi world. In about 1000 CE, he called a synod which decided the following particulars: (1) prohibition of polygamy; (2) necessity of obtaining the consent of both parties to a divorce; (3) modification of the rules concerning those who became apostates under compulsion; (4) prohibition against opening correspondence addressed to another.
See: http://www.jewishencyclopedia.com/view.jsp?artid=172&letter=G.

remains an option (in theory) for *Sephardim* within the religious courts of Israel to this day, the rule against marriage between man and his wife's sister seems motivated by consideration of the wife's feelings and the need to preserve the integrity of the relationship between two sisters. As such it has much more in keeping with the next chapter, Leviticus 19, where the need for right conduct in social relationships is stressed again and again. Indeed, the link in ethical tone between this rule, and the chapter sandwiched between the two dealing with prohibited sexual acts, makes the apparent contrast between the *ethical* preoccupations of Leviticus 19 and the *separatist* agenda of 18 and 20 even more marked.

In my view, the juxtaposition of the chapters is not accidental. Rather, it suggests that just as the sex rules should be understood in the context of the imperative of setting the people Israel apart from the other nations, so they should be understood in the context of the ethical regulation of social relationships. And yet, to this day, Jewish law has failed to consider the implications of this juxtaposition for sexual ethics.

Sex and Love: a New Combination

At the heart of Leviticus 19, a chapter dealing with correct ritual practice and ethical behaviour towards the poor, the stranger, the disabled, the elderly, one's neighbour, lies the famous dictum 'You shall love your neighbour as yourself. I am the Eternal.' (19:18). According to Rabbi Akiva, a leading second century scholar, this commandment was not simply an important rule; it was 'the great principle of the *Torah*'.[11] What does that mean? The *first* principle. The *underlying* principle. You shall love your *neighbour*. Who is your neighbour? The person who lives *next* door to you; the person who is *like* you. You shall love your neighbour as *yourself*: You shall love yourself – then you will be able to love your neighbour. And what is love? It is not merely an emotion; it is an act, a commitment. The phrase 'You shall love your neighbour as yourself' is part of a section of laws dealing with acts of justice, with the myriad material ways in which we must fulfil our responsibilities towards our neighbours and towards God.

None of the various laws relating to sexual behaviour both in

11 *Sifra* 89b.

Leviticus and elsewhere say anything about love. The word is not even used in connection with the story of the first relationship at the beginning of Genesis. And yet there are many love stories in the Bible: Jacob and Rachel, Samson and Delilah, David and Jonathan, Ruth and Naomi.

And then there is the great book of love, *Shir Ha-shirim*, The Song of Songs, traditionally attributed to King Solomon, the child of David's union with Bathsheba, another legendary lover. In contrast to the Garden of Eden narrative, Arthur Waskow points out that '… the sexual ethic of the Song of Songs focuses not on children, marriage, or commitment, but on sensual pleasure and loving companionship.'[12]

The Song of Songs provides a welcome reminder that sex is not just about *who* can do *what* with – or to – *whom*, it is about love and the joys of physical desire and intimacy. Fortunately, the post-biblical codes, while primarily concerned with the reproductive imperative, generally validate pleasure and so include both the 'right' of wives to experience sexual satisfaction,[13] and the permissibility of a wide range of sexual practices – including both oral and anal sexual activity – if it is desired by the couple concerned.[14]

But the implications of love – as understood in the context of Leviticus 19:18, and of loving companionship – as described in the Song of Songs – are not part of the framework of the rules governing sexual conduct. The reasons for this derive from the fact that despite the acknowledgement of women's capacity for sexual pleasure, the rules of sexual conduct are primarily concerned with what *men* do.

Significantly, of the various ethical rules delineated in Leviticus 19, only that concerning the command 'You shall love your neighbour as yourself' deals with the relationship of *peers; of equals; of equal men*. All the others involve ensuring right conduct between those whose relationship to one another is *asymmetrical:* the person with property *vis-a-vis* the one who is poor, the Israelite *vis-a-vis* the stranger, the able-bodied *vis-a-vis* the disabled, the young *vis-a-vis* the old. Similarly The Song of Songs is unique in its egalitarian treat-

---

12 Arthur Waskow, 'Down to Earth Judaism: Sexuality', in Jonathan Magonet (ed.), *Jewish Explorations of Sexuality*, Berghahn Books, 1995.
13 *Talmud K'tubbot* 61bff.; 47b-48a.
14 Maimonides, *Mishneh Torah*, Hilchot Issurey Bi'ah 21.9.

ment of the lovers. In its pastoral paradise, love and desire is expressed equally and actively by both partners. Indeed, it is the passionate female voice present in the poem which has led some scholars to suggest that the text is probably the work of a woman.[15]

For the spirit of Leviticus 19:18 and The Song of Songs to infuse the sex laws would require a huge conceptual shift. It would mean treating both women and men as active *subjects,* peers, equals. It would mean perceiving sex, not as a series of acts perpetrated by one party on the body of another, but as a means of expressing a *relationship.* It would mean seeing the expression of love and desire as one of the *primary purposes* of sexual activity. It would mean recognising all relationships, whether heterosexual or homosexual, with or without children, as *variations* on the theme of human partnership and evaluating them all according to the identical criteria of *love, equality* and *reciprocity.*

The commandment to 'love your neighbour as you love yourself' provides the ethical framework for a code of sexual behaviour. So what happens when we apply the criteria of love, equality and reciprocity to the sexual prohibitions outlined in Leviticus 18 and 20? Clearly all relationships in which the *inequality* of the parties is an inherent feature, for example relationships between adults and minors, are unacceptable. As far as other relationships are concerned, a clue to whether or not they fulfil the criteria emerges from the specific sexual terminology employed in the texts. There are a number of linguistic expressions for sex in the *Torah,* of which the most common are 'to know' – *lada'at* and 'to lie down' – *lishkav.* Both of these terms are morally neutral. The words themselves do not convey the nature of the sexual encounter, positive or negative. By contrast the expression *gillui ervah,* 'uncovering nakedness', which is used in the *Torah* exclusively in cases of incest and in reference to sex with a menstruating woman, suggests not only sexual intimacy, but *vulnerability* and *danger.* Within the worldview of the *Torah,* blood is a powerful substance, and contact with it is taboo. From the vantage point of the present day, the danger associated with 'uncovering nakedness' has more to do with the potential for exploitation involved in 'uncovering' a person's 'nakedness'. In the words of a

---

15 See Sybil Sheridan, 'The Song of Soloman's wife', in Sybil Sheridan, ed., *Hear Our Voice. Women Rabbis Tell Their Stories,* SCM Press 1994, 64-70.

contemporary rabbi quoted anonymously:[16] 'Very simply, it means making a person completely vulnerable and then not taking care of them in their nakedness.'

The implications of this interpretation are clear. Whether or not one abstains from sex during menstruation, most Jews today would probably not put sex with a menstruating woman in the same category as sex with a family member, where the issue of exploitation is much more readily apparent. However, there would probably be general agreement that there is a *potential* for exploitation in *any* sexual context.

But the perspective of *Torah* appears to be much narrower. Interestingly, the expression 'uncovering nakedness' is not used in *Torah* in connection with other categories of prohibited sexual behaviour outlined in Leviticus 18 and 20 – adultery, sex between men and bestiality. In these examples, the more neutral term 'lying down' is employed.[17] Clearly none of these cases entails the danger of blood contact or a built-in asymmetrical power dynamic. Indeed, in the case of two men lying down together, perhaps there may be an implicit assumption that the *independent male subject* is not in a position to exploit his *equal* – another male. But, at a deeper level, 'uncovering nakedness' refers not only to *who* is involved, but to *what* is involved. Even if the parties concerned are equals, any sexual encounter which entails exposing and exploiting another person's vulnerability is 'uncovering nakedness'.

Towards an inclusive, egalitarian Jewish sexual ethic

In recent years, sexual ethics has once again become a topical item on the Jewish agenda – largely in the context of the need to rethink Jewish attitudes towards same-sex relationships.[18] But other issues have also prompted new debate: sexual activity on the part of teenagers;[19] sex

---

16 See Sharon Cohen, 'Homosexuality and a Jewish Sex Ethic', *The Reconstructionist*, July-August 1989, 15f.

17 Note that the reference to bestiality in the case of a woman and an animal says 'You shall not stand before a beast ... (*lo ta'amod lifney v'heimah*)'.

18 See Chapter 7, note 30 for the new approaches that emerged in the 1990s. See, also, the pamphlet, *Jewish and Homosexual* by Dr. Wendy Greengross (Reform Synagogues of Great Britain, London, 1982), for an attempt to grapple with the issues, which pre-dated Jewish lesbian and gay input.

19 See 'Sex. And What Should I Tell My Teenager?', MANNA 26, Winter 1990.

out of marriage;[20] the incidence of extra-marital relationships; the growing phenomenon of 'serial monogamy'; the general diversification of family patterns.[21] The challenge of an inclusive, egalitarian approach rooted in love and reciprocity is that it may be seen to turn heterosexual marriage, monogamy and child-rearing into options among a wide range of other alternatives rather than the essential components of the *model* Jewish family arrangement.[22] On the other hand, the reality of Jewish relationship patterns today is diverse. And indeed, as David Biale has argued, contemporary concerns, like pre-marital sex, are actually not new issues at all and have always been a feature of Jewish life, more or less sanctioned and accepted at different times.[23] An inclusive, egalitarian approach makes it possible to apply ethical criteria to the broad *spectrum* of relationships and does not give *any* individual or group the licence to live outside the law and engage in irresponsible, exploitative or dangerous sexual behaviour.

And so, within the parameters of love and reciprocity, it is possible to specify a range of core ethical values which may be expressed in a *variety* of different relationships. In his article, 'Rethinking Jewish Sexual Ethics',[24] David Teutsch lists twelve values which may be seen as central to Jewish sexual ethics regardless of whether the relationship is between 'two women or two men' or 'a woman and a man': procreation, meaningful relationships, freedom for consenting adults, strong families, fidelity, stable community, protection from violence and abuse, good health, honesty, privacy/modesty, physical pleasure and caring.

Ironically, of all these values, procreation alone – the first sexual imperative of the *Torah* – is clearly *not* a possible feature of all rela-

---

20 Hyam Maccoby, *The Independent,* 12 September 1987, for a discussion of the sources on pre-marital sex. See also *Foresight,* the journal of Progressive Jewish students, September 1990, special issue on *Love and Sex.*
21 See *The Jewish Family Today and Tomorrow,* a pamphlet published by the Reform Synagogues of Great Britain in 1983, for an early attempt to confront social change, its effects on the family and the implications for Jewish life.
22 See Waskow, *Down-to-Earth Judaism* (note 12), and the response to this by Daniel Landes, 'Judaism and Sexuality', in the same volume.
23 See David Biale, *Eros and the Jews,* HarperCollins, New York 1992, for a full treatment of Jewish attitudes to sex 'from Biblical Israel to Contemporary America'.
24 In *The Reconstructionist* (July/August 1989).

tionships: there are loving, committed, heterosexual couples who cannot have children and those who choose not to. Equally, within same-sex relationships, some partnerships include children, others do not.[25] Just as an inclusive, egalitarian approach should inform our understanding of what constitutes a valid intimate relationship, so our definition of *family* needs to be expanded to encompass a variety of different 'familial' living arrangements, including heterosexual and gay or lesbian partnerships – with or without children; 'communal' families encompassing single adults and/or couples – with or without children; and one-parent families.[26]

The impressive *Report of the Reconstructionist Commission on Homosexuality*, published in 1992,[27] includes 'discussion of values fundamental to Reconstructionism', which provides a further contribution to the development of a new approach to sexual ethics. Here in a treatment of fifteen different values, we find a number which do not appear in Teutsch's list: human dignity and integrity; *k'dushah*/holiness; equality; inclusive community; democracy; learning from contemporary sources of knowledge; 'You shall surely pursue justice'. Clearly from the teachings of tradition to the insights of modern scholarship, there are a host of resources out of which to construct the specific details of a Jewish sexual ethic based on love and reciprocity. Contrary to the fear that an inclusive, egalitarian approach will prove too permissive, the reality is that it is extremely challenging and demanding for all Jews – heterosexual, lesbian, gay, bisexual and transgender alike.

Embracing, diversity: *K'dushah* today

An inclusive, egalitarian approach may have its roots in 'Love your neighbour as yourself' and encompass a wide range of Jewish values, but is it really in harmony with the predominantly separatist spirit of Judaism, as expressed in Leviticus, and developed within rabbinic

---

25 See Ariel Friedlander, 'Hundreds of Kids', MANNA 48, Summer 1995, for a sensitive treatment of Jewish teaching and attitudes on fertility and infertility.

26 See Chapter 12 – and for an early recognition of this phenomenon: *The Jewish Family Today and Tomorrow* (note 21).

27 See Ch. 7, note 30. See also the study materials for a course designed for synagogue study programmes, Robert Gluck, Ed., *Homosexuality and Judaism. A Reconstructionist Workshop Series*, (The Reconstructionist Press, 1992).

law? The philosophical framework of Jewish thought is characterised by the making of clear, unequivocal distinctions – that is what *k'dushah*, 'holiness' is all about. At first sight the values of equality and inclusivity seem at complete odds with this dynamic – particularly when it comes to including same-sex relationships and treating them as equal. But, again, as my treatment of *kiddushin* in the preceding chapter, demonstrates, in essence *k'dushah, setting apart*, is paradoxical. The bride and groom are set apart to *be joined* with one another.

What is more, not only are separated elements essentially part of one another, but their unity is *rooted* in diversity. Towards the end of each of the three Jewish daily prayer services, there are two complementary prayers known as the *Aleynu*. In contrast to the *particularistic* tone of the first prayer, the second one includes the *universalistic* hope that all the inhabitants of the world will recognise the Oneness of the Eternal: 'On that day the Eternal will be One and known as One'. The vision of universal unity is a coming together of all the different people. It is a *union of different parts*.

The Jewish concept of holiness sets apart and embraces different elements and remains at the heart of Jewish sexual ethics. 'Homosexuality' is different from 'heterosexuality'. Female sexuality is different from male sexuality. Each individual relationship is different. And sexuality is also a continuum, embracing varying degrees of bisexuality between the two extremes, in which each relationship is also part of the rich texture of possibilities for human love, and as such should be subject to the same ethical rules. Ultimately, that is what an inclusive, egalitarian approach to sexual ethics is all about.

PART THREE

The Struggle with Trouble:
Making Communities Out of Who We Are

The Introduction to Part Three is rather longer than the introductions to Parts One and Two for two reasons: Because 'My Journey' provides a context and explanatory framework for those two sections, but not for Part Three; and also because I want to explore what I mean by 'The Struggle with Trouble'.

Interestingly, although Judaism appears to be overwhelmingly governed by communal norms and the *halachah* and to revolve around the ongoing life of the community, at the heart of the story of the Jewish people are the stories of individuals – individuals, like the patriarch, Jacob. But as it happens, Jacob's story did not remain his story alone. From the time he cheated his twin brother Esau out of the birthright and blessing due to the firstborn,[1] until his death, Jacob's journey became emblematic of the journey of the Jewish people. This was not just because he was the last of the patriarchs, the one who brought his family down to Egypt at the end of the book of Genesis and whose descendants became slaves. It is also because of the transformation he underwent along the way.

Jacob's transformation is related in Genesis chapter 32:23-33, when on the eve of his reunion with his brother Esau, following his twenty year exile, he wrestles that night with an unknown 'man'. We read:

> He rose up that night, and took his two wives, and his two handmaids, and his eleven children, and passed over the ford of the Jabbok. / And he took them, and sent them over the stream, and sent over that which he had. / Then Jacob was left alone; and there a man wrestled with him until the breaking of the day. / And when he saw that he was unable to prevail against him, he touched the hollow of his thigh; and so, the hollow of Jacob's thigh was strained, as he wrestled with him. /
>
> And he said: 'Let me go, for the day is breaking.' / But he said: 'I will not let you go, unless you bless me.' / So, he said to him: 'What is your name?' And he said: 'Jacob.' / And he said: 'Your name shall no longer be called Jacob, but Israel; for you have striven with God and with men, and have prevailed.' / Then Jacob asked him, and said: 'Tell me, I pray you, your name.' And he said: 'Why is this that you ask for my name?' And he blessed him there. /

---

1 See Genesis chapters 25 and 27

And Jacob called the name of the place *P'ni-El*: 'for I have seen God face to face, and my life has been preserved.'[2] / Then the sun rose over him as he passed over *P'ni-El*, and he was limping on his thigh. / Therefore the children of Israel eat not the sinew of the thigh-vein which is on the hollow of the thigh, to this day; because he touched the hollow of Jacob's thigh, even in the sinew of the thigh-vein.

There have been, and continue to be, many interpretations of this passage.[3] As he prepared for his reunion with his brother, did Jacob dream of wrestling with Esau, hoping that his brother would bless him, after all, despite what Jacob had done to him? And: fearful that Esau would kill him, did Jacob hope that he would sustain no more than a bruised thigh? Was Jacob, perhaps, wrestling within himself, his self, including, because he was a twin, his twin brother, Esau?

At the end of the Jacob/Esau narrative, the *Torah* relates 'the generations of Esau – that is Edom'.[4] Later, identifying Edom as the archetypal enemy of Israel, the prophets, who prophesised after the Babylonian exile, interpreted the Jacob-Esau narrative in the context of the political tensions between the kingdoms of Judah, and neighbouring, Edom.[5] Later still, for the early rabbis, traumatised by Roman domination, adopting the tradition of the perennial conflict between Jacob/Israel and Esau/Edom, Edom became identified with Rome.[6] So, the twins, who 'crushed' one another in their mother's

---

2   The Hebrew word *P'ni-El*, means 'the face of God'
3   See, for example, *B'reishit Rabbah*. The term *Rabbah* was first applied to the *midrash* on Genesis, which dates to 400 CE. See also Louis Ginzberg's *Legends of the Jews*, Vol. 1, pp.384-388 (JPS, Philadelphia, 1968), for a compilation of the traditional *midrashim* on 'Jacob Wrestles with the Angel'; and Vol. 5 for the sources of these *midrashim*.
4   See Genesis 36 for Esau's geneology.
5   See, in particular Obadiah and Malachi. However, although the prophets made an absolute contrast between Jacob and Esau – 'Yet I have loved Jacob, but hated Esau' (Malach1:2-3) – they also criticised Jacob's behaviour, e.g., Hosea 12:4.
6   For the rabbinic understanding of Esau as Israel's enemy, Edom see, e.g., *Mechilta d'Rabbi Yishma'el, Shirata* 5 (Vol.2 of edition, edited by Jacob Z. Lauterbach, Jewish Publication Society of America, Philadelphia, p.42), for an interpretation of Exodus 15:5-6: '" Dashes in pieces": '"The enemy" – that is, Pharaoh, as it is said: "the enemy said…" (Ex. 15:9). Another interpretation: that [the enemy] is Esau, as it is said: "because the enemy said…"

womb,[7] become two peoples destined to be enemies: Why?

It seems that there is a binary impulse in the *Torah* from the very beginning, from the moment one human being becomes two, a tragic opposition between the one and the 'other', situated *k'neged* – in relation, but always opposite,[8] forever in a position to oppose and to be an opponent. So, in the first human family, Cain kills Abel;[9] so, Abraham's sons, Ishmael and Isaac are divided from one another;[10] and in the next generation, Esau and Jacob, too.

Yes, it's partly about issues of inheritance. Only one son may inherit, and the *Torah* disrupts the assumption of primogeniture by elevating the second son. But that's not all that is going on. When one human being becomes two, when the two sons separated from one another are, actually, twins, we are confronted with the challenge of the human condition: to be one *and* two, to be singular *and* plural at the same time. When taking their cue from the *Torah*, the prophets and the rabbis perceived an absolute division between Jacob/Israel and Esau/Edom; following the logic of this binary impulse, subsequent generations abandoned the *p'shat*, the plain meaning of the narrative. Yes, Jacob and Esau were separate individuals, each with very different personalities, aptitudes and interests. Yes, the tragic gulf between Rebecca and Isaac was played out in the favouritism each parent displayed to their favoured son,[11] but they were, after all, twins. Perhaps, on the eve of his reunion with Esau, Jacob imagined wrestling again with the twin with whom he had been crushed together in Rebecca's, womb, and finding a resolution?

Whether Jacob strove that night with a man, or with a messenger/angel of God, or with a phantom, he emerged, at sunrise, with a

---

(Ezekiel 36:2)'. For the identification of Edom with Rome, see, e.g. the Babylonian *Talmud Gittin* 57b, quoting, Genesis 27:22b: '"... but the hands of the hands of Esau" – this refers to the wicked government that destroyed our temple, burnt down our sanctuary, and exiled us from our land.'

7 See Genesis 25:22-23. Concerning what was going on in Rebecca's womb: Interestingly, the Hebrew, *Va-yitrotz'tzu ha-banim* (25:22), means, literally, 'The children *crushed one another.*' The root, *Reish Tzadi Tzadi* means to 'crush'.

8 See Chapter 1

9 See Gen. Ch. 4

10 See Gen. Ch. 21

11 See Gen. 25:27-28.

new name, Israel – *Yisrael* in Hebrew. *Yisra-El*: 'he who strives [with] God – *El*; from the root, *Sin Reish Hei*, meaning to strive, persist, exert oneself, persevere. The text, as we have seen, actually gives an explanation for the name: 'your name shall no longer be called Jacob, but *Israel*; for you have *striven with God* and with men, and have prevailed.'[12]

In her perceptive lecture, delivered at the Tavistock Clinic, Alexandra Wright,[13] focuses on the matriarch, Rachel, and explores Rachel's triumphant statement following the birth of her first son: 'Wrestlings of God have I wrestled with my sister, and have prevailed.' (Genesis 30:8). Alexander Wright points out, 'The verse provides the etymological link to the naming of one of Jacob's son, Naphtali, born to Rachel's maidservant, Bilhah.' (p.4). Rachel's 'wrestle' with Leah, from the root, *Pei Tav Lamed*, meaning to twist[14] - reflected in Naphtali's name - is not the same as their husband Jacob's 'striving'. Nevertheless, although the words are different, the underlying concept is similar. Jacob strove with God – and with men – and prevailed. Rachel wrestled with Leah, 'wrestlings of God', and prevailed, when she, finally, had a son – albeit a surrogate son. For both characters, Jacob and his beloved Rachel, life involved struggle, struggle to realise themselves through the struggle with their siblings – which, explicitly in Jacob's case, became emblematic of the struggle 'with God and with men' – and also with others.

In the course of the previous twenty years, since he had left home, Jacob's main protagonist had been his uncle Laban, his mother's brother. Jacob did eventually prevail over Laban, and his reunion with Esau passed without incident, and they went their separate ways.[15] But Jacob did not emerge unscathed from his twenty years exile, or from his night-time encounter. His thigh was so badly sprained that he was limping. Of all the parts of his body that might have been damaged, that Jacob's 'thigh' is strained is very revealing. When Abraham was instructing his servant to return to Haran to find a wife for his son, Isaac, he got him to make an oath by placing his

---

12 Genesis 32:29.
13 Senior Rabbi of the Liberal Jewish Synagogue. 'A fateful contest I waged my sister'. A model for family life? (09.03.05). Unpublished.
14 As in the twisted thread of blue in the *tzitzit*, the tassel, of the ritual fringes described in Numbers 15:38.
15 Gen. Ch. 33.

hand under Abraham's thigh.[16] More specifically, Exodus 1:5 speaks of the seventy people who 'came out of the loins of Jacob'. So, Jacob's thigh/loins – the locus of, both, fidelity and fecundity are now injured. And we can see in his limp, a more contemporary resonance: having been on the run, ever since his personal exodus twenty years earlier, Jacob was now limping home. But he was not home yet. Before he finally arrived there, Jacob's beloved Rachel, losing the final struggle of her life, died giving birth to their second son.[17] So, along with his bruised thigh, Jacob returned home with a broken heart.

Did Jacob learn from his separation from his twin, from his experience of exile, and from his loss of Rachel? Judging by how he handled his relationships with his sons, and the way he made a favourite of Rachel's firstborn, Joseph,[18] the emphatic answer would have to be, no. Even as he was about to die, having suffered the grief of thinking that Joseph was dead for so many years, when blessing Joseph's sons, Jacob insisted on giving the blessing due to the firstborn son, Manasseh, to Ephraim, before confirming Joseph's pre-eminence among his sons.[19]

The story of Jacob takes up seven long portions of the book of Genesis – amounting to half of the whole book. The linchpin between the generations of the ancestors and the story of the emerging people, Jacob is clearly very important. But that strange tale of his night-time struggle, and his renaming as *Yisrael*, father of the Jewish people, transforms his story into something else altogether. So, what do we learn from the Jacob/Israel narrative?

We learn some very obvious things. As we read at Genesis 28:10, *Va-yeitzei Ya'akov* – 'Jacob 'went out'. He experienced a personal exodus[20]. Even for those who do not have to take flight, as Jacob did, life is a journey that involves leaving the familiar for the unknown, and suffering wounds and losses. We are also reminded that human beings have a tendency to go on repeating mistakes, and that life is

---

16 See Genesis 24:1-9.
17 Gen. 35:16-20.
18 See Gen. ch. 37.
19 Gen. 48:22.
20 The Exodus from Egypt came to be known as *y'tzi'at mitzrayim* – literally, 'the going out of Egypt' – see *Birkat Ha-yom*, the Blessing for the Day on *Erev Shabbat*, recited after the blessing for wine.

a continual struggle. The Jacob narrative also teaches us something that is at the core of this book: that life is not only about struggle, it also engenders *trouble* that cannot always be resolved. The troubling plurality and complexity that is at the heart of life: *chayyim* – a plural word in Hebrew.

I have called Part Three, *The Struggle with Trouble* because I think that we – Jews, human beings – struggle to come to terms with the troubling nature of life. We find it very difficult to live with complexity and compromise – and so, we go for easy binary solutions. We might recognise that we struggle, but we see all this as a problem, an aberration, a condition to be overcome and resolved. And as a consequence of our psychological need for simple resolution, Jews, at least, often misunderstand our own teachings. The *kabbalistic*, mystical teaching of *tikkun olam*, 'repair of the world', for example,[21] has become popularised in recent years, in our quest for wholeness and perfection. But the point of the concept of *tikkun olam* is that it is a quest, a goal – not a certain product of our earnest endeavours. In *Pirkey Avot*, the Sayings of the Sages, we find a much-quoted teaching that has also become a popular song (2:16):

It is not for you to complete the work, but neither may you desist from it.

The fact that this wise teaching is expressed in the negative – in *two* negatives – is very instructive: 'It is *not* for you to complete the work'. This doesn't just mean that the work is endless, or that the work will go on, long after we are gone. The point is that it is not possible to achieve complete resolution – ever. Nevertheless, '*neither* may you desist from it'. Just because it is not possible to achieve resolution, doesn't mean we should stop making the effort to effect change.

The prophet Isaiah envisaged a future Messianic time, 'when the leopard shall lie down with the lamb'.[22] Ever the rationalist, the Jewish philosopher and codifier, Maimonides, wrote: 'This, however, is merely allegory, meaning that the Jews will live safely, even with

---

21 See Glossary for an explanation of *Tikkun Olam*.

22 Isaiah 11:6: 'The wolf also shall dwell with the lamb, and the leopard shall lie down with the kid; and the calf and the young lion and the fatling together; and a little child shall lead them.' See also, the 'second' Isaiah: Isaiah 65:25.

the formerly wicked nations. All nations will return to the true religion and will no longer steal or oppress. Note that all prophecies regarding the Messiah are allegorical. Only in the Messianic age will we know the meaning of each allegory and what it comes to teach us.'[23] Another way of interpreting Isaiah is to acknowledge the natural world's troubling realities, like lambs being eaten by leopards in the wild – or by foxes –as they are around where I live, in East Sussex.

To return to the theme of Part Three: in their different ways, the chapters in this section focus on the struggle with the troubles associated with the challenge of engendering Jewish life today, and touch on wider issues concerning the connection between Jewish life and teaching, and the wider world. In Chapter 10, Compelling Commitments and the Impulse for Engagement, the theme is galvanising the human impulse to commitment, in the context of three core commitments that are, both, all embracing and entirely non-prescriptive.[24] In Chapter 11, Empowering Individuals and Creating Community, I use an imaginative retelling of the narrative after Sinai to demonstrate how community may be constructed out of the gifts that individuals bring, using my own experience as rabbi of Brighton and Hove Progressive Synagogue, as an example.[25] In Chapter 12, The Jewish Family is Dead: Long-Live Jewish Families, I suggest that the diversity and plurality of Jewish family structures today is an

---

23 Maimonides, Commentary on *Mishnah Sanhedrin* 10:1.

24 The first version of this chapter was published as 'Bridging Choice and Command'. *MANNA* Essay. *MANNA*, No. 78, Winter 2003. The second version, focussing on the context of Liberal Judaism was published as 'Compelling Commitments: A Radical Re-think of Liberal Judaism?' In *Aspects of Liberal Judaism*. ed. David J. Goldberg & Edward Kessler. (Vallentine Mitchell, Portland, Oregon & London, 2004). More recently, a version of that article, giving examples, was published as a booklet: *Compelling Commitments: a New Approach to Living as a Liberal Jew* by Liberal Judaism. (London, 2007). See also: shorter articles: 'Compelling Commitments' (*LJ Today*, July/August, 2004) and 'The Meaning of a Mitzvah' (Judaism page, *The Jewish Chronicle*,12.03.04).

25 The original version of this chapter was published as 'Creating Community'. *MANNA* Essay. *MANNA*, No.64, Summer 1999. The main revision here is the addition of my experience as rabbi of Brighton and Hove Progressive Synagogue.

expression of Jewish renewal and a cause for celebration.[26] In Chapter 13, Living as a Jew in a Multicultural Society, I suggest a new way of thinking about the six-pointed 'Star of David'– so associated with Jewish identity; and I propose a framework for living positively, as a Jew, in the midst of other peoples.[27]

---

26 This chapter is a revised version of the talk I gave at the Second Bet Debora conference of women rabbis and cantors in Berlin in 2001, which was published as, 'Long Live Jewish families' in *Bet Debora Journal*, 2, 2001.
27 This chapter is based on my *Yom Kippur* morning sermon of 18th September 2010.

CHAPTER TEN

Compelling Commitments and the Impulse for Engagement

What are 'compelling commitments'? Before I explain what I mean by this phrase, I want to begin with a tale from the *Torah*. As the Exodus narrative opens, we find a remarkable, little- known story that marks the start of the process of the liberation of the Hebrew slaves. The Pharaoh 'who knew not Joseph'[1] commands the midwives, Shifra and Pu'ah, to kill the first-born baby boys of the Hebrews, while keeping the girl babies alive. But they do not obey orders. We read at Exodus 2: 15-21:

> The king of Egypt said to the Hebrew midwives – of whom the name of the one was Shifra, and the name of the second was Pu'ah / He said: 'When you are helping the Hebrew women to give birth, and you look at the birthing stones: if it is a son then you shall kill him, but if it is a daughter, you shall let her live.' But the midwives feared God, and did not do as the king of Egypt had said to them, rather they kept the boy children alive. / So the king of Egypt called for the midwives, and said to them: 'Why have you done this thing, and kept the boy children alive?' / Then the midwives said to Pharaoh: 'Because the Hebrew women are not like the Egyptian women; for they are lively, and they give birth before the midwives are coming to them.' / So God dealt well with the midwives; and the people multiplied, and became very mighty. / And it came to pass that because the midwives feared God, he made for them houses.

How did Shifra and Pu'ah find the courage to defy the genocidal decree of the mighty Pharaoh? What impelled the midwives to save life, rather than follow orders and kill the newborn baby boys? Where did their courage and that impulse come from?

If the 20th century, which haunts the world still, were a book, it

---

1 See Exodus 1:8.

would read like a great compendium of horror stories. And yet, in the midst of each terror-tale there are vignettes, which speak of compassion and dignity and the determination of a few courageous individuals to defy the death-dealers and save life. When slaughter is the order of the day, what impels some individuals to separate themselves from the mob, and to take enormous risks on behalf of those who are supposed to be their enemies?

Rather than respond to these questions directly, I want to turn to a form of Judaism that emerged in Britain at the dawn of the 20th century – before the monstrous events of the First World War and the *Sho'ah*. A true daughter of Enlightenment and Modernity, Liberal Judaism fashioned a new framework for Jewish life in a world in which tyrants like Pharaoh seem to be banished forever. What is more, from its inception in 1902 in the form of the Jewish Religious Union, Liberal Judaism not only acknowledged that Judaism is dynamic and changing, but also empowered individuals to make choices and take responsibility for their own Jewish lives. From the outset, the three principle founders and exponents of Liberal Judaism, Claude Montefiore, Lily Montagu, and Rabbi Israel Mattuck, were determined, not only that Judaism should progress to meet the challenges of the modern world, and make a contribution to the task of creating an ethical and just society, but also that reason and intellectual integrity should be the hallmarks of the new progressive form of religion.

As early as 1899, Lily Montagu, writing about 'Spiritual Possibilities of Judaism Today', declared[2]:

Together we must sift, with all reverence the pure from the impure in the laws which our ancestors formulated in order to satisfy the needs of the age…

In one of his early sermons at a Jewish Religious Union *Shabbat* service, Claude Montefiore argued[3]:

Religion needs the mind; it needs thought and study, as well as ardour and love… Where Jewish students, or rather Jewish teachers, so often fail is that they learn the answers of past ages to past

---

2 Published in the *Jewish Quarterly Review*, 1899.
3 Entitled 'Religious Education'.

problems, but hide their ears and envelop their minds from the questions and problems of today.

Forty years later, Israel Mattuck, who became the rabbi of the newly-established Liberal Jewish Synagogue in 1912, wrote[4]:

Judaism cannot for all time be confined in a form given it in the past. It must develop as life changes and human thought grows... Judaism... was always a developing religion. Rabbinic Judaism developed out of Biblical Judaism; the Bible itself records a development of Judaism. Liberal Judaism is its latest development.

Unlike Orthodox Judaism, which regards the *Torah* as God's word, pure and simple, *min-ha-shamayim* – 'from heaven', Liberal Judaism understands the *Torah* as the work of human beings – that is why the founders of Liberal Judaism felt able to teach about the necessity of adapting our Jewish inheritance to meet the needs of the age. What is more, they taught their co-religionists to look not only to the *Torah* for guidance, but also to the insights and wisdom of generations of our people from Sinai until this day. And so, in searching for guidance rather than instruction, from the inception of Liberal Judaism, Liberal Jews have made the assumption that it is up to individuals to decide what we will and will not do. God, the Creator of the world and the Liberator of our ancestors, may continue to address us in myriad ways, but the God Liberal Jews apprehend is neither a Dictator nor a Commander.

It follows that unlike Orthodox Jews, who bear *ol ha-mitzvot*, 'the yoke of the commandments', Liberal Jews are free to choose. But is it as simple as that? Some years ago now I argued that, 'the Progressive debate on the performance of *mitzvot* seems strangled in a false dichotomy. On the one hand there are God's commands – the preserve of the Orthodox. On the other hand there is "personal choice" – the privilege of the Progressive Jew. But what does "personal choice" mean? Why do individuals "choose" one practice or another... what impels me to perform this ritual and not that one?'[5].

---

4 *The Essentials of Liberal Judaism.* (Routledge & Kegan Paul, London, 1962), p. 140. First published in 1947.
5 'Wearing my *Tallit*: Thoughts on the hidden agenda'. In *Women and Tallit.* Working Party on Women and Judaism. (RSGB, London, 1987), p. 27.

The terms Liberal Judaism and Progressive Judaism are more or less interchangeable – although, in Britain, Liberal Judaism tends to designate a particular denomination in Jewish life, and the term, 'Progressive' encompasses a range of forms of Progressive Judaism, which, in Britain, include two specific movements, Liberal Judaism and Reform Judaism. In 1993, leading British Reform rabbi, Tony Bayfield, published his second statement on 'Reform Judaism and the Halakhic Tradition', *Sinai, Law and Responsible Autonomy*[6]. In this statement, he explains the way in which the Jewish individual stands in the centre of an 'inner triangle', and negotiates his/her personal autonomy in relation to 'Our God', 'Jewish Tradition', and 'Jewish Community'. There is no such thing as absolute autonomy. No one chooses in a vacuum. Modern Jews make Jewish choices by reflecting on the choices s/he wishes to make in the context of the *particular* responsibilities that define Jewish life.

Having explored this inner triangle, Bayfield goes on to acknowledge 'that there is a second, outer triangle reflecting Jewish existence in a larger world and the theology of our relationship to humanity'[7]. So, standing in the centre of an 'outer triangle', the Jewish individual's autonomy is also mediated by his/her *universal* responsibilities in relation to *'Ein Sof'* – the ineffable mystery of the Eternal One, the human family's shared store of 'Wisdom and Knowledge', and 'Humanity'. Taken together, these two triangles form a *Magein David* – what Bayfield calls 'The Star of Responsible Autonomy.' [8]

Tony Bayfield's 'Star of Responsible Autonomy' offers a framework for negotiating the apparent 'dichotomy' between 'personal choice' and 'God's commands'. But is the constraint on individuals solely external? In my view, we can only begin to build a bridge to span the void between 'command' and 'choice', when we recognise not only that our choices are constrained by *external* forces, but that they are also impelled by *internal* ones: We carry our Jewish inheritance not only *on our backs*, but also *in our mouths and hearts*.

Let me explain what I mean. Even if we do not think there's a big Commander – *M'tzavveh* –in the sky forcing us to bear *ol ha-mitzvot*,

---

Second edition, with a new introduction by Dee Eimer and Elizabeth Sarah, published in 1997.

6   *Sinai, Law and Responsible Autonomy.* (RSGB, London, 1993).
7   ibid. p. 21.
8   ibid. p. 23.

'the yoke of the commandments', in my experience, many of us do *feel compelled* to keep, if not all, then certainly, a number of key *mitzvot*. Before we jump to considering what those key *mitzvot* might be from a Liberal/Progressive/Reform Jewish perspective, I would like us to spend a little time exploring what I mean by saying that many of us 'feel compelled' when the compulsion is not connected to any notion of an *external* force.

On the last *Shabbat* of the year, we read the *Torah* portion, *Nitzavim*. In Liberal communities on *Yom Kippur* morning, and in Reform communities on *Yom Kippur* afternoon, we re-read a couple of passages from *Nitzavim*. The second of these passages is in my *Torah* 'Top Ten' of profound teachings. Every time I read it, I feel moved beyond words, and I experience the sense deep inside me that what I'm apprehending is 'true' – in a way that has nothing to do with any rational, factual notion of Truth. So, we read in Deuteronomy chapter 30, verses 11 to 14:

> For this commandment, which I command you today is not too complex for you, nor too remote. / It is not in heaven that you need to say: 'Who will go up to heaven for us, and fetch it for us, that we may hear it and do it?' / Neither is it across the sea that you need to say: 'Who will cross the sea for us and fetch it for us, that we may hear it and do it?' For the matter is very near you, in your mouth and in your heart to do it.

Note: The text talks of *'this commandment*, which I command you today', not *'these commandments'*. According to the medieval 13th century commentator, Nachmanides[9] 'this commandment' is a specific reference to the command to repent, since the previous passage begins with the exhortation to return to God[10]. For Ya'akov Tzvi Mecklenburg, born in 1785, on the eve of the Enlightenment, on the other hand, 'this commandment' refers to the whole of the *Torah* – and most commentators up to the present day agree.

These are reasonable explanations. My approach is radically differ-

---

9 Rabbi Moshe ben Nachman, who was born in Gerona in Spain in 1194. Also known as the Ramban. He was a *Talmudic* jurist, and also very interested in *Kabbalah* – the mystical dimension of Judaism, and so his comments frequently offer mystical insights.
10 Deuteronomy 30:2.

ent – and my starting point is the very last phrase: *'Ki-karov eilecha ha-davar m'od; b'ficha u'vilvav'cha la'asoto'* – 'For the matter is very near to you in your mouth and in your heart to do it.' Although animals communicate with one another in various ways, human beings, alone among the creatures of the earth, attempt, using language, to *make sense* of our existence. Not content simply to live and reproduce ourselves, we want to shape the world around us to our own design. Each one of us has that power within us – a power that we discern as we watch a baby learning to speak, a power that centres on our ability to think and feel - 'the matter is very near you, in your mouth and in your heart to do it.'

To do *what*? Human beings don't just talk, think and feel. Our talking, thinking and feeling leads to action – and we don't act alone. Biologically driven, certainly, we are also fashioners of Culture. We formulate rules and regulations and ethical codes, and impose them on ourselves, building complicated social structures. And alongside, all our utilitarian pursuits, our mouths and our hearts crave and create beauty in every place.

We do not know what the author intended, but, for me, what the passage suggests, so evocatively, is that the feeling of command comes from *within* us. It is neither complex nor remote; it is neither up in heaven, nor somewhere else across the sea, it is neither the responsibility of God, nor of a leader who will fetch it for us, rather 'the matter is very near you, in your mouth and in your heart to do it.'

As human beings, we feel compelled to act. But where does acting *as Jews* come into the equation? While all humanity thinks and acts, the concept of *mitzvot* is Jewish. Jews not only have a love affair with words, we have a very particular sense that we must translate words into deeds, into *mitzvot* – the actions that we feel compelled to perform. But what determines *which* actions we feel compelled to perform? The key to answering this question lies in the very next section of text:[11]

See, I have set before you this day life and good and death and evil... therefore you shall choose life, that you and your descendants may live.

---

11 ibid. 30: 15; 19b.

U'vacharta ba-chayyim – 'therefore you shall choose life'. *What else can we do?* 'The matter is very near you, in your mouth and in your heart to do it.' What could be nearer to us, in our mouths and hearts, than the matter of choosing life? And, of course, it begins in our mouths: For a suckling baby, choosing life is a simple biological urge. A new baby, born prematurely to friends of mine, spent the first few weeks of his life sucking and sucking because his life depended on it, and he gained ounces of weight every day. So, what does it mean for us to choose life? And what makes choosing life a *mitzvah*, a specifically *Jewish* compulsion? Perhaps, what makes choosing life Jewish is simply the fact that, having looked death and evil in the face so often, we continue to feel compelled to choose life and good – which doesn't mean that, like everyone else, we don't sometimes choose death and evil instead.

Many of the *mitzvot* we find in the *Torah*, which have been incorporated into codes of law the world over, originate in a Near Eastern Code, formulated by Hamurabi, an enlightened king of Babylon, who reigned between 1945 and 1902 BCE, and undertook the codification of Babylonian law. As I indicated earlier, the compulsion to create rules and regulations is common to all humanity. The Jewish version of this universal phenomenon is born of our *particular* adventures and ordeals as a people. And so, for example, while the Ten Commandments may be shared by humanity, for Jews, there is an 11th – a specifically Jewish commandment, the *mitzvah* to *remember everything*: the joy as well as the torment. The *mitzvot* have emerged out of our experience: 'Justice, justice you shall pursue'[12] because we have known injustice. 'Seek peace and pursue it'[13] because we have been destroyed many times. 'When a stranger resides with you... you shall not wrong him... you shall love him as yourself, for you were strangers in the land of Egypt'[14]. We haven't been strangers in the land of Egypt for millennia. But there have been other furnaces, other houses of bondage. Again: In the face of death and evil, what can we do but choose life and good?

What can we do, but be ourselves? No one is simply a human being. Each one of us is a *particular* human being, with particular charac-

---

12 Deuteronomy 16: 20.
13 Psalm 34:15.
14 Leviticus 19:33-34.

teristics – and being Jewish is part of our particularity – *if we so choose*: So! Whatever the circumstances of our birth, *we are all Jews by choice today*. But it is not a free choice. Jews today are caught between the demands of the world, indifferent to our particular Jewish compulsions, and the demands of Jewish particularity, which seem to require us to see the world exclusively through Jewish eyes.

So what do Liberal/Progressive/Reform Jews feel impelled, compelled, to do? If we look back one hundred years to the establishment of Liberal Judaism in Britain, it is clear that the founders of that movement, intoxicated with the gifts of the Enlightenment and Modernity, felt compelled almost exclusively, by the drive to transform society into an oasis of reason, truth, justice, compassion and peace. For them living as a Jew was primarily a matter of acting on the ethical principles of Judaism, set down in key sections of the *Torah*, and highlighted by the prophets. Ritual was a secondary matter only, and only those ritual acts that 'made sense', or which 'enhanced life' – principally, those associated with study, prayer, and the celebration of *Shabbat* and the festivals – became integral to Liberal Judaism.

But after the *Sho'ah*, Progressive Jews – both Liberal and Reform – in common with our sisters and brothers throughout the Jewish world felt compelled by other concerns. Not only had Modernity let us down big time, but also, tasting the acrid smoke of the ovens in our mouths, and our hearts breaking with grief, we longed to savour the flavour of particularity once more, our hearts beating to a Jewish rhythm all of our own. The compulsion to choose Life – to choose *Jewish* life – after our journey through the 'valley of the shadow of death' became almost overwhelming. We were all survivors now. Jewish ethics were no longer enough to sustain us. Liberal/Progressive/Reform Jews, too, needed to nourish our souls by participating in uniquely Jewish acts.

Over sixty-five years have elapsed since the *Sho'ah*. During that time, the Jewish world has been undergoing a process of transformation triggered by a number of developments, including the establishment of the State of Israel, the collapse of Communism in the East, and the liberation of women in the West. And so, too, Progressive Judaism – in both its Liberal and Reform incarnations – has been changing. More than that, Progressive Judaism has been in the forefront of change in the Jewish world, because of all the different Jewish denominations, Progressive Judaism alone acknowledges that Jewish life is connected with the world and our responsibilities as Jews extend beyond the needs of our people to encompass, not only humanity, but God's creation as a whole. Moreover Progressive Judaism recognises that Life makes demands on us *now*, impels us to *continue to* work out how we should live *today*. We may not feel commanded by an external force, but we do feel compelled not only to *cherish our inheritance*, but also to *engage in recreating it in the context of the needs of the present, and in relation to the world around us*.

Progressive Judaism is not only, like Orthodox Judaism, a response to Modernity, to the consequences of intellectual Enlightenment and political Emancipation. Progressive Judaism provides a framework for working out how to live Jewishly in the modern – and now post-modern – world; an attempt to re-interpret and re-engage with our Jewish inheritance in the context of the needs of the present.

In *Sinai, Law and Responsible Autonomy*, Tony Bayfield presents a 'Star of Jewish Responsibility' – a combination of intra- and inter-relationships, which together encompass the arena of Progressive Jewish life. In *Pirkey Avot*, the Sayings of the Sages, included in the *Mishnah*, edited around the 2nd century CE, we find two teachings that pre-figure the two triangles of 'responsibility'[15]. First (1:2):

The world stands on three things: Teaching (*Torah*), Divine Worship (*Avodah*) and Loving Deeds (*G'milut Chasadim*).

Then a few paragraphs further on (1:18):

The world stands on three things: Justice (*Din*), Truth (*Emet*) and Peace (*Shalom*).

---

15 The *Mishnah* is the first post-biblical code of Jewish law reflecting the deliberations of the early rabbis, who gave themselves the task of interpreting the teachings of the *Torah*. One section of the six 'orders' of the *Mishnah* is *Pirkey Avot*, which is devoted to the rabbis' philosophical teachings. This particular teaching is attributed to Simeon ben Gamliel II, Principal of the Rabbinic Academy in Usha, in the lower Galilee, from 140-170 CE, whose son, known as *Y'hudah Ha-Nasi* – 'Judah the Prince' – was responsible for editing the *Mishnah* around the year 200 CE.

16 See Chapter 13 for an exploration of these two texts, as two interlocking

Torah, *Avodah* and *G'milut Chasadim*: the three pillars that uphold Jewish life; Truth, Justice and Peace: the three pillars that uphold the world as a whole. Just as the *Torah* presents God as both, the Creator of the world, and the One who brought the people Israel into being at Mount Sinai, Rabbinic Judaism, encompasses both the particular and the universal dimensions of Jewish responsibility – while emphasising the particular. Likewise, Progressive Judaism encompasses both dimensions. However, while Classical Liberal Judaism emphasised the universalistic teachings, contemporary Liberal Judaism gives equal weight to both.[16] But perhaps more important than this, from its inception Progressive Judaism has embraced the most important blessing of Modernity, the acknowledgement that individuals – and not just communities – have a role in defining and perpetuating Jewish life.

And so, as Progressive Jews we have evolved, and are evolving what I like to call *compelling commitments*, which frame the choices we make each and every day. Of course, emerging out of our on-going experience these *compelling commitments* are not set in stone, but at their heart, I believe, we find these three – each one with a particularist and a universalist dimension:

Compelling Commitment One: Embracing Jewish Teaching and engaging with knowledge in the wider world

The commitment to nurture and cultivate our own Jewish lives and the life of the Jewish people as a whole, by continuing to learn and engage with the *Torah*, with our Jewish stories, teachings and traditions, and by participating in the various ritual acts, which celebrate life with Jewish flavours, colours and tones.

And:

The commitment to engage with the accumulating wisdom of the world, to study and to learn about the major developments in human knowledge, and to find ways of ensuring that the developing wisdom of humanity in all its dimensions connects with and informs Jewish teaching.

---

triangles, forming a new six-pointed 'Star of David', proclaiming a message that is, both, universalist and particularist.

17 See my pamphlet, *Compelling Commitments. A New Approach to Living as a*

Compelling Commitment Two: Sustaining the Jewish Community and repairing the world

The commitment to honour both those that have gone before us and those who are yet to be born, by becoming links in the chain of the generations of our people, and by maintaining, restoring and re-creating Jewish communal life in Britain, in Israel, and throughout the world.

And:

The commitment to love not only our neighbours, but also the stranger in our midst; to liberate the oppressed, protect the vulnerable and support the fallen; to pursue justice and to seek peace; to participate in the great task of *Tikkun Olam*, the repair of the world.

Compelling Commitment Three: The Eternal is our God and The Eternal is One

The commitment to explore the meaning of existence, to journey, to search, and to *listen* out for the voice of the Eternal, who calls each Jew to become part of *Am Yisrael*, the people who 'struggle with God', and to strive to sanctify Life each day through our actions and our relationships.

And:

The commitment to acknowledge that the Eternal is One, and to work together with all the peoples of the world to recognise the essential unity of existence in all its diversity.

Unlike the contemporary Orthodox approach to Jewish life, these Compelling Commitments remind us that our Jewish inheritance concerns not only the particular life of the Jewish people, but the life of humanity and the world as a whole. Unlike the Orthodox understanding of the 'Commandments', these Compelling Commit-ments offer a framework for our lives, without spelling out exactly what each and every Liberal/Progressive/Reform Jew should be doing each and every moment of the day. It is the responsibility of each and every individual to decide for themselves and in relation to those around them, how to put their sense of commitment into practice.[17]

Let us now return to the story of the defiant midwives. Who were these midwives? Interestingly, their names reflect the noisy nature of their work with women in labour: Shifra, from the root, *Shin Pei Reish*, is related to the noun, *shofar*, 'horn'; while *Pu'ah* comes from the root, *Pei Ayin Hei*, to 'groan'. But a *remez*, a 'hint', in the Hebrew tells us more: that Shifra and Pu'ah were Hebrews themselves, not simply 'midwives of the Hebrews' - *Va-yomer melech mitzrayim la-m'yal'dot ha-ivriyot* - 'The King of Egypt said *to the Hebrew midwives*'.[18] If Shifra and Pu'ah had been simply, *'midwives of the Hebrews'*, the Hebrew would be: *lim'yal'dot* (preposition only) - not *la-m'yal'dot* (preposition plus definite article). So, these Hebrew women chose to defy the command of the mighty tyrant, Pharaoh. Moreover, although the midwives 'feared God'[19], neither God, nor any other power told them to save the baby boys - the matter was in their mouths and their hearts to do it. Despite the order to kill, what they felt compelled to do was save life.

When we speak about 'taking action', we often use the metaphor of our 'hands'. In the case of midwives - any midwives - speaking of the 'the work of their hands' is not a metaphor. Literally, with their hands they bring new life into the world. The story of Shifra and Pu'ah's defiance transforms a striking image in the *Torah* portion *Nitzavim* into a profound *truth*: Compelling Commitments begin in our mouths and hearts and become manifest in the work of our hands. The time has come for Liberal/Progressive/Reform Jews to develop a *holistic* approach to living Jewishly today that engages *every dimension* of our complex humanity, as we grapple with the challenge of ensuring that *Judaism lives in our lives*: 'For the matter is very near to you in your mouth and in your heart to do it.'

Liberal Jew (Liberal Judaism, London, 2007) for an array of examples of ways of putting each of the commitments into practice.
18 Exodus 1:15.
19 ibid. 1:17.

CHAPTER ELEVEN

Empowering Individuals and Creating Community

Picture a desert scene: a massive mountain of rock towers over a bewildered rabble of ex-slaves, necks straining, as they gaze upwards. Just a short while ago, the mountain had quaked with thunder and they had been dazzled by lightning and flashes of fire. Now, everything is silent and still – but although the drama has ceased and the mountain is shrouded in cloud, they cannot turn their heads away.

Finally, exhaustion overtakes them. One by one they fall where they stand, until the entire camp is asleep in the rubble and dust.

For six days the whole world is a stony wilderness dwarfed by that mountain and the dense, fiery, smoking cloud. The people stumble around in a daze like the survivors of an earthquake unable to recognise the new terrain they now inhabit. All that remains of the shattered life they once knew are the three people responsible for taking them away from it all: that Egyptian prince turned Hebrew liberator-god, Moses; Aaron, his smooth-talking brother; and Miriam, the elder sister, who danced a pathway into freedom through the midst of the sea.

And then on the seventh day, the exultant joy of deliverance a distant memory overwhelmed by the eruption of God, Moses leaves them, goes up the mountain and disappears into the cloud. Day after day, they wait for his return. As they wait, they begin to emerge from their shock and survey the landscape beyond the mountain. Where are they? Where are they going? Moses started it all but he is nowhere to be seen. The mountain shuddered, but now it is still. What next?

The people wait. But then, overcome with anxiety, the men of the camp approach Aaron in a huge huddle of fear: 'Get up, make us a god who will go before us. For this Moses, the man that got us out of Egypt, we don't know what's become of him'. Sensing the danger of the moment, Aaron responds quickly: 'Break off the golden rings which are in the ears of your wives, of your sons, and of your daughters, and bring them to me.' And so all the people break off the golden rings that are in their ears and bring them to Aaron who takes them and fashions the gold with an engraving tool into a molten calf. When the people see the molten calf, their panic ebbs away in a wave of relief and they say in one voice: 'This is your god, Israel, which brought you up out of the land of Egypt.'

A familiar tale.[1] A shadow story that fills the void after the dramatic moment of Revelation. What does it teach us about human behaviour? That, in the face of the unknown and the unexpected, people are fearful, weak and gullible? That those who have no experience of taking responsibility for their own lives crave authority and security? That people reared in a world of tangible, material gods, can only believe in what they can see, hear and touch? That a large collection of people is a monolithic, undifferentiated mass?

Instead of responding to these questions directly, let us consider another version of this *Torah* tale. So, picture again the desert scene: the same overwhelming after-shock of Revelation. But then on the seventh day, something starts to change. As if emerging from a haze, people begin to see their new world in a different light. Fear and dread give way to awe and wonder as they look at the mountain. Then, slowly, they gather together in small groups to speak about their experience of that momentous day. As they talk together, excitedly at first, calm gradually descends upon the camp. And then, in the midst of this special new day, Moses announces that God has called him and that he must ascend the mountain once more. The people watch attentively as Moses climbs, until he disappears into the cloud.

The next day, with Moses gone, the people turn their attention from the mountain to their makeshift camp. 'We don't know how long Moses will be gone', someone says, 'so it would be a good idea to make this place more habitable'. Over the next few days, the area at the foot of the mountain is transformed from a gritty heap of rubble to a proper encampment, complete with clearing and tents made from the coarser materials they had brought with them from Egypt. And the homemaking doesn't end there: 'Why don't we decorate it with the treasures we took from the Egyptians?' a youngster

---

1 Exodus chapter 32. My account paraphrases the text, with direct quotations indicated.

suggests. A short while later, people emerge from their tents with gifts: gold and silver and brass; cloths of blue and purple and scarlet; fine linen and goats' hair; rams' skins dyed red; sealskins; acacia-wood; oil and spices; onyx stones and stones for setting. Some carry their offerings grandly on their heads, others wear them, dancing to display their splendour. Soon the whole camp is ablaze with colour and light. They gaze at one another in astonishment. For the first time in their lives, in the midst of the new habitation they have created together with their own hands, each person feels special and shines with pride.

A naïve fantasy? Well, actually, like the 'molten calf' scenario, it also follows on from the scene in the immediate aftermath of Revelation – in fact, the picture of the Israelites bringing their splendid offerings is where the *Torah* takes us *next*. The *Torah*'s account of the scene after Revelation forms the conclusion of Exodus chapter 24 at the end of the *parashah*, the *Torah* portion, *Mishpatim*, and the narrative of the 'molten calf' doesn't appear until Exodus chapter 32, in *Parashat Ki Tissa*. The intervening chapters and *parashiyyot* – portions – focus on the instructions for the construction of the tabernacle. So we read at Exodus 24 (:16-18):

> The glory of the Eternal dwelt upon Mount Sinai, and the cloud covered it six days; and the seventh day God called Moses out of the midst of the cloud. / And the appearance of the glory of the Eternal was like devouring fire on the top of the mountain in the eyes of the Israelites. / Then Moses entered into the midst of the cloud, and went up into the mountain; and Moses was in the mountain forty days and forty nights.

And the *Torah* continues with *Parashat T'rumah* (Exodus 25:1-19):

> The Eternal One spoke to Moses, saying: /Speak to the Israelites, that they take for Me an offering; from everyone whose heart makes them willing you shall take My offering. / And this is the offering that you shall take from that which is theirs: gold, and silver and brass; / and blue, and purple, and scarlet, and fine linen, and goats' hair, / and rams' skins dyed red, and sealskins and acacia-wood; / oil for the light, spices for the anointing oil, and for the sweet incense; / onyx stones, and stones to be set, for the cape and for the breastplate. / Then let them make Me a sanctuary, that

I may dwell among them. / According to all that I show you, the pattern of the tabernacle and the pattern of all its furnishings, just so shall you make it.

So what did the people do during Moses' absence? I am not asking a question about the 'facts' of the story. We do not know what happened in the wilderness – not any of it. What we have is a document which reflects varied traditions transmitted, first orally and later as written texts, and finally edited into the form of the 'Five Books'. *Torah* means 'teaching'. The *Torah* is teaching us something with this interrupted narrative. A plain, chronological reading of the text would suggest that the theme of the construction of the tabernacle does not form part of the narrative. And so the narrative resumes once more, after this 'interruption', with the episode of the molten calf. Interestingly, from the time of the first *midrashim*, commentaries, through the mediaeval period, the rabbinic commentators did not go for a chronological approach to these texts, and the prevailing view was that the instruction to build the tabernacle came *after* the sin of the molten calf and not before. Indeed, the sages saw the tabernacle as God's response to the people's frailty, to their need for a tangible sign of the Divine Presence in their midst. But, whether or not the instructions preceded or followed the molten calf, the early rabbinic commentators were in no doubt that what the Israelites did while Moses was away from them was resort to idolatry.

Perhaps they did. But the insertion of the tabernacle theme also raises other possibilities. Perhaps ex-slaves would have slavishly recreated the idolatrous practices that they knew, but these ex-slaves had experienced Revelation. Perhaps the eruption of God at Mount Sinai was more than a thunderous spectacle – perhaps it generated a real transformation. The *Torah* offers two alternative profiles of the Israelites following God's Revelation. The Israelites who collude in the creation of the molten calf remain leader-dependent. They act as a mass, without any sign of individual volition – and so they offer only gold which is melded into one huge object; they are only able to believe in a god that they can see and feel; they have no faith in the covenant into which they have just entered. By contrast, the Israelites who cooperate in the building of the tabernacle are a new breed: self-motivated. They value their gifts and offer them willingly.

They share a vision of a community in which the God who had roared on the top of the mountain would come down and dwell in their midst.

The two alternative profiles are not given equal weight in the *Torah*. The *Torah* implies that the molten calf tale describes what *was*; the subject of the tabernacle is inserted into the narrative, interrupting the continuity, to present as image of what *might have been* – and what *could be*. So perhaps my musings about the newly-formed people are a naïve fantasy after all. But still, it is the possibility that it could have been different that is all important. Unless we are prepared to consider that it could have been different *then*, how can we hold out the hope that it can be different *now* or in the *future* - that change is possible?

The molten calf narrative of fear has left a deep legacy. Priests, prophets, judges, sovereigns and rabbis: the history of mainstream Hebrew/Jewish leadership is a fascinating one. But what does that history teach about the led? Is there anything to counter the prevailing biblical view of a dependent mass? In theory, the rabbis made Judaism more participatory. They promoted universal education (for males) and enabled the home and the synagogue to become centres of Jewish life and worship in place of the priestly arena of the Temple. In practice, the authority of the rabbis to decide the law and determine the practice of the community has been absolute. While Jewish life has never been monolithic, within any given community, the prerogative of the rabbi and the established local *minhag* (custom) combine to control what any individual member within it may or may not do.

This state of affairs is most true in the context of orthodox communities. But it also pertains within the progressive world. In theory, Progressive Judaism is a daughter of Enlightenment and Emancipation, of an age which liberated the individual from absolute communal power. In practice, many progressive communities – i.e. both Reform and Liberal in the British context – have become very set in their ways. Progressive congregations may not attempt to control what their members do in their own homes, but how easy is it for individuals to try and modify established synagogue practices? Within most progressive communities as with orthodox ones, the individual member is expected to conform to 'the way we do it here'. Very few progressive synagogues seem able to

EMPOWERING INDIVIDUALS AND CREATING COMMUNITY

create an environment in which individuals may contribute their gifts and express their individuality within the context of community activities and religious services.

Concern for the individual is not a modern invention. In the very first chapter of Genesis (1:27), we learn that the human being is created *b'tzelem Elohim* – 'in the image of God', and the *Torah*'s laws concerning the just treatment of people, all refer to the individual: the neighbour; the stranger; the poor; the worker; the widow; the orphan; the elderly person; the deaf; the blind. But recognising the rights of individuals to just treatment is one thing, incorporating the needs of individuals within the community is very difficult – which is why even progressive congregations do not seem to manage very well. And then, in recent years, a huge reaction against excessive 'individualism' seems to have taken place. Both the compassionless Thatcherite 'I'm all right Jack' 1980s and the more benign 'liberal' 60s and 70s have been set aside in favour of an emphasis on the individual's responsibility towards the community. The philosophy of Communitarianism, which owes much to the German-born Israeli-American sociologist Amitai Etzioni,[2] had a huge impact on social thinking during the 1990s. As a result, many institutions and groups, including, 'New Labour', the Churches, and a number of Jewish organisations, began to stress the primacy of community over the needs of the individual.

Individual responsibility without individual rights is highly dangerous – as the human rights organisations Liberty and Amnesty International, keep trying to remind us. So the challenge is to create forms of community which include individuals and the differences individuals bring. But how? That is the big question.

---

2 A prolific writer, Amitai Etzioni's books, include: *My Brother's Keeper: A Memoir and a Message.* (Rowman & Littlefield, Lanham, MD, 2003); *From Empire to Community: A New Approach to International Relations.* (Palgrave Macmillan, New York, 2004);*The Monochrome Society.* (Princeton University Press, Princeton, 2001); *The Limits of Privacy* (Basic Books, New York, 1999), *The New Golden Rule* (Basic Books, NY, 1996); *The Spirit of Community* (Crown Books, New York, 1993); *The Moral Dimension: Toward a New Economics* (Free Press, New York, 1988). In 1990, Etzioni founded the Communitarian Network, a non-profit-making, non-partisan organisation, and he was the editor of *The Responsive Community: Rights and Responsibilities*, the organisation's quarterly journal, from 1991-2004. For information about Amitai Etzioni, see: http://www.amitaietzioni.org/

By getting away from the idea, in the first instance, that community is only about what we share in common, that it necessarily involves everyone conforming to a monoculture. Once a community agrees on its core values – mutual respect, compassion, peace, integrity, equality, justice, lifetime learning – and each individual member agrees to express and act on those values, it should be possible to devise ways of facilitating individuals to contribute their unique qualities, gifts and interests to the life of the community. If the synagogue building is alive with people on a *Shabbat* morning, does it matter that they are engaged in a variety of activities, from dance to social action – including different forms of service – and only come together for *Kiddush*? And even within an individual service, once we get away from the notion that 'we've always done it like this' or ' it has to be like this', is it not possible to create a format for services which incorporates variations and makes space for creativity, meditation and individual preferences?

So far I have used the words 'individual' and 'community' quite uncritically, without defining what they mean. But if we are going to move beyond trying to negotiate around what appears to be a problematic tension between the individual on the one hand and the community on the other, it is essential that we explore the interface between the two more closely. In their article, 'Between persons: the narrow ridge where I and Thou meet',[3] Harriett Goldenberg and Zelda Isaacson highlight the distinction which Martin Buber made between the *individual* and the *person* in a way which clarifies not only what makes dialogue possible between people, but also what makes *community* a living reality. In *I and Thou*, Buber distinguished between individuals and persons: '*Eigenwesen* [individuals /egos] appear by setting themselves apart from other *eigenwesen* … Persons appear by entering into relation to other persons.'[4] And in *The Knowledge of Man*, he wrote: 'An individual is just a certain uniqueness of a human being … But a person, I would say, is an individual living really with the world. And with the world I don't mean in the world - just in *real* contact, in real reciprocity with the world ….'[5]

---

3 *Journal of the Society for Existential Analysis* 7:2 July 1996.
4 Charles Scriber's Sons, New York, pp. 111-112.
5 Humanities Press International Inc., Atlantic Highlands, New Jersey, 1998, pp. 173-174.

'Then let them make me a sanctuary, that I may dwell *among them*' – V'*asu li mikdash, v'shachanti b'tocham*'. Issachar Ber Eilenburg, Rabbi of Gorizia in Italy, who wrote *Tzeidah La-derekh*, the 16th century super-commentary on Rashi, has this to say about the fact that the verse says *b'tocham*, '*among them*', and not *bo*, '*in it*':

> The Divine Presence does not rest in the sanctuary on account of the sanctuary, but on account of Israel, for they constitute the Temple of God.

And we might add, *b'tocham* also suggests Israel, not as a singular entity, but as a people encompassing all the different persons living in relation with one another who constitute 'Israel'. When each person brings their offering for the building of the *mishkan*, then God dwells amongst *them*. In this sense, the *mishkan* is not a *building*, it is the *community* itself. When each person contributes their gifts for the creation of the community, then God dwells among *them*. And as *T'rumah* clearly states, each gift is needed. The *mishkan*/community cannot be complete if any particular contribution is missing. Of course, the gifts we give are not the same, and it might appear that gold is better that goats' hair, but they are all of equal value in the eyes of the Eternal. What makes my gift *special* is the fact that it is *my* gift, given willingly. I do not want to live alone; I want to live with others. What makes my gift *essential* is the fact that I recognise that the community cannot exist without me; I am called upon to give.

The emphasis on the value of the individual is not in conflict with the value of community. On the contrary, individuals realise their value, become persons, by interacting and creating community out of the gifts they bring. The same *parashah, Ki Tissa*, which includes the narrative of the molten calf, opens with a text in which Moses is to take a census of the community and then require each male to give a half-*shekel* for the upkeep of the sanctuary.[6] As 'poll taxes' go, it was a modest one; not demanding too much from the poorer members of the community. On another level, it provides a vivid illustration that individuals become *persons* and make a 'whole' offering only when they bring their gifts *together*. And it is when these

---

6 Exodus 30:11:16.

individual gifts are brought together that the community becomes possible.

So what is the 'possible' community? Unlike the half-*shekel*, no two individuals are alike, and each one of us is infinitely precious. And so the community is not simply the sum of its individual members: it is what happens when persons meet and share and live with one another.

In *Between Man and Man*, Buber distinguished between *community* and *collectivity*. Within the *collectivity*, the person 'ceases to have complete responsibility. The collectivity becomes what really exists, the person becomes derivatory ... Collectivity is not a binding but a bundling together: individuals packed together, armed and equipped in common ... But community... is the being no longer side by side but with one and another of a multitude of persons. And this multitude ... experiences everywhere a turning to, a dynamic facing of, the other, a flowing from *I* to *Thou*. Community is where community happens.'[7]

Community is the creative encounter of persons – each one of whom is endowed with special gifts:

> Our deepest fear is not that we are inadequate; our deepest fear is that we are powerful beyond measure. It is our light not our darkness that most frightens us. We ask ourselves; "Who am I to be brilliant, gorgeous, talented, fabulous?" Actually who are you not to be? You are a child of God. Your playing small doesn't serve the world. There's nothing enlightened about shrinking so other people won't feel insecure around you. We are meant to shine as children do. We were born to make manifest the glory of God that is within us and it's not just within some of us, it's in everyone. And as we let our own light shine we unconsciously give other people permission to do the same. As we're liberated from our own fear our presence automatically liberates others.

Who wrote this? When I was in the process of writing this essay in 1999, one of the rabbinic students in the spirituality programme, which I co-taught with Rabbi Marcia Plumb at the Leo Baeck College, brought to class, one day, a passage that he understood to be taken from Nelson Mandela's inaugural Presidential Address. I checked the

7 Collier Books, Macmillan, New York, 1965, p.80, p.31; p.31.

address, but could not find the passage. Perhaps it was from Nelson Mandela's autobiography? I scoured the book, but could not find it. A few years later, I discovered on the internet that it was written by Marianne Williamson, described on the web as 'a motivational speaker and author', and that it is an excerpt from her book, *A Return To Love*. But that's not all. According to the internet, this passage 'is a cultural phenomenon as it is quickly becoming one of today's most well-known sagacious quotes from an author who is still living.'[8] Indeed, the passage is so well-known that it is quoted in the 2005 film, *Coach Carter*. And yet, many people – including the homeopath I went to for a while, who has it written in beautiful calligraphy on her bathroom wall – still believe it was said by Nelson Mandela during his inaugural address![9]

Does it matter who wrote it, if it has something to teach us? I can understand why so many people wanted to believe that Nelson Mandela, arguably the most inspirational figure of our age, had said those words. In London a few years ago, Steve Greenberg of CLAL, The National Jewish Centre for Learning and Leadership in the United States, posed a challenge: 'Treat yourself and everyone you meet as an image of God, and see what a difference it makes to you, to them, to the world.'[10] In a nutshell that is what Marianne Williamson is saying. Ultimately, the *mishkan* is nothing other than the product of the gifts of each and every 'brilliant, gorgeous, talented, fabulous' image of God, letting 'our own light shine' and making 'manifest the glory of God' in the community we create together.

It is not easy to recognise ourselves as 'brilliant, gorgeous, talented, fabulous' because 'It is our light not our darkness that most frightens us'. But the fear and the self-hatred is part and parcel of our loneliness and isolation. When I encounter another and experience

---

8 See: www.squidoo.com/our_deepest_fear

9 Having revised my original article to acknowledge that Nelson Mandela did not say those now famous words, as I prepared the manuscript of this book for publication, I was interested to read an article by Oliver Burkeman (Guardian Weekend, 29th October 2011), in which he discusses the phenomenon of the misattribution of the Marianne Williams quotation to Nelson Mandela.

10 Paraphrase of a remark in a talk by Rabbi Steve Greenberg at The Sternberg Centre, April 1996.

their beauty, I may also discover my own and together we become more beautiful. 'You shall love your neighbour *as yourself*';[11] when we love ourselves we are able to love our neighbours. But further, reciprocity is mutually reinforcing. I learn to love myself more through my love for others and my love for others is ultimately inseparable from their love for me.

Picture a contemporary 'desert' scene. The mainstream Jewish community in Britain is diminishing steadily and increasing numbers of individual Jews whose parents were synagogue members are choosing not to join themselves and are disappearing off the communal map. Like any arid wilderness, there are a few lush oases scattered around. The only revelation is that it's taken us so long to notice.

But a report published by the Institute for Jewish Policy Research in February 1996 on the 'Social and Political Attitudes of British Jews', which summarised the findings of a postal survey,[12] found that while 36.9% of respondents did not belong to a synagogue (with the figure rising to 'close to half' for those under 35 years old), only 8% were completely uninvolved in Jewish life 'using a strong definition [of non-involvement] based on a lack of social, religious, organisational or cultural contact with Jews or Jewish events'.[13] And even uninvolved Jews expressed some level of Jewish identification: 60% felt they had been influenced by their Jewish background, 'nearly always positively', 81% believed that it is 'important that Jews survive as a people'... 55% had a 'moderate or strong attachment to Israel' ... and 17% 'expressed a desire to become more involved'.

What was this report saying? Growing numbers of Jews seem to be choosing to express their Jewishness outside the mainstream Jewish community – which includes all the different mainstream Jewish denominations. While the JPR report found that 15% of those who were affiliated to a synagogue had moved to a more progressive congregation to that to which their parents belonged, the unaffiliated were disproportionately the children of Reform (56%) and Liberal (59%) members, with the percentage for the children of the

---

11 Leviticus 19:18.
12 *Social and Political Attitudes of British Jews* by Stephen Miller, Marlena Schmool and Antony Lerman.
   http://www.jpr.org.uk/Reports/PJC_Reports/no_1_1996/index.htm
13 ibid. p.10.

Orthodox members being quite a bit lower at 27%. Perhaps the notion of 'personal choice' that is a feature of Progressive Judaism may have something to do with these figures. But the fact that the children of progressive Jews may feel free to choose is not the issue. The issue is that, like smaller numbers of their orthodox peers, many are choosing *not* to participate in mainstream communal life.

And it seems that mainstream synagogues and denominational organisations are doing very little to persuade them to choose otherwise. The JPR report suggested that relationships with non-Jews may be a factor in people disaffiliating: 62% of 'uninvolved' Jews (8% of the sample), compared to 30% of the sample as a whole, were married to non-Jews (p.11), and 64% of those who had disaffiliated, compared with 39% who stayed members of their parents' synagogues, agreed that 'Rabbis should be more helpful in welcoming non-Jewish members into the community' (p.15). This information underlines the failure of synagogues to meet individual Jews where they are and acknowledge diversity. And if one adds to the 30% of Jews married to non-Jews, another 30% who are single, including 9% widowed and 7% separated and divorced, (p.13), and the 6-10% of lesbian and gay Jews, both single and coupled, who currently live on the side-lines,[14] it becomes glaringly apparent that the inability of synagogues to address Jewish individuals has the effect of marginalising between 60% and 70% of the Jews in Britain.

Of course, 1996 is a long time ago. A more recent JPR report on, 'Synagogue Membership in the United Kingdom', published in May 2010,[15] produced even more challenging statistics. As of 2010, synagogue membership by denomination, shows that of the total 82,963 synagogue members by household, affiliated to a total of 409 synagogues, 54.7% belong to Central Orthodox congregations, 19.4% to Reform, 10.9% to the strictly Orthodox, 8.7% to Liberal, 3.5% to Sephardi and 2.7% to the Masorti – the relatively new centrist movement in British Jewry. However, the most interesting statistics concern the change in synagogue membership from 1990 to 2010, which shows that mainstream Orthodox membership has declined

---

14 There is a consensus that in any given population, 6-10% of people are lesbian or gay.

15 The authors of the report are David Graham and Daniel Vulkan. See: http://www.jpr.org.uk/publications/publication.php?id=233

by 31.4%, Reform, by 4.2%, Liberal by 7.6%, and Sephardi by 9.5%. Meanwhile, the Masorti movement has increased by 85.1% and the strictly Orthodox by 101.6%.

With the exception of the small but growing Masorti movement, which in 2010 had 2,269 members, and the slightly larger, strictly Orthodox section of the Jewish community, which by 2010 had increased to 9,049 members, outstripping the Liberals by almost 2000, Jewish communal life in Britain seems to be in steady decline. So what is the solution? The increase in strictly Orthodox affiliation would suggest that some Jews, at least, are attracted to a more authoritarian brand of Judaism. The increase in Masorti affiliation would suggest that increasing numbers of Jews are drawn to the blend of traditional practice with liberal theology. So, what are the lessons for Liberal and Reform Judaism? What can Liberal and Reform congregations do to reverse the decline in synagogue affiliation?

I can only speak for a relatively small out-of-London congregation, but since I began working as rabbi of Brighton and Hove Progressive Synagogue in December 2000, I am pleased to report that there are signs of new life. Firstly, the membership has been increasing. As a south coast congregation, we have a disproportionate number of elderly, and, as a result, I conduct between 10 and 15 funerals per year. And yet, in recent years, there has been modest growth, with an average of 20 to 25 people joining the congregation each year – including non-Jewish friends.

But, of course, it is not just about numbers. Why are people, going against the trend, and choosing to join the synagogue? There are as many reasons as there are individuals. In 2002, deciding to transform director/actor/writer/critic, Sir Jonathan Miller's dismissive remark about being 'Jew-*ish*' rather than Jewish,[16] into something much more positive, I suggested to the synagogue council that we hold an open morning, with the heading, 'Are you Jewish, or Jew-ish?' We made it clear in our publicity that we welcome all-comers, and especially those on the margins: patrilineal Jews, Jews living in mixed households, with a non-Jewish spouse or partner, secular Jews, lesbian and gay Jews. We had no idea how many people

---

16 I could not remember when Jonathan Miller made the, now famous remark about being 'Jew-ish', so I googled it, and got 222,000 results ...

would come, so volunteers prepared thirty bagels – half smoked salmon, half cream cheese – and I made sure we had plenty of copies of the synagogue magazine and diary and all the various Liberal Judaism leaflets. Seventy people turned up! Of course, they did not all decide to join – but a handful did – and some of the others, return from time to time. One of the people who did stay, a Dutch Jew, who described herself as 'secular', when we first met, subsequently, attended my adult study programme, *Access to Judaism*. Not long afterwards, she began to be the editor of the synagogue magazine, *Open Door*, for seven years, during which time, she celebrated her *Bat Mitzvah* at the age of 60, and became with her sister, an overseas member, who still lives in the Netherlands, one of our lay readers of *Shabbat* services and Director of the High Holy Day choir.

In addition to holding these open mornings most years, the synagogue has also become more open in other ways. For example, my partner, Jess, an artist,[17] gathering artists together from both within the congregation and beyond it, has put on two major exhibitions at the synagogue in recent years – in 2005 and 2008 – which have drawn in scores of people. In fact, the second exhibition, which was held under the auspices of the Artists Open Houses during the Brighton Festival, attracted 660 visitors over four Sundays. Again, some of those visitors decided to stay. One of them, made the decision to become Jewish, and since making that journey, marked her 40th birthday by becoming *Bat Mitzvah*. She is now a regular lay reader of *Shabbat* services, a warden, chair of *Avodat Ha-Lev*, the synagogue rites and practices committee, and a member of both the council and the executive.

Just two examples of two different congregational initiatives and of two very different individuals, with different backgrounds and life-experiences – out of the two dozen or so, who decide to join the synagogue each year – including non-Jews, without Jewish partners, who are attracted to the warmth, informality and learning opportunities we offer. And there is a paradoxical lesson we have learned. By diversifying what we do, and making efforts to reach out to more people – those who are Jewish, those who are Jew-ish, and those were not Jewish at all – we have found, not only that a wider variety of people have joined the congregation, but that a number of these

---

17 See: www.jesswoodpainter.co.uk

same people have involved themselves in the synagogue's core activities – that is, have decided to participate actively in education, in religious services, and, even, in pastoral care.

When it comes to the core activities of the congregation, the way in which these are organised has also made a difference to levels of participation, and to the range of people, who come along. To take the example of *Shabbat* celebrations, I lead just 50% of *Shabbat* services. It is up to each lay person to choose how she or he will lead the service, how much will be in Hebrew, how much will be sung, and so on. In addition to this built-in variation, we also mark each Friday evening differently. The first *Erev Shabbat* of the month, we hold a home-style *'chavurah'* meal, with table songs, and participants bringing a vegetarian or permitted fish dish and/or desert to share; on the second, there is a shorter service, followed by a home-grown speaker; on the third, there is a creative service, focussing on poetry and reflection, with participants sitting in a circle; and on the fourth of the month, there is, simply, a regular service. While some regulars attend all these celebrations, each one also attracts different people.

Starting off with a book club twice a month led by one of our members, who is a writer, and fair-trade coffee tea and biscuits each week at 10:30 am, *Shabbat* mornings services are also various: the first of the month is conducted by one – or two – lay readers; on the second, I lead what I call a *'Beit Midrash'* service,[18] which involves a shortened liturgy and an extended study of the *Torah* portion, and on the fourth, I give a sermon; on the third, the young people of our *Beit Lameid*,[19] which is held every *Shabbat* morning, guided by their teachers, and the post-*Bar/Bat Mitzvah Kabbalat Torah* students,[20] lead what

---

18 *Beit Midrash* means 'House of Study'. The three traditional names for synagogue – *k'hillah* in Hebrew – are *Beit K'nesset* – House of Meeting, *Beit Midrash*, 'House of Study', and *Beit T'fillah*, House of Prayer.

19 *Beit Lameid* meaning, House of Learning – the name coined for our young peoples' education programme by *Beit Lameid* teacher, Andy Cable, who studied at the Leo Baeck College for a Certificate in Religion School Education, an Advanced Diploma in RSE and a Masters in Education.

20 *Kabbalat Torah*, which means, literally, 'receiving of the *Torah*', is Liberal Judaism's name for post-*Bar/Bat Mitzvah* education for 13 to 15-year-olds, which concludes with a special service, led by the KT students, and the receiving of a certificate by each student. That certificate also functions as an affirmation of status for those young people with only one Jewish parent.

we call the *Tikkun* service for the whole congregation.[21] Apart from a themed creative service written by the young people once a term, the monthly *Tikkun* service follows the regular liturgy, while including contemporary music, and a short play in place of the *haftarah* reading from the prophets. As a result of the experience of leading the *Tikkun* service, the young people are all very confident, when it comes to becoming *Bar* or *Bat Mitzvah*, about conducting the entire service until the *Torah* reading, and giving a *d'var Torah*, their own commentary on the portion – apart from reading the scroll and the *haftarah* reading.

In addition to celebrating young people when they become *Bar* or *Bat Mitzvah*, as I have already indicated, we also like to celebrate people of all ages at different times. A number of people have marked their *Bar* or *Bat Mitzvah* (or *Bat/Ben Torah*)[22] as adults – including, so far, two women in their mid-80s. On one occasion, a congregant celebrating her 50th birthday, and reading the *Torah* scroll for the first time, marked the occasion as her *Yoveil*, her Jubilee.[23] In addition to these celebrations, there are many other occasions when I am called upon to recite a *Mi Shebeirach* – the blessing which begins, 'May the One who blessed our ancestors, bless…'. These occasions include someone marking a special birthday, or celebrating some other significant milestone, like completing a Ph.D., or having a book published as well as for couples celebrating a special anniversary. And then there are the individual baby blessings, which also take place on *Shabbat* mornings – usually on the third *Shabbat* of the month, when the young people are leading the service.

Another very important aspect of the diversity that has become a feature of the congregation is our deliberate practice of inclusion. The synagogue website, the synagogue leaflet, all our publicity mate-

---

21 *Tikkun*, meaning, 'Repair'. The name for our monthly, young-people led *Shabbat* morning service – is also the brainchild of Andy Cable, and is currently led by another teacher, Eileen Field.

22 Some adults, feeling they became *Bar/Bat Mitzvah* when they were 13, even though they didn't celebrate their coming of age at that time, choose to call the occasion when they read the scroll for the first time and give a sermon, a *Bat/Ben Torah* – 'Daughter/Son of the *Torah*'.

23 The *parashah* – *Torah* portion – *B'har*, in Leviticus chapter 26, describes the 50th year following the seven cycles of seven, as a year of *d'ror*, 'freedom', a special *yoveil*, jubilee, marked with a sounding of the *shofar*, the ram's horn.

rials make clear that we are open to Jews whose only Jewish parent is their father, to Jews and their non-Jewish partners, to lesbian and gay Jews. I am very proud that the council of BHPS was among the first within Liberal Judaism to ratify the LJ policies on same-sex relationships and mixed-faith relationships and to take the unanimous decision that ceremonies for same-sex couples and for couples where one partner is not Jewish – both same-sex and heterosexual – could take place on the *bimah* – the platform, where services are led and the *Torah* is read.

Has there been a reaction against this openness and inclusiveness? During my first year and a half as rabbi of BHPS, six couples left the synagogue. In the advent of the adoption of the Liberal Judaism policy on same-sex commitment ceremonies, one family decided to go elsewhere. Since then, apart from deaths and people moving home, we have slowly grown.

Is it possible to reverse the trend of an overall decline in synagogue membership? Who knows? Different synagogues and different denominations will have different strategies. Of course, it is not possible to generalise from the experience of one rabbi and one congregation. Nevertheless, I would say that if a relatively small, out-of-London congregation, that employs a rabbi on a 60% contract, has an administrator working 50% time, and relies on volunteers to organise its activities, can manage to draw in a wide variety of individuals, sharing their diverse gifts for the benefit of the community – and in this connection, it's worth mentioning that our members and friends come to us from a very wide geographical area[24] – then other congregations can do likewise. All that it takes is the willingness to open the doors of our synagogues, of our hearts and of our minds and the generosity to welcome newcomers and embrace the offerings which they bring.

---

24 Although centred in Brighton and Hove, in East Sussex, our main membership covers a wide geographical area: stretching west to Winchester in Hampshire, eastwards to Folkestone in Kent and as far north as the Sussex/Surrey border –not including a few odd members, who live in other parts of the country altogether – and one in the Netherlands.

CHAPTER TWELVE

The Jewish Family is Dead: Long Live Jewish Families!

What constitutes a family? For several decades during the post-war period, one single notion of the family held sway in Britain. Census data and surveys contributed to the popular perception of the average, normal family as a nuclear unit composed of a father, a mother and two point four children. This perception persisted in British society despite important ways in which it did not fit the experience of a number of different cultural, ethnic and religious minority communities – extended families from the Indian sub-continent, matriarchal families of Caribbean origin, *Chasidic* families with large numbers of children. It also persisted long after the reality had changed – even in the heart-land of average middle England.

During the last forty years, however, a new awareness has emerged, as the so-called normal family has broken down (some would say, shattered) in the face of sexual liberation – via the widespread availability of contraception and abortion – donor insemination, and a liberalisation of the divorce laws. And in place of a *singular* mould, *multiple*, perplexing, shards: serial monogamy; complex multi-parent families, following second and third marriages; teenage pregnancy; partnerships out of wedlock; marriages and partnerships without children; increasing numbers of single adults, with and without children – including those who have never been partnered, and those who have survived several years following the death of their partner.[1] Into this heterosexual mêlée, has been added the consequences of closet doors flung open: lesbian and gay communities based on non-biological bonds and friendship networks; lesbian and gay partnerships; lesbian and gay parenthood and adoption; lesbian and gay marriages and families.

---

1 See *The Jewish Family Today and Tomorrow*, a pamphlet published by the Reform Synagogues of Great Britain in 1983, for an early attempt to confront 'Social change, its effects on the family and the implications for Jewish life.'

Family life has changed and transmuted into a heterogeneous phenomenon – but what about *Jewish* family life? Well, it seems that on the ultra-orthodox front – particularly within the *Chasidic* world – there has been very little change since *shtetl* days.[2] But what about those Jews - the vast majority - who don't live apart from the mainstream society?

Each year, my congregation, Brighton and Hove Progressive Synagogue, holds a *seder* on the first night of *Pesach* (Passover).[3] My experience of conducting the *shul seder*[4] for the first time back in April 2001, demonstrated clearly to me the extent to which Jewish family life is changing. It was a lovely, lively occasion celebrated by a very diverse group of members and friends of the congregation of different ages: Jews by birth and Jews by choice; non-Jewish partners and family members; nuclear families; extended families; singles; couples – including at least one lesbian family, and two lesbian couples. Into this mix came a group of regular guests at the synagogue's festival celebrations - some adults with learning disabilities, who are part of a small Jewish residential project in the area called 'Sussex Tikvah'.[5]

As we say in England, 'a good time was had by all'. But the subtext of this happy gathering was a little more complex. And as I facilitated the proceedings, I was conscious, on that great night for asking questions, of some insistent questions of my own. What were we all doing here on the *first* night of *Pesach*? Why weren't people at

---

2 *Shtetl* is the name given to the small Jewish villages that once populated pre-war Eastern Europe. The largest *Chasidic* communities in England cluster in Stamford Hill, North London, North Manchester and Gateshead.

3 *Seder*, Hebrew for 'order': the name given to the order of the ritual on the first night of the festival of Passover (the first two nights in Orthodox practice - in Israel, only one night is observed), which involves the telling of the tale of the Exodus and includes key symbols of slavery and springtime (see note 7).

4 *Shul* – a *Yiddish* word, related to the German, *schule*, school – the most common name Jews use when referring to the synagogue – which reflects the primary role of education in Jewish congregational life.

5 *Tikvah*, Hebrew for 'hope'. Sussex Tikvah is an Edwardian house in a residential area in central Brighton, where six Jewish adults, with varying ages and learning disabilities have been living together for several years. Set up, thanks to private funding, in the name of Rachel Mazzier, in 2009 Sussex Tikvah came under the auspices of Norwood, a Jewish charity, which focuses on responding to the social needs of the Jewish community in Britain.

home conducting their own *s'darim*? Why weren't people attending a family *seder* in someone else's home? Of course, the answers to these questions were bound to be as diverse as the gathering itself, and led me to ponder on further questions. Did some people lack the necessary knowledge and confidence to organise their own *seder*? Did others simply not have a family to invite, or to go to?

Since I didn't actually give voice to my questions, I could only guess at the possible responses. But one thing was clear: for a variety of reasons, seventy people – between about 20 and 25% of the congregation – had chosen to come along to the *shul* and celebrate the *seder* together. In fact – as the waiting list indicated – the gathering could have been bigger, but the fire safety regulations did not permit more than seventy people to be seated in the synagogue hall.

My comments about the diversity of the gathering are a little misleading. While there were children present, there were, in fact, just ten youngsters there altogether, and though the age range spanned over eighty years, there was a yawning age-gap between twelve and thirty plus. As I surveyed the scene, my observations about the age pattern, of course, prompted further unspoken questions: were the young nuclear families who weren't there, celebrating the *seder* at home, or with other nuclear families? Were the young adults, who were absent at the communal *seder*, with their families, or, perhaps, doing their own *Pesach* thing somewhere else?

In the 1950s and 60s when I was growing up, communal *s'darim* were rare – and rarer still was a *first night* communal *seder*. So what has changed since then? There are several ways of responding to this question. I have already referred to changes in family patterns in the wider society. Perhaps it might also be important to acknowledge the impact of increasing prosperity and secularisation on traditional family values. In addition, I could make reference to demographic studies which demonstrate how extended families, which used to live side by side in close-knit communities, have become geographically dispersed across countries – even across the globe. Moreover, I could draw on both sociological and demographic evidence to examine the decline in active Jewish affiliation and observance and the increase in out-marriage.

However, rather than analysing societal change over the last three decades, I want to look more closely at the phenomenon itself – that first night communal *seder* that prompted my questions. But before

I do, I want to turn to the *seder* I conducted that year on the second night of *Pesach*, organised by the Jewish Lesbian and Gay Group based in London – founded in 1972 – the oldest Jewish lesbian and gay group in the world, which is celebrating its 40th anniversary in 2012. That *seder* was specifically arranged to provide a space for lesbian and gay Jews – who are often excluded, ignored or marginalised within their families – to celebrate together, in the spirit of *Pesach*, as free people. But this *seder* was more than this. As a group spokesperson put it, in an article published in the *Jewish Chronicle*, the previous week, 'we consider our group to be a family ... our *seder* reinforces the fact that we are an alternative family.'[6] During the past four decades since lesbian and gay Jews have begun to emerge from the hidden nooks and crannies of their otherwise 'normal' Jewish families, the emerging communities of lesbian and gay Jews have become alternative families, offering love, support, and a deep sense of kinship. The most interesting aspect of this development is that the sense of family has become greater as the diversity of the Jewish lesbian and gay community has become more evident. Contrary to what some might imagine, that second night *seder* was a very *heterogeneous* gathering, encompassing Jews of all denominations and none, women and men of different ages, singles and couples – and two children as well. In fact, the similarities between the gatherings on the first and second night were as notable as the obvious contrasts. On the one hand, at both *s'darim* there were many more adults than children and there was an absence of teenagers and young people in their twenties and thirties. On the other hand, at both *s'darim*, the individuals had made an active choice to be there and there was a tangible sense of a diverse group of people celebrating together as a family.

Individuals making active choices; diverse groupings celebrating together as a family. It is important to hold these two concepts, these two realities, together in our minds as we consider the implications of what may seem, at first sight, to be an unlikely combination. The observance of *Pesach* throughout the generations, like the observance of all the practices that define Jewish life, is rooted in an obligation to serve God who liberated our people from Egyptian bondage. This means, of course, that the obligation to keep *Pesach* is, in some sense,

6 The *Jewish Chronicle* 6th April 2001.

the obligation that defines our existence as the Jewish people. Quoting *Torah*, the *Haggadah*, the rabbinic 'telling' of the Exodus story, read at the *seder*, sets out the obligation in no uncertain terms: 'You shall tell your child on that day, this is because of what the Eternal One did for me when God brought me out of the land of Egypt.'[7] Each parent is obligated to tell their child - that is the model. But now we have a new phenomenon: individuals making choices, individuals choosing to celebrate together with others with whom they share a sense of kinship that is not rooted in a biological bond.

Those who choose to participate in communal *s'darim* are not the only ones doing the choosing. There are also those who choose, still, to celebrate in their own homes or in the homes of relatives or friends. And, there are those who choose *not* to celebrate. Some of the choosers, no doubt, still feel obligated, but they are making choices none the less. And it is in the nature of choosing, that a choice is not made once and for all; choosing is a dynamic process. We can all make choices either way as far as participating in *Pesach* is concerned. And the same is true of the biological ties we make and break and of the alternative families we join and leave. Despite an established tradition, codified by the early rabbis almost two thousand years ago, with the family, *l'dor va-dor*, 'from generation to generation', at its heart, the continuation of Jewish life is in the hands of choosing individuals.

But that does not mean that Jewish communal structures are redundant. It is clear to me, on the basis of my experience, that the communal *seder* is not only a metaphor for Jewish life today, and a setting in which the changes in Jewish family patterns are played out for all to see, it also provides a dramatic demonstration of the ways in which congregations are transforming themselves in *response* to changes in Jewish families. The home is no longer the cornerstone of Jewish life for increasing numbers of Jewish people. With the biological family no longer the locus of strong Jewish connections for many Jews, individuals and couples and families are turning to

---

7 The *Haggadah* – 'Telling' – from the Hebrew root, *Nun Gimmel Dalet* to 'tell' is the liturgical text, combining passages from *Torah*, with rabbinic commentaries, that narrates the Exodus from Egypt, and is read during the *seder*. The original text of the *Haggadah* is found in the *Mishnah*, the first rabbinic code of law, edited c. 200 CE in the tractate, *Mo'eid*, 'Seasons'. Here the *Haggadah* is quoting Deuteronomy 6:23.

congregations, communities and *chavurot* – friendship groups[8] – to fulfil these nurturing, nourishing and connecting functions.

The *chavurot*, which have taken off among young Jews in London in recent years, as a way of providing accessible, informal, non-prescriptive alternatives to established congregations and denominations, are demonstrating that while synagogue numbers may be dwindling in the mainstream denominations, young Jews are finding new ways of living as Jews, creating community, and expressing their Jewish identity.

Meanwhile, synagogues, whose activities traditionally revolve around prayer, study and meeting, are now being challenged to develop new roles as *extended families* and Jewish *homes* for their members and friends. Which means that the family and home demands on congregations are extending way beyond providing an annual communal *seder*. One of the best examples, from my experience, is the development of *Erev Shabbat* shared meals, taking place not only in the synagogue itself, but in peoples' homes. I know of one particular weekly gathering, which includes single people and couples in the sixty plus age group, who belong to all four congregations in Brighton and Hove. Held in a different home every week, each person who comes contributes a dish. In addition to sharing an *Erev Shabbat* meal, those who meet together, also support and care for one another. As one person put it to me, 'we're there for one another; we are like a family – like a family should be'.

---

8   *Chavurot* (singular: *chavurah*) are groups of friends/like-minded people, who celebrate *Shabbat*, the festivals and other key Jewish moments together. First established in the USA in the 1970s, they are also multiplying in Britain. I used to attend *Shabbat* gatherings of the *Ru'ach Chadashah* ('New Spirit') *Chavurah*, based in Muswell Hill, north London, in the early 1990s, and a couple of my friends are long-standing members of the *Ru'ach Chavurah*, inspired by the Jewish Renewal movement in the US, also based in North London. In recent years, young Jews, disenchanted with what they regard as divisive denominational Judaism, have been creating new initiatives, such as, Wandering Jews, a *chavurah* that makes *Shabbat* together in each other's homes, and empowers the host for the evening to decide how *Shabbat* will be celebrated – with study, meditation, prayer, etc. The Carlebach *Minyan* is a traditional, egalitarian *chavurah*, inspired by the melodies of Shlomo Carlebach, and on Friday evenings participants bring food to share. These *chavurot* are part of Grassroots Jews, a loose coalition that embraces Jews of all backgrounds and Jewish persuasions.

As a rabbi I experience on a daily basis the changes that are taking place in the wider society— through my pastoral responsibilities. A significant proportion of people in my congregation are elderly and live on their own, without any immediate family members nearby. They are mostly widows, but there are some widowers, too. The social care system provides some support. But it's the regular visits and phone calls and lifts to synagogue activities made by volunteers, as part of the congregation's *L'Chayyim* project,[9] that provide the sense of being part of a family. Every couple of months, there is the opportunity to come together for lunch and entertainment at the synagogue. And so, for those who are elderly and alone, the sense of the synagogue as a family is heightened by a feeling of kinship with one another.

And it is not only congregations, communities and *chavurot* that are beginning to provide new forms of Jewish family and home. In recent years, young Jews have begun to set up shared homes together, called '*Moishe* Houses', which are part of an international movement, providing social hubs for young Jews, mostly in the 21-30 age group. While a small group will actually share a house, many more will be linked to it. At the *Moishe House* in Willesden Green, in London, founded in October 2007, for example, a huge crowd will gather to celebrate *Erev Shabbat* together, as I am reliably informed by two young members of my community, who were associated with it when they lived in London.[10]

The annual *Limmud* Conference[11] held each year as a Jewish cultural alternative to Christmas, which attracts more than 2000 participants – and is run largely by young Jews – is also establishing

---

9 *L'Chayyim*! is the Jewish toast, 'To Life!' Initially set up with the support of a grant from Age Concern, the *L'Chayyim* project is co-ordinated by a volunteer, who liaises regularly with me, and reports to a steering committee that includes people with expertise in the area from outside the synagogue. The project includes regular training opportunities for the volunteers.

10 *Moishe* is the Hebrew for 'Moses'. The Willesden Green *Moishe* House is funded by the Pears Foundation. See www.moishehouse.org/houses.

11 *Limmud* means, 'Learning'. *Limmud* has now been running for thirty years. Started by teachers involved in Jewish education, it has broadened into a celebration of Jewish learning, arts and culture with hundreds of workshops, lectures and performances. Participants come from all over the world. In recent years, *Limmud* activity has expanded to include a summer *Limmud*-Festival, as well as regional biennial *Limmud* days. See www.limmud.org

a family-like nexus for the young Jews, who organise it. And the event itself is also creating a context in which new bonds and new connections are being forged between diverse individuals with differing backgrounds and personal circumstances. The development of *Limmud* demonstrates that many Jews, who are attached to particular congregations and particular denominations, nevertheless, are interested in sharing and learning and making connections with others across the Jewish spectrum.

The examples of all the forms of extra-denominational Jewish life that have emerged in recent years indicate that Jewish life in Britain is vibrant and dynamic, and that far from the family being broken beyond repair, Jews are living in, creating, and connecting with multiple families.

So, to return to the question with which I began: what constitutes a family? The fact that the picture of family life in general – and Jewish family life in particular – is so complex today does not mean that it is not possible to provide a coherent response. On the contrary; while there are many types of family – biological, non-biological and a mixture of the two – all of them, including synagogues, like mine in Brighton & Hove, and social phenomena like the *chavurot*, *Moishe* Houses and *Limmud*, share crucial elements in common: each family – regardless of its profile – provides a context in which people may form bonds and make connections with one another; each one provides a locus for shared concerns, mutual support and *belonging*; each one engenders Jewish life. The Jewish family has not disappeared, it has transmuted into myriad forms. The only thing that is surely gone forever – I hope – is the myth that the family – Jewish or otherwise – is a singular, monolithic entity. And so, we can say – with confidence, I think: *The* Jewish family is dead; long live Jewish *families*!

CHAPTER THIRTEEN

Living as a Jew in a Multicultural Society

Since 2005, and the launch of the Make Poverty History campaign to coincide with the G8 summit in Edinburgh, I have worn a white Make Poverty History *kippah* (skullcap) that was created and marketed by the cross denominational Jewish coalition that participated in that campaign.[1] I have worn that *kippah* (actually, to ensure that I've always got a clean one, I have a half dozen), for three main reasons – two of which are connected: to remind people that campaigns may come and go, but the need to 'make poverty history' remains; to make people aware that making poverty history is a Jewish goal; to let people know, that the middle-aged woman they see before them, is Jewish.

I am sure no one would dispute the first reason. And if you knew how many people come up to me and say, and I quote, 'do Jews want that/believe that, too?' – you would not question the second reason. But you might wonder: why do people need to know that the middle-aged woman standing in front of them in the supermarket queue, or at the next table, or walking along the street – all the various places where I am accosted by strangers curious about my *kippah* – is Jewish?

Significantly, 2005 was the year when, on July 7th, the London morning rush hour was overtaken by murder and mayhem, as British-born Islamist suicide bombers, detonated their devices, killing 55 people. In the aftermath of the bombings, a few friends questioned why I would want to go out in public, identifying myself as a Jew: wouldn't that make me an easy target for anti-Semites? I thought about it, and then came to the conclusion that, just as it was important that Muslims in Britain continue to go out into the world as Muslims, despite the increase in Islamophobia after 7/7, so it was important for Jews to do likewise, despite anti-Semitism.

---

1   The coalition included: Liberal Judaism, the Movement for Reform Judaism, the Masorti Movement and the United Synagogue. *Tzedek* – Jewish Action for a Just world – and JCORE, the Jewish Council for Racial Equality were also part of the campaign.

But, of course, when the Jew being a Jew in public is a Jewish woman, displaying a sign of Jewishness, usually associated with Jewish men, something more complex is going on. If I did not wear my *kippah*, those who notice me wearing one and approach me to ask me about it, wouldn't learn many things: that engaged, observant Jews are not just the orthodox; that there is a progressive branch to Jewish life which practices gender equality; that most Jews look, more or less, like everyone else – which is very important when it comes to people whose awareness of Jews is confined to stereotypes. Believe it or not, in reserved England, people do come up to me and ask about my *kippah* – all the time; at least two or three times a week. And they always say, more or less, the same things: 'Excuse me, I hope you don't mind my asking, is that a Jewish hat you're wearing?' And then, when I say yes: 'Isn't that what Jewish men wear?' And then I tell them about Progressive Judaism – and maybe, that I'm a rabbi too, if they're particularly interested. But I try not to say this straight away, because when I have, the response is, invariably, 'oh, so that's why you're wearing one' – which, is frustrating because it's not why I choose to wear a *kippah*.

The point about my wearing a *kippah* is very simple: it is about being a Jew in the world – my kind of Jew in the world - not just at home and in the synagogue. And for those who might be worried about being so conspicuous. I've only been attacked once – given a hard push at Victoria Station. And the two occasions, when I've been verbally assaulted, both involved Jews taking exception. Once, on the Bournemouth seafront, when a group of *Chasidic* boys started shouting abuse and once on the Brighton seafront, when an Israeli man in shorts and a T-shirt, with a tattoo of the Israeli flag on his arm, told me that 'a woman shouldn't wear a *kippah*'!

Of course, I am not just a woman and a Jew – so walking around with a *kippah* on my head, I could be accused of distorting the complexity of who I am, as a unique individual – a bearer of multi-identities; a Jew, who is a woman, a lesbian and a congregational rabbi; a wife, a sister, a niece, a cousin – and, although my parents are no longer alive, still a daughter, carrying their complex legacies within me. The reality is, I embrace all these dimensions and inhabit multiple communities as a result – which confounds any attempt to contain me – and might be quite troubling for those who would rather a 'rabbi' was simply a 'rabbi'.

But this isn't about me – I am using myself as an example. So let me take another – very different – example. A *Bat* or *Bar Mitzvah* at my synagogue is always deeply moving to witness – and very impressive. I am always impressed by two things, in particular - how each *Bar* or *Bat Mitzvah* stands in the pulpit and summons up the courage to lead the congregation in prayer and to read the sacred scroll of the *Torah* for the first time and what they have to say, when they comment on their *Torah* portion. I will never forget, for example, what one *Bar Mitzvah* said in his *D'var Torah*, his commentary on the *Torah* portion. When, reflecting on the setting up of the Tabernacle in the wilderness,[2] he talked about *belonging to several different communities* – including the *shul* community.[3] It was a fact of his life that he was sharing with us, and it was also a very profound insight. We all inhabit different communities – although, we may not always recognise and acknowledge that we do. We inhabit the community that is our family of birth or our family of choice – or both. We inhabit the community of our friends. We inhabit the community of the synagogue – and may be part of several sub-communities within it. We inhabit the community of our neighbourhood, our city, or town, or village.

As Jews, we belong to the wider Jewish community of our locality, our denomination, of British Jewry and world Jewry as a whole. Some of us choose to belong to a variety of other communities of shared activity as well – from our workplace, to the bowls club, to the orchestra we play in, the political party we support and the causes and activities we are committed to.[4] The list is as long and varied as all the different Jews who inhabit contemporary society. For many of us, daily life is a complex nexus of connections and of journeys that take us in different directions.

So, how do we make sense of our personal identity in the midst of all this diversity and plurality? What does it mean to be a Jew, who carries the experiences and history of our people together *with* her or his own particular bundle of life experiences and personal history *and* whose personal bundle may also include experiences and legacies that are *not* Jewish? Complicated, isn't it?

2 *Va-yakheil-P'kudey* – Exodus 35-40.
3 Jacob Swirsky, Brighton & Hove Progressive Synagogue, 13th March 2010.
4 This rather eclectic list includes some of the commitments of the diverse membership of BHPS.

Quite apart from all our *individual* differences, it is not as if 'the Jewish people' is singular: our people, inhabiting for thousands of years, so many different geographical settings and cultures, is also extremely complicated. When my partner, Jess, and I were living in Israel for four months during 2006 – 2007, what struck us most was how incredibly culturally diverse a place it is. Of course, the history of that land has made it so: shaped, as it has been, by its millennia long experience of occupation by successive empires, including, most recently, the Ottoman Turks in the 19th century and the British in the 20th century. And then, there are the different people, who live there: the Muslim and Christian Palestinians, the Bedouin and Druze communities, as well as the various Jewish communities, with roots, not only in the land, but also in, Germany, France, Eastern Europe, Russia, North Africa, Iraq, Syria, the Yemen, South and North America – and many more places besides these.

While we were in Tel Aviv, we used to make a daily visit to a green-grocer nearby to where we were staying. High on one of the walls of his shop he had a large, colourful poster with pictures of all the different fruits that grow in Israel. On the day we were leaving Tel Aviv, we went into the shop and asked him if he knew where we could buy the poster. His response was, simply, to take it off the wall and give it to us. When we got it home, we noticed that in addition to giving the Hebrew names for each fruit, the names were also printed in Arabic, English and Russian. Framed and now hanging in our kitchen, the poster reminds us of all the wonderful, varied 'fruits' of Israel – both actual and symbolic – and of what a complex soci-ety it is.

So, what are the implications for our Jewish lives and practice, of all the diversity that we encompass between us? What are the impli-cations for our congregations and for the various Jewish denominat-ions? What are the implications for Jewish life as a whole?

Many different people have come to see me over the past decade since I became rabbi of Brighton and Hove Progressive Synagogue: secular Jews, lost Jews, marginal Jews, patrilineal Jews, lesbian and gay Jews, new Jews, Jews who have recently discovered their Jewish inheritance, ex-Christians looking for God, ex-atheists looking for spiritual meaning, long-time searchers, who have explored many religious paths and have not yet found a home, non-Jews, whose journey to Judaism began several years earlier, when they first learned about the *Sho'ah*, non-Jews, who are simply drawn to Jewish life and want to become part of it. Each person has a unique history and set of experiences and very particular needs and questions. But, curiously, significantly, they have all shared the same, basic quest. Having approached the synagogue because they already knew that there was a good chance of receiving a warm welcome – having heard about us from a friend, or checked out our website – they want to experience the *distinct* qualities of Jewish life and participate in the *particular* ways of Judaism.

Of course, it is important to them that the congregation is liberal, progressive, inclusive, egalitarian, and, open to, and, engaged with, the wider world – that is why they approach this congregation and not the other synagogues in the area, or, in some cases, come to us having tried one or two of the other synagogues. But what these seekers want more than anything else is to savour and explore all the particular elements that make Jewish life, *Jewish*. So, they have made their way to Brighton and Hove Synagogue – and most of them have stayed.

There has been much debate in recent years in Britain about the pros and cons of living in what is called a 'multicultural society'.[5] As a member of a minority – a very small minority – I am more than aware that despite the burgeoning numbers of minority communities in Britain, British society remains predominantly white and Christian – even if allegiance to Christianity is nominal as far as most people are concerned. Nevertheless, many peoples and cultures now inhabit this island, and what it is to be British, has expanded to include those who were previously excluded. At the same time, a multicultural society can only be genuinely multicultural if each one of the many cultures it encompasses is distinct, active, and vibrant. And so, alongside all the other cultures which inhabit these shores, Jews face the challenge of making our own particular contribution to the mix.

For Jews who define themselves as Orthodox, the challenge is reasonably simple because their principal raison d'être is to follow the traditional teachings first formulated by the Sages centuries ago

---

5 The point of this piece is to examine the challenge of living as a Jew in a society where there are many other peoples, religious groupings and cultures, rather than to contribute to the current British debates about the pros and cons of living in a multicultural society and whether or not Britain may be described as a multicultural society.

in the pre-modern world, and to continue the practices that have been enshrined in the *halachah,* in Jewish law, for hundreds of years. For Progressive/Liberal/Reform Jews, on the other hand, the challenge is more complex. Having defined ourselves as the children of the Enlightenment, and embraced the gifts of emancipation, and become passionate exponents of the values of the modern world, like, democracy, freedom and equality, some progressive Jews have also defined themselves *against* the Jewish traditions of the past, and, indeed, rejected, both, the worldview of pre-modern Jewish life, and those rituals, such as *kashrut,* the dietary laws, which set us apart from other peoples.

So how do we, who call ourselves 'Progressive/Liberal/Reform Jews', express the *Jewish* dimension of our identity? Well, we can walk around, as I do, wearing a Make Poverty History *kippah* – or any *kippah,* for that matter – which is what some 'Progressive/Liberal/Reform Jews' are choosing to do. Another response to this question would be to regard our Jewish identity as a sub-category – I'm a Jew of the Progressive/Liberal/Reform persuasion – and adopt only those Jewish practices that cohere with a commitment to Progressive/Liberal/Reform principles rooted in reverence for reason and democratic values – or, at least, which do not conflict with these principles.

That was the classical Progressive Jewish response – but, actually, even for classical Progressive Jews it was not quite that simple. 2010 was the 200th anniversary of the first ever Progressive/Liberal/Reform service, which took place on 17th July, 1810 at the Temple of Jacob in Seesen, Westphalia, in Germany – the country which was the first home of Liberal Judaism. Curiously, while keen to excise those Jewish traditions, which were out of step with modern ideas, many of the pioneers of the new movement, nevertheless, wanted to keep the practice of circumcision.[6] Why?

What is clear from the early debates among Liberal Jews back then is that 'reason' and the other 'liberal' criteria did not always win the day when it came to deciding which practices should be maintained and which should be rejected. The example of circumcision is obviously quite extreme. The point is that Progressive/Liberal/Reform

---

6 See *Response to Modernity: A History of the Reform Movement in Judaism* by Michael Meyer. (Oxford University Press, 1988,) p.190; p.211.

Jews are not motivated to maintain less controversial rituals, like candle-lighting and making *kiddush*[7] on *Shabbat* and festivals, because these rites express Progressive/Liberal/Reform principles, we continue to do them because they express what is *distinctive* about Jewish life and make us *feel Jewish*.

Not long after I first became rabbi of Brighton and Hove Progressive Synagogue, I produced a booklet about celebrating *Erev Shabbat*, the Sabbath Eve, on Friday night, in the home. The booklet includes explanations and annotations, as well as the text in Hebrew and English accompanied by transliterations. I give it to all the seekers who come and see me, who want to begin to engage in Jewish practice. I also put it out every *Erev Shabbat* at *Kiddush*, when I'm leading the service. It has proved to be the most popular resource I've ever produced since I became a rabbi. I have lost count of the number of times I have had to re-photocopy it because it has run out; and we do not get that many people at the synagogue on Friday evenings! Liberal Judaism produces a wide range of pamphlets on issues ranging from Jewish status to Zionism to Lesbian and Gay Jews.[8] Interestingly, one of the most popular pamphlets produced by the rabbis of the movement in recent years is *Ethical Eating* written by Rabbi Janet Burden, which provides guidelines for eating Jewishly, which encompass fair trade, ecological concerns and animal welfare.

So, it seems that the time has come for Progressive/Liberal/Reform Jews to explicitly articulate our commitment to maintaining and developing *Jewish* life in today's multicultural society. What do I mean by this? I am suggesting that in addition to continuing to promote and champion the *universalist* agenda, and continuing to participate in social justice activities, we also champion a Progressive/Liberal/Reform approach to the *particular* concerns of Jewish

---

7 *Kiddush* means 'sanctification' – the acknowledgement of the 'sacred' character of the seventh day, which is set apart from the six days of the working week. The Hebrew root for sacred – *Kuf Dalet Shin*, means to 'set apart'. The ritual of *Kiddush* involves the blessing of the fruit of the vine. This blessing is followed, on Friday evening, by *birkat ha-yom*, 'the blessing of the day' – after which, a small glass of wine/grape juice is drunk.

8 Liberal Judaism leaflets are available from The Montagu Centre, 21 Maple Street, London W1T 4BE. See also: www.liberaljudaism.org. At the time of writing, I am currently working together with Rabbi Rachel Benjamin to produce the first Liberal Judaism booklet on *Shabbat*, due to be published in 2012, which will include the LJ approach to *Shabbat*, as well as *Shabbat* rituals and songs.

life. I am suggesting that we do *both* and we value both, *equally*.

Interestingly, there is an important rabbinic precedent for this approach, which precedes the development of all the different denominations of Jews by 1600 years. I'm referring to the two passages from the first chapter of *Pirkey Avot*, The Sayings of the Sages, which I explore in the context of 'Compelling Commitments' in chapter 10. So, to return to those two passages; first (1:2):

> *Al sh'loshah d'varim ha-olam omeid* – The world stands on three things: on *Torah* – Teaching; and on *Avodah* – Divine Worship; and on *G'milut Chasadim* – Loving Deeds.

And then (1:18):

> *Al sh'loshah d'varim ha-olam omeid* – The world stands on three things: on *Din* – Justice; on *Emet* – Truth; and on *Shalom* – Peace.

The world stands on these six pillars, these two sets of three. What a wonderful idea! Without them, the world will collapse. And, *both* sets of three are needed. The three pillars that uphold the core features of Jewish life are not complete without the three pillars that express more universal values.

I prefer to think of these two sets of three, as two *interlocking triangles*, forming together the 'six pointed star' we call the *Magein David*, 'the Shield of David'. During the *Sho'ah*, Jews were forced to wear the yellow star as a badge of shame that set our people apart as shunned and despised and facilitated our persecution. Since that devastating time, the *Magein David* has become a badge of pride, emblazoned in blue on the flag of the modern State of Israel, and is worn by hundreds of thousands of Jews across the world, proud, once again, to claim their Jewish identity. But as yet, the 'six pointed star' that has become so familiar as a sign of Jewishness, has not been invested with a *universalist* meaning alongside its *particularist* meaning. Living as we do now in a multicultural society, participating as we do in the wider world, hasn't the time come for the *Magein David* to become a symbol of the complete interconnectedness of universalist and particularist concerns that are, after all, as our Sages taught us, the foundation of the world? And: who else to proclaim those two interlocking triangles of commitment than Progressive/ Liberal/ Reform Jews?

On *Yom Kippur*, in place of the traditional readings from the

Torah,[9] both Liberal and Reform congregations in Britain read from the 'Holiness Code', Leviticus chapter 19, which sets out the ethical rules governing social and economic relationships. We also read a passage in the Book of Deuteronomy, which speaks about the covenant between the Eternal One and the people Israel. This text begins (Deuteronomy 29:9a):

> *Atem nitzavim ha-yom kul'chem lifney Adonai Eloheychem.*
> You are standing today, all of you, before the Eternal your God.

The *Torah* usually uses the singular form when addressing the people – for example, most famously, in the declaration, *Sh'ma! Yisrael, Adonai, Eloheinu, Adonai Echad* – 'Listen! Israel, the Eternal is our God, the Eternal is One',[10] but in some places, as here, it employs the plural – again:

> *Atem nitzavim ha-yom kul'chem lifney Adonai Eloheychem.*
> You (plural) are standing today, all of you (plural), before the Eternal your (plural) God.

Kul'chem – all of you: that is, *each one of you*. Although the covenant is between the Eternal and Israel – Israel is *kul'chem* – all of you: that is, *each one of you*. Each one of us – with our bundle of identities, experiences, hopes and dreams. Living as a Jew in a multicultural society means *living as the Jew each one of us is*, in a multicultural society. Each one of us will have our own reasons for identifying as a Jew. All of us together, with all our differences: individuals on a journey; compatriots and fellow travellers. Just as our ancestors, with all their differences, including their different backgrounds – some, *b'ney Yisrael*, the descendants of Jacob; some, descendants of the *erev rav*, the 'mixed multitude'[11] – escaped slavery in Egypt for the freedom and challenges of the wilderness, so Jews today, with all our differences, including our different backgrounds, face the challenge of living *as Jews* in the wilderness of the world.

---

9 In Orthodox congregations, Leviticus 16 (the rite for the Day of Atonement during the Second Temple period) and Numbers 29:7-11 (the offerings brought on *Yom Kippur* in Temple times) are read in the morning and Leviticus 18 (the sexual prohibitions) in the afternoon.

10 Deuteronomy 6:4. The word *Sh'ma!* – Listen! – is the masculine singular form of the simple imperative.

11 See Exodus 12:37-38.

PART FOUR

The Struggle with Israel:
Taking a Step Back for the Sake of Peace

Lofty Symbols[1]

Yad Va-Shem
stationed
high on a hilltop
like *M'tzadah*
the twin-souls of Israel
guardians of the
collective memory
the murdered millions
and the defiant remnant
hovering over the land

I wrote this poem while on a four-month sabbatical in Israel[2]. It says something about Israel; it also says something about me. It is not self-evident why an engaged Jew might also engage with Israel. Despite the inclination of critics of Israel, of various hues, to conflate 'Israeli' with 'Jew', being Jewish does not infer anything about any particular Jew's relationship with Israel. At one end of the spectrum, there are those Jews, who call themselves Zionists, and feel passionately committed to and identified with Israel. And at the other end, there are those who call themselves anti-Zionists, who do not support the existence of a Jewish state. In between, the range of perspectives is vast. The space between the extremes encompasses

---

1 *Yad Va-Shem*, meaning 'Hand and Name', is Israel's national Holocaust commemoration museum and centre. *M'tzada*, meaning 'fort', 'stronghold' – known as 'Masada'; formerly King Herod's fortress stationed on a tabletop hill by the Dead Sea, which became the refuge for the Zealots, who held out against the Romans for four years after the destruction of the Temple in Jerusalem in 70CE. As their conquest by the Romans became imminent, the Zealot leader, Eleazar ben Yair, decided that the community – 960 people in all – should die by their own hand rather than be captured and killed (see the imaginative account of the contemporary Jewish-Roman historian, Josephus, *The Jewish War*, Penguin Classics, 1959, pp.357-367, and the report of Yigal Yadin in *Masada: Herod's Fortress and the Zealots' Last Stand*, 1966).

2 My sabbatical started in early December 2006, and finished towards the end of March 2007. During this time, not one for keeping journals, I documented my stay by writing one, sometimes two – reflections each day in my own form of Jewish Haiku - using multiples of seven syllables, up to 49.

those who are totally indifferent to their Jewish identity, as well as those whose Jewish identity is expressed, wherever they choose or happen to live – be it Berlin or Hackney.[3]

I am one of those 'in between' Jews – of another, particular kind. I am a committed Jew, who dedicates my energies to enabling Jewish life to flourish in Britain, and who also feels deeply committed to Israel. I care passionately about the achievement of a just and peaceful settlement to the conflict between Israeli and Palestinian peoples, and the creation of a Palestinian state – which is why I walk around with a lapel badge displaying both the Israeli and Palestinian flags, and the caption: 'Peace, Justice, Life'. I am one of those Jews, who does have a relationship with Israel, so let me tell you a little about it.

I visited Israel for the first time, when I went there for a holiday in July 1978. Everything about that experience – being a Jew in a country where Jews form the majority; the landscape; the collision of Jewish cultures; the clash between peoples and religions – was so extraordinary, that I decided to return as soon as possible. And so, a few months later, in November, I went to work as a volunteer on a very small, secular and radical *kibbutz* called *Adamit* in the Western Galilee, very close to the Lebanese border, where my sister-in-law lived. I loved being immersed in agricultural tasks that included long hours in the citrus and avocado groves. It was wonderful working the land, but I also got a bit of a feel for life 'underground'. At that time, *k'tushah* rocket attacks from Lebanon were quite frequent, so I became quite familiar with the *kibbutz* bomb shelters – although most of the missiles went over the top of us and landed on the *kibbutzim* in the valley below. While I was living on *Adamit*, Israel signed a peace treaty with Egypt, which involved leaving the Sinai desert, which had been occupied since the Six-Day War in 1967 and evacuating the settlements there. Meanwhile, the rockets from the North kept coming.

---

3 After the East End, Hackney in East London, has also been, and remains, an important centre of Jewish life. I lived in Clapton Common, just off Stamford Hill, the heartland of London's *Chasidic* community, for six years in the 1980s. In recent years, increasing numbers of Jews have been moving back to Stamford Hill and Dalston and Stoke Newington - the North London Progressive Jewish community, for example, has been revitalised as a result. See Brian Klug, 'Next Year in Hackney', in his book, *Being Jewish and Doing Justice: Bringing Argument to Life*. (Vallentine Mitchell, London, 2010).

Although in many ways I felt at home on the *kibbutz*, as an emerging lesbian, living in what was, at that time, an intensely hetero-normative society that only welcomed Jews, who were hetero-sexual, I knew I could not make a home there.[4] So, I left the *kibbutz* after seven months and returned to England, and became actively involved in the Women's Liberation Movement. But then, three years later, just a few months after getting involved in the development of a Jewish feminist community in Britain, and beginning to engage with my Jewish inheritance, the Israeli invasion of Lebanon in 1982 changed my life.

Strange as it may seem, living on the *kibbutz* had not really impinged on my sense of Jewish identity because although most of that small community were Jewish, like me they expressed their Jewishness by being passionate about socialism. When I returned to the *kibbutz* four years later in 1983, I felt a new atmosphere – a certain tension. All Israeli men do a month's reserve duty in the army every year until they are fifty or so – but for those who had served in Lebanon over the past year, the experience felt very different. They did not want to participate in a new occupation. Everyone was pleased that the rocket attacks had ceased, but meanwhile relations with the Israeli Arab villages close by, formerly very genial, had cooled. Perched on the top of a rugged hill, facing Israel to the South and Lebanon to the North, the place really felt like it was on an edge.

Having felt the impulse to heed the commandment not to give Hitler a posthumous victory,[5] the Israeli incursion into Lebanon forced me to take responsibility for my Jewish identity. After I got back from my holiday I struggled with two choices: should I go and live in Israel and participate in the burgeoning peace movement, *Shalom Achshav* – Peace Now – which had burst onto the political scene following a massive rally in Tel Aviv, involving hundreds of thousands of people, or should I start learning more about my Jewish heritage, so I could begin to understand what Judaism was about; what Jewish life was about – and, more importantly for me at the time, why Israel? Not to mention, why the diaspora?

I decided to become a student again. In one sense it wasn't a hard choice, but in other ways it was the most challenging of the two

4 See 'My Journey', note 5.
5 See 'My Journey'.

options. I had left *cheder* – synagogue classes for children – at the age of eight, when my elder brother became *Bar Mitzvah*. I knew nothing and had to begin right at the beginning with the *Alef-Beit* – the Hebrew equivalent of ABC. What is more, I had no experience of Jewish communal life because my parents had chosen not to participate in it – which meant that I would have to venture into an entirely new terrain. And, there were two other factors involved that other people thought might create a few difficulties: I was a lesbian, and rather than simply pursue a little Jewish study in my spare time, I felt what I really needed to do was become a rabbi.

Much has happened since then. I have been a full-time professional Jew now since 1984 – including five years rabbinic training – and I've visited Israel many times. During the past seven years, my experience of Israel has been particularly intensive: In February 2005, I was part of a delegation of rabbis involved in a Rabbis for Human Rights mission, meeting with Jewish and Arab Israelis and with Palestinians who are working for peace. Then for four months, from December 2006 to March 2007 I spent my sabbatical there. I returned again for three-week long trips in January 2008 and January 2009, and, in October 2010, I co-led a Liberal Judaism tour, with Rabbi Charley Baginsky, bringing together the members of our synagogues.[6] Shortly after this book is published, I will be participating in another Rabbis for Human Rights mission.[7]

The greater part of this book focuses on troubling with Judaism: the struggle for Jewish life and meaning; the struggle with trouble for Jews and within Jewish communal existence. In Part Three, in chapters 10 and 13, I have drawn on a key Jewish teaching, in the context of thinking about, the Compelling Commitments of Jewish life, on the one hand (Chapter 10), and the implications of living Jewishly in a multicultural society (Chapter 13), on the other. In chapter 14, I return to that teaching, investigating it in greater depth. I explore how words live, how concepts relate with one another, and how by making connections between words and concepts, we may also understand how to make connections between peoples, partic-

---

6 That is BHPS and Kingston Liberal Synagogue
7 5th to 12th February 2012.

ularly those peoples who are in conflict with one another.[8]

In Chapter 15, For Israel and For Palestine, I draw on this teaching to make the case for a complex embrace of both Israel and Palestine that recognises the divisiveness of a binary approach to the conflict, and that acknowledges that a just peace demands mutual acknowledgement and compromise on both sides.[9]

In Chapter 16, Remembering Isaac and Ishmael, I draw on the tale of the two sons of Abraham recounted in the book of Genesis, and re-read in synagogues on the first day of the Jewish New Year, in the context of a particular event involving a particular Palestinian family, and a particular Palestinian, in order to highlight the importance of acknowledging the individuals behind the labels.[10]

In Chapter 17, Remembering we were Strangers, I connect the *Torah's* frequently repeated injunction, 'remember you were strangers in the land of Egypt', which is the focal point of the celebration of the Festival of *Pesach* (Passover) each year, to the continuing power imbalance between the Israelis and Palestinians, which demands a return to the Jewish ethical values, articulated in the *Torah* and expounded by the prophets.[11]

Part Four concludes with the prayer for peace between Israelis and Palestinians that I wrote in 2000 and recite during *Shabbat* morning services after the reading from the *Torah*.

---

8 This chapter includes some of the themes I have discussed at various speaking engagements including: at the St. Ethelburga's Centre for Reconciliation and Peace in the City of London, 15th June 2005; at a Jewish-Christian-Muslim Seminar at Sussex University, 3rd March 2009; at The Headstrong Club, Lewes, 3rd November 2009; and, at Worthing Theological Society, 28th September 2010.

9 This chapter also also draws on my sermon 'Many Israels', 5th March 2005, the sermon I gave on Pesach morning on 30th March 2010, and, my articles in the *Jewish Chronicle*: 'For Israel and for Palestine', 2nd May 2008 and 'A Palestinian state will give us peace of mind', 9th September 2011.

10 The substance of this chapter is the sermon I gave on the morning of *Rosh Ha-Shanah*, the Jewish New Year, on 28th September 2011.

11 The substance of this chapter is the sermon I gave on the first day of *Pesach*, 30th March 2010

CHAPTER 14

The World Stands on Justice, Truth and Peace

The Hebrew Bible is full of powerful statements about *shalom*, peace. Both Jews and Christians often quote the text found in the Book of Isaiah[1] and also in the Book of Micah,[2] which looks to a time in the future when 'they shall beat their swords into ploughshares and their spears into pruning hooks; nation shall not lift up sword against nation, and they shall learn war no more.' These famous words express an *ideal* state – but they also say something very *real* about what it takes to create peace: That, like making war, it demands *energy* and *effort* – all that beating of metal – and involves *learning* the ways of peace. And Micah adds something else – a vision of the peaceful life that is also very instructive: 'Rather, everyone shall sit under their vine and under their fig tree and none shall terrorise them'.[3] Creating peace involves making it possible for everyone to create prosperity and to live in security. Peace is not an end but a new beginning.

Significantly, many of the references to peace in the Bible connect peace to justice. Several passages in the biblical Book of Isaiah, for example, indicate that peace and justice are inextricably linked. We read, for example, in Isaiah chapter 32, verse 17:

> *hayah ma'aseh ha-tz'dakah shalom; va-avodat ha-tz'dakah hashkeit va-vetach ad olam.*
> For the work of justice shall be peace; and the service of justice, quietness and security forever.

And so, working for peace involves working for justice – and indeed, pursuing both: in the *Torah*, in the Book of Deuteronomy, in a section dealing with the laws of justice, we read at chapter 16, verse 20: *Tzedek, tzedek tirdof* – 'Justice, justice, you shall *pursue'.* And the

---

1 Isaiah 2:2-4.
2 Micah 4:1-3.
3 Mic. 4:4a.

Psalmist declares in Psalm 34, verse 15: *Sur mei-ra va-aseih-tov; bakeish shalom v'rodfeihu* – 'Turn away from evil and do good; seek peace and *pursue* it.' In Hebrew, nouns, adjectives and verbs are all derived from three-letter roots: That is, each word is rooted in three consonants. The word 'pursue' in Hebrew, indicated by the three consonants, *Reish, Dalet* and *Pei*, conveys a sense of urgency, as it does in English. In Hebrew syntax, it is usual for the verb to come first, and so, in the verse, *Tzedek, tzedek tirdof* – 'Justice, justice, you shall pursue', the tone of urgency is heightened, not only by the repetition of the word, *tzedek*, justice, but also by the word order: *Justice, justice, you shall pursue.'* Meanwhile, the repetition of 'justice' suggests something else, impartiality: where two parties are involved, pursuing justice for the one also necessitates pursuing justice for the other.

So, peace cannot be separated from justice – and both require us to pursue them actively. To understand the relationship between the two more deeply, and the conditions necessary for people to make peace, I now return to that key teaching that I reflected on in different contexts in chapters 10 and 13. Here again is the text from *Pirkey Avot* 1:18:

> *Al sh'loshah d'varim ha-olam omeid: al ha-din, v'al ha-emet, v'al ha-shalom.*
> The world stands on three things: on justice, and on truth and on peace.

This brief statement reminds us that from a Jewish perspective, the *TaNaKh*, the Hebrew Bible, was not the last word on the subject of peace. It also deepens our awareness of the connection between peace and justice, while making another powerful assertion. Both peace and justice are inextricably connected with truth. Indeed, the world stands on all three together – conjuring up an image of pillars, which suggests that if just one pillar were removed, the world would collapse.

'The world stands on three things: on justice, and on truth and on peace' – and so, there can be no justice without truth and peace, no truth without justice and peace, and no peace without justice and truth. That is the challenge before all of us – before all humanity. To understand the challenge more fully, it helps to have a sense of the Hebrew meanings of these three pillars of the world.

Justice

There are four words for justice in the Bible and rabbinic literature. The text before us speaks of *'din'*. In biblical Hebrew *din* means 'judgement', and the early rabbis extended this meaning of the word, by using it to denote 'law', a law-suit' and a 'claim', as well as 'justice'. *Din* conveys justice in the sense of the legal system for executing justice, and in the Bible we also find another word that plays a similar role, *mishpat* – based on the three consonants, *Shin, Pei* and *Tet*, meaning to judge. The 'judges' of the Bible were the *shof'tim*.

The Bible also uses two other related words for justice, *tzedek* and *tz'dakah*, which are both based on the three-letter root: *Tzadi Dalet Kuf*. And so, as I indicated a moment ago, we read in Deuteronomy chapter 16, verse 20, in the context of a passage dealing with how the system of justice is to be administered: *Tzedek, tzedek tirdof* – 'Justice, justice you shall pursue'.

And then, in Deuteronomy chapter 24, in a section dealing with economic justice, we read at verse 13 that when giving a loan, returning a garment taken as a pledge before sunset is an act of *tz'dakah* – justice. While the words *tzedek* and *tz'dakah* relate to the individual's responsibility to act justly, the words *din* and *mishpat* focus on the legal system that creates a framework governed by rules of impartiality, which regulates the conduct of individuals, and attempts to ensure that the stronger members of the society come to the aid of the more vulnerable and dependent members of the society – designated in the *Torah*, in particular, as 'the stranger, the orphan and the widow'[4] (in that order).

In British society we speak of a fair system of justice. From a Jewish legal point of view, fairness is not only about impartiality – for example, as it says in the *Torah*, not favouring the rich on the one hand or the poor on the other[5] – it is also about correcting inequalities. And so the pursuit of justice, *tzedek*, involves what we now call 'redistributive justice'. While charity – from the Latin word *caritas* – suggests an act of kindness that expresses our loving feelings towards others, the Hebrew equivalent, *tz'dakah*, connotes an act of justice that we are *obligated* to perform in favour of the poor and the needy. The point about *tz'dakah* is that we are supposed to do it even when we don't *feel* charitable.

---

4 Deuteronomy 24:17.
5 Deut. 16:19; Leviticus 19:15.

Truth

And what of truth? As soon as we use the word truth in our post-modern society, we are aware that truth is not quite as absolute as it once seemed. In a British Court of Law, a witness must speak 'the truth, the whole truth and nothing but the truth' – but nevertheless truth is subjective as well as objective, and the witness speaks the truth as she or he understands it. The Hebrew word for 'truth' – and, interestingly, there is only one word – is *emet*. *Emet* is based on the same root from which we derive the word 'Amen' – pronounced *'Amein'* in Hebrew. The three-letter root, in question – *Alef Mem Nun* – means to *confirm* or *support*. And so, when we respond to a prayer with the word 'Amen', we are basically indicating our support or affirmation for the sentiments expressed – as if we were saying: 'I agree!' Or: 'So may it be!'

Similarly, the word *emet* has a sense of affirmation about it. Truth becomes firm and solid when we affirm it. Just as justice requires action and a system of regulation, so truth requires *acknowledgement*. And so, where there are competing truths, the challenge becomes: how can I affirm my own truth and also, acknowledge the truth of the other person? Justice is not possible while we remain unable or unwilling to acknowledge that we are not the sole guardians of 'The Truth'.

Peace

Like truth and justice, peace is a much-used word that carries with it a significant, additional freight of meaning in Hebrew. The word we translate as 'peace' – *shalom* – is based on a three-letter Hebrew root, *Shin Lamed Mem* – meaning to be *complete* or *sound*. And so, a related word, *shaleim*, means 'whole.' Peace is not the same as 'tranquillity', *shalvah*, or 'quiet', *sheket*; and peace is not simply the absence of war or violence: peace is a state of completeness. A passage in Leviticus – chapter 5, verse 16 – speaks of a person committing a wrong, being obliged to make restitution, or reparation, using a verbal form of the root – *y'shalleim*. And so making peace involves putting right what is wrong, in order that what is broken may be repaired and become whole again.

The notion of 'making whole', reinforces the connection between peace and justice. In the *Torah*, in the books of Exodus, Leviticus and Deuteronomy, the rules of justice, encompass all aspects of society, including economic behaviour. Interestingly, in this regard, while Leviticus chapter 19 speaks of the need for 'just' balances, weights and measures – using the word *tzedek*, Deuteronomy chapter 25, expresses the same teaching, emphasising the requirement of justice, by adding the word, *sh'leimah*, 'whole'. And so we read at verse 15: 'You shall have whole and just weights; whole and just measures' – *Even sh'leimah va-tzedek yihyeh lach; eifah sh'leimah va-tzedek yihyeh lach.* Incidentally, the verb to 'have' doesn't exist in Hebrew, so the literal translation of the verse is: 'a weight whole and just [there] shall be to you; a measure whole and just [there] shall be to you.'

So, peace, *shalom*, suggests, 'wholeness' – and so, also, 'well-being' and 'welfare'. That is why the Hebrew greeting, when people meet is '*shalom*'. There is a telling example in the *Torah* that centres on the greeting of 'peace', which illustrates beautifully the potential for peaceful relationships of respect and integrity between different peoples. When Moses is about to leave Midian and return to Egypt on a mission to persuade Pharaoh to liberate the slaves, his father-in-law, Jethro, the Priest of Midian, says to him, *lech l'shalom* – 'go in peace'[6] – or, rather, more literally, 'go *for* peace' *l'shalom* – that is, for the sake of peace. Later, after the slaves have made their grand Exodus, Jethro comes to Sinai – the site of the impending Revelation – to wish Moses well, before returning again to his own land. We read that when 'Moses went out to meet his father-in-law, he bowed low, and kissed him; and each man enquired about his friend's welfare' – *Va-yishalu ish-l'rei'eihu l'shalom* – or, rather, more literally, 'They enquired, each man of his friend, for the sake of peace'.[7]

Yes, Moses and Jethro were 'friends'. But more than this: the word *rei'a* friend, also means 'neighbour' – as in, 'you shall love your neighbour as yourself'.[8] And even more significantly: Jethro – as all the references to him emphasise – was Moses' father-in-law. When Moses became the 'groom' – *chatan* – of Tzipporah; Jethro became his 'father-in-law', *chotein*. Both words *chatan*, 'groom', and *chotein*, 'father-in-law', are based on the root, *Cheit Tav Nun*, which means to 'make an alliance'. When Moses married Tzipporah, the Israelites

---

6 Exodus 4:18.
7 Ex. 18:7.
8 Leviticus 19:18.

and the Midianites entered an alliance, a relationship rooted in establishing peace between them. Indeed, the Israelites and Midianites entered a covenant – as the curious tale of Tzipporah circumcising her second son on the journey back to Egypt suggests: 'A bridegroom of blood, you are to me!' Tzipporah proclaims to Moses, adding: 'A bridegroom of blood because of the circumcision.'[9] The root *Cheit Tav Nun* meaning to 'make an alliance' is also related to an Arabic root meaning to 'circumcise.'

Justice-Truth-Peace

Of course, marriage is not the only way to build bridges between peoples and alliances need not be sealed in blood. What this narrative about Moses, Jethro and Tzipporah teaches us, above all, is that it is possible to forge relationships of respect and integrity across the cultural, religious, ethnic and racial divide and so create the conditions for justice, truth and peace to flourish.

It is possible – but it is also a tall order! We only have to think about the major conflicts raging in the world today. But nevertheless, the Hebrew meanings of justice, truth and peace, both, help us to identify the connections between these three pillars of the world, and also suggest the steps we need to take to be in a position to make peace – or, rather, suggest how we might go about hewing the stones for the pillars, and preparing the foundations to set them in place.

9 Exodus 4:25-26.

CHAPTER 15

For Israel and For Palestine

As I point out in the Introduction to Part 3, the binary impulse in Jewish thinking is highly problematic. Life/death; blessing/curse; good/evil; love/hate; peace/war; left/right; right/wrong – the list of binary oppositions is endless.[1]

On the face of it, it may seem entirely reasonable to make sense of the world in binary terms, but the trouble with these stark choices is that sometimes they force us to choose between right – and right. The logic of binary thinking dictates that when there is only one singular right possible, the other contender must be wrong.

And so it is with Israel/Palestine. If I am 'for' Israel, I cannot also be 'for' Palestine but the fact is I am *for* Israel *and* Palestine – and for *bona fide* Jewish reasons. The binary impulse found in Jewish teaching as elsewhere, is not, as it happens, the dominant motif. Indeed, Jewish teaching embraces both particularistic and universalistic issues – that is, concern, both, for the particular life of the Jewish people, and for the world as a whole. The problem is, Jewish individuals and denominations often choose to emphasise *either* the particularistic *or* the universalistic: either/or – another binary affliction.

But we can be among those who challenge binary thinking. We can promote a new 'for Israel *and* for Palestine' consciousness. The case for Israel is well-rehearsed. Equally, the case for Palestine – made on the part of those caught up in the flip side of the binary trap – is also well-rehearsed. But there is another approach, and, rather than 'taking sides', we can actively promote an awareness that acknowledges the just claims of *both* Israelis and Palestinians.

Ever since I became an engaged Jew in the early 1980s, I have been struggling to articulate my orientation to Israel and Palestine, and find a framework, which might be useful for approaching the

---

1 See for example, Deuteronomy 30:19. Also, verse 15 of the same chapter: 'See, I have set before you this day life and good, and death and evil.'

conflict between Israelis and Palestinians in such a way that I/we acknowledge fully both peoples, and find a way to be, both, for Israel and for Palestine.

In the preceding chapter, I explored Simeon ben Gamliel's pithy statement, 'The world stands on Justice, Truth and Peace'[2]. Here I want to see the extent to which this formulation about the world has something useful to contribute to an understanding of the conflict between Israelis and Palestinians, and how both peoples might find a way of standing upright with integrity.

Let us first explore the issue of Justice. In chapter 14, I examine the short verse in Deuteronomy chapter 16 – verse 20: 'Justice, Justice you shall pursue' – *Tzedek, Tzedek tirdof.* It is clear to me that for there to be peace between Israelis and Palestinians, both sides of the conflict deserve Justice and both sides must pursue Justice – not only for themselves but for the 'other', as well. The repetition of *tzedek*, 'Justice', provides a powerful lesson to Israelis and Palestinians alike.

In 1939, before the outbreak of the Second World War, Martin Buber, best known for his philosophical work, *I and Thou*, wrote a letter to Mahatma Gandhi, who had taken the position that 'Palestine belongs to the Arabs'. Yes, in 1939, *before* the Nazi regime had transformed its evil vision of a 'Jew-free' Europe into gruesome reality, and the Jewish quest for a nation state in the land of their ancestors became an issue of Jewish survival. In this letter, Buber not only makes the best case I have ever heard for the just claims of both peoples to the strip of land, between Lebanon and Egypt, on the eastern seaboard of the Mediterranean, he also helps us to see what nonsense it is to speak of *any* people being the rightful owners of a piece of land – unless they are, genuinely, an aboriginal people. Buber wrote:[3]

> I belong to a group of people who from the time Britain conquered Palestine have not ceased to strive for the concluding of a genuine peace between Jew and Arab.

> By a genuine peace we inferred and still infer that both peoples

---

2 *Mishnah Pirkey Avot* 1:2

3 From: Martin Buber's 'Open Letter' to Gandhi Regarding Palestine (February 24, 1939) in Arthur Hertzberg, ed.,*The Zionist Idea.* (Jewish Publications Society, 1997), pp. 463-464.

together should develop the land without the one imposing its will on the other.... We considered it a fundamental point that in this case two vital claims are opposed to each other, two claims of a different nature and a different origin which cannot objectively be pitted against one another and between which no objective decision can be made as to which is just, which unjust.

We considered and still consider it our duty to understand and to honor the claim which is opposed to ours and to endeavour to reconcile both claims. We could not and cannot renounce the Jewish claim; something even higher than the life of our people is bound up with this land, namely its work, its divine mission. But we have been and still are convinced that it must be possible to find some compromise between this claim and the other, for we love this land and we believe in its future; since such love and such faith are surely present on the other side as well, a union in the common service of the land must be within the range of possibility. Where there is faith and love, a solution may be found even to what appears to be a tragic opposition.

In order to carry out a task of such extreme difficulty – in the recognition of which we have had to overcome an internal resistance on the Jewish side too, as foolish as it is natural we have been in need of the support of well-meaning persons of all nations, and have hoped to receive it. But now you come and settle the whole existential dilemma with the simple formula: "Palestine belongs to the Arabs."

What do you mean by saying a land belongs to a population? Evidently you do not intend only to describe a state of affairs by your formula, but to declare a certain right. You obviously mean to say that a people, being settled on the land, has so absolute a claim to that land that whoever settles on it without the permission of this people has committed a robbery.

But by what means did the Arabs attain the right of ownership in Palestine? Surely, by conquest, and in fact a conquest with intent to settle. You therefore admit that as a result their settlement gives them exclusive right of possession; whereas the subsequent conquests of the Mamelukes and the Turks, which were conquests with a view to domination, not to settlement, do not constitute such a right in your opinion, but leave the earlier conquerors in rightful ownership. Thus settlement by conquest justifies for you, a right of ownership of Palestine; whereas a settlement such as the Jewish — the methods of which, it is true, though not always doing full justice to Arab ways of life, were even in the most objectionable cases far removed from those of conquest — does not justify in your opinion any participation in this right of possession.

These are the consequences which result from your axiomatic statement that a land belongs to its population. In an epoch when nations are migrating, you would first support the right of ownership of the nation that is threatened with dispossession or extermination; but were this once achieved, you would be compelled, not at once, but after a suitable number of generations had elapsed, to admit that the land "belongs" to the usurper. . .

It seems to me that God does not give any one portion of the earth away, so that the owner may say as God says in the Bible: "For all the earth is Mine" (Exodus 19:5). The conquered land is, in my opinion, only lent even to the conqueror who has settled on it - and God waits to see what he will make of it.

Buber's attitude to the other inhabitants of the land reflected his philosophy of 'I and Thou'. But Buber's approach was also rooted in the *Torah*'s insistence on justice and acknowledgement of the needs and the rights of others[4]. At the time that he was writing, before the *Sho'ah* and the establishment of the State of Israel, Buber was part of a group of Zionists called *B'rit Shalom* (Covenant of Peace), founded in 1921, who hoped that Jews and Palestinians would be able to live together and argued for a bi-national state.[5] If he were alive today, after everything that has happened, I have no doubt that the compromise Buber would be advocating would be a two-state solution.

Since that memorable day in September 1993, when President Clinton facilitated a handshake between Yitzchak Rabin and Yasser

4 Leviticus 19
5 See *A Land of Two Peoples, Martin Buber on Jews and Arabs*, ed., Paul R. Mendes-Flohr, (Oxford University Press, New York, 1983) p.73.

Arafat on the White House lawn, the hope for a two-state solution has been dashed again and again. And yet, despite the fact that many have given up that hope and some are arguing, once more, for a bi-national state, the majority of Israelis and Palestinians remain committed to the goal of two states for two peoples. The basic issue is one of justice. To repeat what Buber said way back in 1939: '... two vital claims are opposed to each other, two claims of a different nature and a different origin which cannot objectively be pitted against one another and between which no objective decision can be made as to which is just, which unjust.' And still today: there can be no *peace* between Israelis and Palestinians without *justice* for both peoples. Perhaps one day, both peoples will choose to share one nation together. For the time being, securing peace depends on an equitable division of the land into two sovereign democratic states.

But there is still something missing from the equation. In order for there to be peace, both peoples must acknowledge each other's cause – and to do this *both* Israelis and Palestinians must find a way of acknowledging the other's experience and learn to make sense of the other's experience – their narrative and their *truth*.

Unless the Israelis are able to acknowledge that for the Palestinian people, the rebirth of the Jewish nation on May 14th 1948, marks *naqba*, catastrophe, how can there be peace?

Unless Israelis acknowledge that Palestinians did not simply flee, they were actively displaced from many places[6] – how can there be peace? And unless Israelis acknowledge that for Palestinians, who lived *inside* the Green Line[7] *before* 1948, a Palestinian state on the other side of that Green Line is a huge compromise, how can there

---

6 The most infamous example concerns the former Palestinian-Arab village of Deir Yassin, which was situated near Jerusalem, but no longer exists. Between April 9th and 11th 1948, Deir Yassin was attacked by the commandos of a joint Irgun-Lehi force led by Menachem Begin, as part of Operation Nachshon, an Israeli military offence to fend off the siege of Jerusalem. Estimates at the time put the number of dead at around 250. Examination of the evidence suggests that between 110 and 120 villagers were killed (See Uri Milstein, *History of the War of Independence IV: Out of Crisis Came Decision*, chapter 16, Deir Yassin – edited and translated into English by Alan Sacks. (University Press of America, Lanhan, Maryland, 1998).

7 The 'Green Line' is the ceasefire line agreed between Israel and Jordan, after the 1948-49 war that followed the establishment of the State of Israel on 14th May 1948. During the Six-Day War that began on June 5th 1967, the land to

be peace?

At the same time, it is not only the Israelis who must make the effort to acknowledge uncomfortable truths. Because the Zionist enterprise was imposed on the Palestinians without consultation, we might conclude that as an oppressed people, they cannot be expected to acknowledge the Jewish narrative – either the Jewish need for a homeland, or the Jewish claim to this particular land. But such acknowledgement is essential for there to be peace. The notion that the Zionists were and are 'western imperialists', intent on gaining a foothold in the Middle East simply does not align with how Jewish Israelis understand Zionism as a movement for national determination that developed in the 19th century in response to European anti-Semitism. What is more, the *Sho'ah*, has demonstrated beyond doubt that Jewish people still need a home of their own, a refuge, free from persecution – and the most obvious place for the Jewish people to be at home is in their own ancestral homeland.

So, how do both peoples begin to acknowledge each other's truths? How do both peoples, find a way not just to acknowledge each other's narratives, but also to accommodate each other's narratives? How might they begin to make space for the other, not only physically, but also psychologically? Such acknowledgement, such accommodation cannot happen in the absence of justice. Again – as Simeon ben Gamliel said: 'The world stands on three pillars: Justice, Truth and Peace' – *in that order*.

Justice demands that the Israeli and Palestinian leadership negotiate together concerning the withdrawal of Israel from the Palestinian territories occupied following the Six-Day War in 1967 in Gaza and the land on the West Bank of the Jordan. Justice demands that following withdrawal, Palestinian militants who continue to launch attacks against Israel are pursued and brought to justice by the Palestinian leadership. Justice demands that the Palestinian territories become a sovereign state, with a democratic system of government, guaranteeing equal rights and equal opportunities to all its citizens – including lesbian and gay people, who are currently

---

the east of the Green Line was occupied by Israel. Israel also occupied the walled Old City of Jerusalem (just east of the Green Line) in order to have access to the ancient Jewish quarter, including the Western Wall of the Temple destroyed in 70 CE by the Romans and the Temple Mount.

persecuted. Likewise, justice demands that Israel undergoes a process of democratic reform in order to ensure that each and every Israeli citizen, regardless of religion or ethnicity, enjoys equal rights and equal opportunities.[8]

'The world stands on three pillars: Justice, Truth and Peace'. Later on in *Pirkey Avot*, we read: 'The sword comes into the world because of justice [*ha-Din*] delayed and justice denied'.[9] There is no doubt that when it comes to the issue of the establishment of a Palestinian state, justice has been delayed and denied – and that there has been much violence directed by Palestinians against Israel and Israeli citizens as a consequence. But how can we be sure that once there is justice, violence will cease and peace will be possible? It comes back to the question of both peoples acknowledging each other's truths – and also something else that I learned when I participated in the Rabbis for Human Rights mission in February 2005.

I arrived in that troubled strip of land filled with despair and I saw much that echoed my worst fears – but I also met with several individuals, who gave me cause for hope, on both sides of the conflict: *Rabbi Arik Asherman*, Director of Rabbis for Human Rights, who courageously stands in front of Army bulldozers intent on destroying Palestinian houses, which don't have building permits, and spends his days not only advocating the cause of the Palestinians, but taking action on their behalf; *Anat Hoffman*, Director of the Israel Religious Action Centre, which challenges discrimination in every place across the religious and ethnic spectrum; *Saeb Erekat*, the chief Palestinian negotiator, based in Palestinian-controlled Jericho, who has continued to keep faith with the peace process, through all the setbacks; and *Yasser Abed Rabbo*, the Head of the Palestinian Peace

---

8 As we read in the Declaration of the Establishment of the State of Israel – paragraph 13: 'The State of Israel will be open for Jewish immigration and the Ingathering of Exiles; it will foster the development of the country for the benefit of all its inhabitants; it will be based on freedom, justice and peace as envisaged by the prophets of Israel; it will ensure complete equality of social and political rights to all its inhabitants irrespective of religion, race or sex; it will guarantee freedom of religion, conscience, language, education and culture; it will safeguard the Holy Places of all religions; and it will be faithful to the principles of the Charter of the United Nations.' (*Official Gazette*: Number 1; Tel Aviv, 14.05.48, p.1).

9 *Pirkey Avot* 5:8.

Coalition, which has its headquarters in conflict-battered Ramallah, working to achieve an independent Palestinian state by peaceful means.

Meeting with these two Palestinians leaders, in particular, showed me how peace was a real possibility, despite all the obstacles. Both men were furious about the way in which the recently constructed separation barrier deviated from the Green Line and cut into swathes of Palestinian territory. At that time, Ariel Sharon was Prime Minister of Israel, and both men were angry about Ariel Sharon's unilateral, patronising approach and the way he delivered ultimata without entering into negotiation. Both men were frustrated by the reluctance of the Israeli authorities to change some of the facts on the ground to make the life of ordinary Palestinians a little easier. Both men were well aware that in deciding to withdraw from Gaza, Sharon was planning to hold onto as much land in the West Bank as possible. And yet both men remained totally committed to a peaceful solution.

Saeb Erekat and Yasser Abed Rabbo were impressive – but the stature of another Palestinian, who lives in a small village on a hill in the midst of the territories, was even more compelling: Nawaf Suf spent thirteen years in an Israeli jail for his involvement in a Palestinian militant group. When he was released he vowed to pursue the Palestinian cause by peaceful means – despite the fact that his brother, Issa Suf, was shot in the spine by a rubber bullet while looking after his older brother's children, and was paralysed. As we sat on comfortable chairs and sofas in their bright living room, drinking, first, mint tea, and then thick, black coffee, listening to Nawaf Suf talk, I watched Issa Suf's impassive face as he sat in his wheelchair. At the end, one member of our group asked him if he was also committed to peace. He smiled slightly, a small resigned smile, and said simply, 'yes. I agree with him'. Nawaf Suf finished his comments by telling us that his son – who was only one and a half years old when his father went to prison – was being detained by the Israeli authorities because one of his acquaintances was suspected of planning a terrorist attack.

What struck me most during that visit was how impossible it was to speak simply of 'Israelis and Palestinians'. From an *external* vantage point, all you see when you look at Israel is the conflict between these two peoples. When you visit Israel it becomes clear just how *diverse* Israeli society is – and it's not just a matter of *Jewish* diversity. More than one and a half million Palestinians live inside Israel – because many resolutely remained in their villages and towns in 1948 and stayed thereafter. Mostly Muslim, but also Christian, these Palestinian Israelis – who until recently have been called 'Arabs' – have no intention of leaving their homes and going to live in the State of Palestine when it is established. Their attachment is to the place where they live and have lived for generations. What they want is to receive equal treatment as Israeli citizens within Israeli society.

It makes sense. It sounds simple. But, in fact, ensuring full equality for Israel's Palestinian citizens will be far more difficult to achieve than creating a Palestinian state. I hadn't really thought about the issue much – until our whirlwind tour took us to the Jewish-Arab Center for Peace,[10] near Haifa. There we met three people – two Jewish and one Palestinian Israeli – who talked to us about a variety of different projects that bring Palestinian Israelis and Jewish Israelis together, encompassing encounter groups, peace education, teacher training, community leadership programmes, Arabic Studies, a bi-monthly young people's magazine, called 'Crossing Borders' and a twenty-four hour Internet Radio Station, called 'All for Peace' – which you can find by following a link from our synagogue website.

It was fascinating, inspirational and challenging. Mohammad Darawshe the main spokesperson for the Centre, responsible for public relations, summed up the challenge: 'We want Israel to be a state for all of its citizens. Of course, Israel must be the Jewish homeland. Every Jew must be able to come here. But once here, we must all be treated as equal citizens with equal rights and responsibilities.' A simple message – but the implications are massive. For some Jews both inside and outside Israel, the binary solution to the conflict between Israelis and Palestinians, the 'two-state solution', is attractive because it seems to preserve the 'Jewish character' of the State of Israel. But what kind of *Jewish* state is it, where twenty per cent of its citizens are non-Jews? In what ways will the concept of the 'Jewish

10 The Jewish-Arab Center for Peace was established in 1963 at Givat Haviva, the Institute for Advanced Studies of the Kibbutz Artzi Federation, which is situated just a couple of miles from the Green Line, in the narrow strip, south east of Haifa.

state' have to adapt to encompass the reality of Palestinian Israeli existence? And what about the symbols of the state: the seven-branched *Menorah* emblem, the flag with the blue *Magein David* at its centre? Won't new symbols that reflect Palestinian Israeli identity also need to be incorporated? Perhaps one day, the flag might include an olive tree as well as a six-pointed star? Of course, the answers to these questions lie far in the future – but we should begin to ask them now.

Towards the end of our meeting with Saeb Erekat, he said something I will never forget: 'It's a win, win, or, it's a lose, lose situation; either: both Israelis and Palestinians have a chance to *live*, or: both Israelis and Palestinians continue to *die*.' The *Torah* proclaims that, faced with 'life and death', 'choose life!' – *u'varchata ba-chayyim*.[11] And, indeed, the Jewish toast is *L'Chayyim*! –'To Life!' Courage, tenacity, commitment to humanitarian values – these were the qualities I have encountered among both Israelis – Jewish and Palestinian – and Palestinians. And more than this: the determination that both peoples should *live*.

Ultimately, it is that determination that is enabling all those involved in working for peace to hew the stone for the pillars, and do everything in their power to put them in place, despite the back-breaking labour and the shattering setbacks.

But even more than determination is needed if there is to be a just peace between Israelis and Palestinians. The central prayer of Jewish thrice-daily worship – called, simply, 'The Prayer', *Ha-T'fillah*, by the rabbis of old – ends with a blessing for peace, followed by a passage of personal meditation, which concludes with a prayer that speaks of 'making peace'. It is traditional to take three steps back as one recites these final words. I remember one of my teachers, Rabbi Jonathan Magonet, former Principal of the Leo Baeck College, telling us about an insight into this practice that he had learned from one of his teachers. In order to make peace between people or peoples, it is essential to step back from one's own position to make space for the other. This insight seems counter-intuitive – doesn't making peace with others involve moving towards them? When we step

---

11 In Deuteronomy 30:19, we read: 'I call heaven and earth to witness against you this day, that I set before you life and death, the blessing and a curse; therefore choose life – that you may live, you and your descendants'.

forward, towards another or others, *justice* requires that we must also step back to allow space for her, him, or them to speak and express their *truth*. This is what it takes to begin to make *peace*. So, what is needed more than anything else in the tragic conflict between the Israeli and Palestinian peoples is for both sides to take at least one step back from their positions, to make space for the other.

Creating justice and peace is very hard work – not least because it involves both sides in the conflict recognising that they cannot have everything they want, and that compromise is essential. The hard relentless work of creating a just peace continues, and will continue – even after the establishment of the state of Palestine. Again: 'The work of Justice [*Tz'dakah*] shall be Peace; and the service of Justice, quietness and security forever.'[12]

So, what can a Jew, who is not an Israeli, do? Very little, except support the efforts of the peacemakers, and add our voices to the call for a just and peaceful resolution to the conflict that fulfils the needs of *both* the Israeli and the Palestinian peoples – and does not promote the needs of one at the expense of the other.

Actually, this is not 'very little'. We may not be able to change the facts on the ground, but we can actively promote a different kind of consciousness – not least, in our own backyard, in the diaspora. In recent years it seems that there has been a growing division within the diaspora Jewish community between the supporters of a 'secure' Israel, on the one hand, and the promoters of a 'just' Israel, on the other. But the landscape of Jewish attitudes has been changing. According to the initial findings from the Israel survey conducted by the Institute for Jewish Policy Research, 78% of the 4,000 respondents supported a two-state solution – and 72% described themselves as Zionists.[13]

In his book, *Future Tense*, the Chief Rabbi of the United Hebrew Congregations, Lord Sacks, an ardent Zionist, writes: "The broad shape of a solution to the problem of Israel and the Palestinians has never been in doubt. It was implicit in the Balfour declaration in 1917, explicit in 1947 United Nations resolution on partition, and set out in detail in all peace proposals since: two states for two

12 Isaiah 32:17.
13 *Committed, Concerned and Conciliatory: The Attitudes of Jews in Britain towards Israel. Initial Findings from the 2010 Israel Survey.* Report by David Graham and Jonathan Boyd, July 2010.

peoples, a political solution to a political problem."[14]

So it seems that perhaps we can talk of 'new' Zionists – and a 'new Zionism' that embraces recognition of the need of the Palestinians for statehood. But what is the substance of this new Zionism? Is the two-state solution simply, 'a political solution to a political problem'? Or, is the new Zionism inspired by Jewish values? The kind of Jewish values articulated by Martin Buber; a new Zionism that is, actually, an 'old' Zionism that has been marginalised since the establishment of the State of Israel in 1948. The Jewish community is united in its longing for peace. On the ground, peace between Israelis and Palestinians cannot be achieved in the absence of justice because the Palestinians will not give up their struggle until they have secured a state. But the longing for peace on the part of diaspora Jews is also about something else: peace of mind. New Zionism creates the possibility of congruence in the hearts and minds of those who love Israel, and want the Jewish state to thrive and survive – and who love justice, too.

Diaspora Jewry needs a new Zionism – and so does Israel. According to the rabbis, the root cause of the destruction of the second Temple by the Romans in 70 CE was *sinat chinam* – 'senseless hatred' between the warring factions of Jewish society at that time.[15]

It is unthinkable that the State of Israel, like its previous incarnations, might be consigned to history – but it is possible. What would be the cause this time? The *haftarah*, the 'concluding' scriptural reading, on the *Shabbat* prior to *Tishah B'Av*, the day that commemorates the destruction of the first and second Temples – the third of three '*haftarot* of affliction' – is taken from the first chapter of the book of Isaiah. There, berating the 'sinful nation'[16], the prophet proclaims: 'Cease to do evil, learn to do good; seek justice; relieve the oppressed'[17]. Isaiah preached during the second half of the 8th century BCE, during the years before and after the northern Kingdom of Israel was wiped out by the Assyrians – and more than a century before the Babylonians destroyed King Solomon's Temple in 586 BCE and devastated Judah.

---

14 *Future Tense: A Vision for Jews and Judaism in the Global Culture* by Jonathan Sacks. Schocken Knopf, 2010. p.150.
15 *Talmud Yoma* 9b
16 Isaiah 1:4
17 ibid.16c-17a

In recent months, a new Jewish grassroots movement called *Yachad* has been launched, determined to raise awareness of the 'growing numbers within Israel, including former army generals, heads of intelligence and leading academic and cultural figures, who believe that a Palestinian state based on 1967 borders, with mutually agreed land swaps, is urgent for Israel's long term survival and security'.[18]

The vote taken by the General Asssembly of the United Nations on the establishment of an independent State of Palestine, following Mahamood Abbas formal presentation on 23rd September 2011, demonstrated that the majority of the world's nations support the Palestinians' bid for statehood. How long can the Security Council veto the will of the majority? Now that the State of Palestine has also been recognised by UNESCO,[19] is it tenable that the United States will be able to continue to justify withholding their contribution to UNESCO's budget, thereby putting programmes, which benefit the poorest of the poor around the world, in jeopardy? And: what about the continuing intransigence of the Israeli government? If the demand of moderate Palestinians for a sovereign state alongside Israel is thwarted, how long before the Palestinian extremists hold sway – not just in Gaza, but throughout Palestine? Is it not in the interests of Israel for the Palestinians to re-direct their energies from rage and protest to State-building and political order? Again we read: 'The sword comes into the world because of justice delayed and justice denied.' (5:11). The time is now. The *haftarah* prior to *Tishah b'Av*, concludes: 'Zion shall be redeemed *by justice* (*b'mishpat*), and its repentant people *by righteousness* (*bitzdakah*)' (1:27).

---

18 www.yachad.org.uk
19 On 31st October 2011, UNESCO voted to admit Palestine as a member. Of the 173 votes cast (from among 194 member states), 107 voted, 'yes', 14, 'no' and there were 52 abstentions. France voted 'yes', the UK abstained and the US, Germany and Israel voted 'no'. (*The Guardian*, 01.11.11)

CHAPTER 16

Remembering Isaac and Ishmael

When speaking about Israelis and Palestinians, it is easy to forget the human beings behind the labels. But, ultimately there will be no future for the Palestinian and Israeli *peoples*, unless Israelis and Palestinians see one another as *people* – as individuals.

Let me begin with a story. A man is walking along the seashore as the tide ebbs, revealing a multitude of stranded starfish. Soon he comes upon a young girl, who is picking up the starfish one by one and returning them to the sea. So he asks the girl, "What are you doing?" And she replies, "They will die if I don't get them back into the water." "But there are so many of them," the man says. "How can anything you do make a difference?" The girl picks up another starfish and carries it to the sea. "It makes a difference to this one."[1]

The man who tells the story is a living example of an individual, who impelled by his own personal experience, is determined to do what he can to make a difference, and create a new future. His name is Izzeldin Abuelaish. Born in 1955 and brought up in poverty in the Jabalia refugee camp in Gaza, Izzeldin Abuelaish trained as a doctor in Cairo, and went on to work in Israel as a gynaecologist, helping infertile Israeli and Palestinian couples to conceive. In 2009, he left Gaza for an associate professorship in public health at the University of Toronto. Yet another Palestinian professional joining the ranks of the expanding Palestinian diaspora? Yes and no: when Dr Izzeldin Abuelaish left for Toronto, only half his family went with him: two of his older daughters, Dalal and Shatha, and his youngest children, daughter Raffah, and sons Mohammed and Abdullah. This was because his wife, Nadia, died of cancer in December 2008, and then, thirty-five days later, on January 16th 2009 at 4:45 PM, an Israeli tank shell killed his other three daughters, Bessan, Aya and Mayar, and his niece, Noor. Meanwhile, his daughter, Shatha, his

---

1 Story told by Izzeldin Abuelaish, *I Shall Not Hate: A Gaza Doctor's Journey on the Road to Peace and Human Dignity.* (Bloomsbury Publishing, 2011), p.232.

niece, Ghaida and his brother, Nasser were all gravely wounded.[2]

Wherever destructive events are being played out across the world, we are usually told that '400' people died here, '2000' people died there. So, in normal circumstances there would not be any reason why anyone living outside Gaza would have learnt about the experience of a particular family during the three-week incursion at the end of 2008 and the beginning of 2009 that the Israeli government called, 'Operation Cast Lead'.[3] But this particular incident drew the attention of the world. In his book, *I Shall Not Hate*, Izzeldin Abuelaish explains how this happened: 'Because the Israeli military had forbidden access to journalists and everyone wanted to know what was happening in Gaza, I had been doing daily interviews with Shlomi Eldar, the anchorman on Israel's Channel 10. I had been scheduled to do one that afternoon. Minutes after the attack occurred, I called him at the TV station; he was doing the live newscast, and he took the call on air'. [4] And so, the story of this man and his family was broadcast across the world.

As it happens, I was in Israel at the time. Needless to say, like everyone else, when I watched the television news that day I was shocked and stunned – not least, by the tragic irony, that a man who spent his life bridging the gulf between Israelis and Palestinians through his humanitarian work as a doctor, should have suffered this terrible personal tragedy. My imagination was also caught by the bizarre series of conjunctions: a man born and brought up in Gaza, who was also a specialist in gynaecology working in Israel, had briefly become an ad hoc news reporter, and was providing a unique window on events in Gaza for the outside world. When I heard that he had written a book entitled, *I Shall Not Hate*, and was going to speak about his experiences at an event during the Brighton Festival, I knew I had to go along and hear him.[5]

I do not know what I was expecting. I still had the image in my mind of that broadcast; his anguished voice; his desperate plea to his Israeli friend for help. Now here he was, a big man, with a loud resonant voice, speaking passionately about his vision of peaceful

2   ibid. p.18.
3   'Operation Cast Lead' began on December 27th 2008 and ended on January 18th 2009.
4   *I Shall Not Hate*, p18.
5   The Brighton Dome, 28th May 2011

coexistence, about how important it is for Israelis and Palestinians to see each other as human beings, and about how 'medicine can bridge the divide between people and ... doctors can be messengers of peace.'[6]   Sharing his reflections about his beloved daughters, Izzeldin Abuelaish also spoke of his conviction that the education and empowerment of women in the Middle East is an essential component in the task of breaking the cycle of violence, and told us about 'Daughters for Life', the educational foundation he has set up in memory of Bessan, Mayar and Aya.

A few people asked Dr Abuelaish questions, but his responses demonstrated that he was not prepared to indulge in political rhetoric. Leaving no one in any doubt that he thought that the only solution to the perpetual conflict was the establishment of an independent, sovereign State of Palestine alongside the State of Israel, he also made it clear that, although he was angry about the perpetuation of the Israeli occupation, he did not just refuse to hate, he considered Jewish Israelis to be his brothers and sisters. Yes, this is how he felt, despite the terrible events of January 16th 2009 – and despite having shared with his fellow Gazans, for years, the daily indignities of long waits at Israeli checkpoints. Yes, however much he was loved by his medical colleagues, as well as by his appreciative patients, both Israeli and Palestinian, nevertheless, when travelling between home and hospital, and back home again, Dr Izzeldin Abuelaish was always just another Palestinian to the soldiers on patrol.[7]

There is no doubt that Izzeldin Abuelaish is a very special, even exceptional individual. And he was fortunate, that when he was young, a teacher noticed him, and he managed to get out of Gaza to go to Cairo and study medicine. But before that move changed his life, Izzeldin Abuelaish was just another young Palestinian in Gaza. Gaza is full of them – how many more might become doctors, might develop their skills and abilities, and make a positive contribution to their people and to the wider society, to the efforts towards peace, if given half the chance?

Of course, we do not know the answer to that question. The point

6   ibid. p. 7
7   See pp. 149-152 for a particular account of dealing with Israeli security checkpoints when his wife was dying of cancer.

I am making by writing about Izzeldin Abuelaish is that, yes, he has an exceptional story to tell, which should shock us, and a vision of peaceful coexistence, which should inspire us. Even more important, his personal testimony also reminds us - when we are talking in global terms, about 'Israelis', or 'Palestinians', or 'Jews', or 'Muslims', or 'Arabs' – that each member of any ethnic group or nation or people or religious community is an individual human being, with their own experience, their own story to tell, their own attitudes and aptitudes. And so, while listening to Izzeldin Abuelaish was inspiring, reading his book was a revelation. In its pages the reader learns his life story, meets his parents, his wife and his children, and discovers their personalities and their dispositions, their interests and their talents, their hopes and their dreams. Just imagine what a picture of 'Israelis' and 'Palestinians' we might have if every Israeli and Palestinian child got a chance to tell their own personal story, and those stories were collected into a book – a book of several volumes – together with photographs of themselves and their families, or broadcast on the internet.

Izzeldin Abuelaish is a dedicated doctor and humanitarian. He is also a faithful Muslim, whose religion has been a source of comfort and strength to him, enabling him to make sense of his loss, and remain hopeful about the future. He writes:

> I want this book to inspire people who have lost sight of hope to take positive action to regain that hope and have the courage to endure that sometimes long and painful journey to peace and a peaceful life. I learned from the Quran that the whole world is one human family. We were created from a man and woman and made into nations and tribes so we may know one another and appreciate the diversity that enriches our lives....
>
> I hope my story will help open your mind, your heart and your eyes to the human condition in Gaza and help you avoid making sweeping generalisations and forced judgements. I hope to inspire people in this world, afflicted with violence, to work hard at saving human lives from destructive hostilities. It's time for politicians to take positive actions to build, not destroy. Leaders cannot be leaders if they are not risk-takers; the risk they must take is not sending in the soldiers, but finding the moral courage to do the right thing to improve the world's human face in spite of criticism

from the haters...

If we want to spread peace throughout this planet, we should start in the holy lands of Palestine and Israel. Instead of building walls, let us build bridges of peace. I believe the disease affecting our relationships – our enemy – is ignorance of one another. Judging others without knowing anything about them is what causes tension, apprehension, distrust, and prejudice ... By knowing one another on a personal level, we can begin to respect each other's differences, but more important we can begin to see how truly similar we are.[7]

Izzeldin Abuelaish wrote those words after the terrible events of January 2009. I wonder what he has to say about the prospects for a peaceful and just resolution to the Israeli-Palestinian conflict – as the blockade of Gaza and settlement expansion continues, and just after the leadership in Israel has pointedly failed to seize the opportunity to support the Palestinian Authority's bid for United Nations' recognition as a sovereign state. Probably, he is very angry. I doubt he is surprised. But I have a feeling that if he were speaking to us now, he would reiterate his message – and counsel us not to give in to cynicism or despair.

The *Torah* portion set aside for reading on the first day of the New Year was selected by the rabbis because it tells the story of the birth of Isaac, to Sarah and Abraham, as related in Genesis chapter 21. The story also relates the expulsion of Abraham's first son, Ishmael, and his mother, Hagar, Sarah's Egyptian maidservant. Sarah says to Abraham: 'Cast out this servant-woman and her son; for the son of this servant-woman shall not inherit with my son, with Isaac'.[8]

At first glance, it looks as if the *Torah* is only concerned with ensuring the succession of Isaac: 'And God said to Abraham: "Let it not be grievous in your sight because of the lad, and because of your servant-woman; in all that Sarah has said to you, listen to her voice; for in Isaac shall descendants be called to you"'.[9] But then the text continues: 'And also of the son of your servant-woman will I make a nation, because he is your offspring.'[10] Further, this promise is reit-

---

7 ibid. pp.228-9
8 Geneses 21:10
9 ibid. 21:12

erated to Hagar, when she and Ishmael are abandoned to the wilderness. In fact, the *Torah* makes the point of underlining the meaning of Ishmael's name: 'Then God *heard* the voice of the lad; and the Messenger of God called to Hagar out of heaven, and said to her: "What ails you, Hagar? Fear not; for God has *heard* the voice of the lad where he is. / Get up, lift up the lad and hold him fast by your hand; for I will make him a great nation"'.[11] As we learn in Genesis 16, when, pregnant, Hagar flees from her mistress's cruel treatment, *Yishma'el* means, '*God will hear*': 'The Messenger of the Eternal said to her: "Behold, you are with child, and shall bear a son; and you shall call his name Ishmael, because the Eternal One has *heard* your affliction."'[12]

Why does the *Torah* make it clear that both Isaac and Ishmael were heirs to a Divine promise, and that each son of Abraham would be the father of a nation? In the *Mishnah*, the first code of rabbinic law, edited around here 200 CE, we read: 'it was for the sake of peace among us that creation began with a single human being: so that none might say to another: my ancestor was greater than your ancestor.'[13] One God means one humanity. This is what Judaism teaches. This, as we have seen from the words of Izzeldin Abuelaish, is what Islam teaches. But there is more that we should learn from the story of Isaac and Ishmael, as recounted in the *Torah*. When we find ourselves making generalised statements about 'Palestinians' or 'Muslims', we need to remember the individuals behind the labels – individuals like, Izzeldin Abuelaish. As the *Torah* introduces humanity by talking about a single human being, so the *Torah* introduces us to the nations, by telling the stories of individuals and families: Abraham and Sarah and Hagar and Ishmael and Isaac. And so, as we read about the brothers, Ishmael and Isaac, Abraham's two sons, we are prompted to remember that Jews and Muslims are sibling peoples – as are Israelis and Palestinians – some of whom are Christians. Even when disagreeing, even when hurting one another, even when taking separate paths and going in different directions, the past of these two sibling peoples is shared, and their

10 ibid. 21:13
11 Geneses 21:17-18.
12 Gen. 16:11.See also Ch. 6.
13 *Mishnah Sanhedrin* 4:5

destinies are linked.

As each New Year seems to drag in its wake the freight of old unresolved problems, we can give in to cynicism or despair, or, even at a distance, we can continue to *hope*, and *support* and *promote* the efforts of all those individuals and groups, among the Israelis and Palestinians, who are working for a just and secure resolution of the conflict between them. The national anthem of the State of Israel is *Ha-Tikvah* – 'The Hope'. To the hope of the restoration of the Jewish people to Zion, let us add the hope that maybe this year, certainly *one* year, we will yet see the descendants of Isaac and Ishmael, living side by side in peace. *Bimheirah b'yameinu*. Speedily in our own day. And let us say: Amen.

CHAPTER 17

Remembering that we were Strangers

My studies of Jewish texts have enabled me to find a vocabulary and a framework, which challenges the prevailing binary oppositional culture that forces people to take sides, and to deny the reality of the other, whoever the 'other' happens to be.

At the same time, we have a responsibility, as Jews, to recognise that the current conflict between the Israeli and Palestinian peoples is also a conflict between an established state and an oppressed people, and that our Jewish tradition teaches us to challenge oppression in every place. When we were travelling with Arik Ascherman on his Rabbis for Human Rights work, he said: 'the real Zionism today involves working for an Israel that is morally strong because it lives up to the highest Jewish values'.

What better time for Jews to remind ourselves of the highest Jewish values than at *Pesach* – Passover – the Jewish people's annual festival of liberation. Here is the sermon I gave at Pesach in 2010, which explores the implications of remembering the Exodus:

'For you were strangers in the land of Egypt'. How many times does the *Torah* repeat that phrase? And, of course, *Pesach* is the season for remembering our misery in 'the house of bondage' *par excellence*. As the first rabbis taught, *Pesach* is Z'*man Cheiruteinu* – the 'Season of our Liberation'.

I don't know how often the *Torah* reminds us of our slavery in Egypt – I've never counted. I do know that having read the *Torah* year after year, since I first began my rabbinic studies, my main thoughts about that constant repetition have gone in two, interconnected, directions. So, even before we stood at the foot of Mount Sinai, the experience of slavery *defined* our existence as a people. And the imperative to remember our experience *then*, acts as the principle rationale for Jewish ethical conduct *now* – that's why being reminded that we were 'strangers in the land of Egypt' invariably follows an injunction about our obligation to act justly towards the vulnerable and marginal in our midst.

But there is one very obvious thing that I've never really noticed about the *Torah*'s insistence on remembering our bondage in Egypt – or maybe just taken for granted: The *Torah* is addressing a people, not only liberated from slavery a long time before anyone can actually remember but, even more significantly, a people with power over their own lives – and, perhaps, more important, power over the lives of others. Alongside the key narratives about the journeys of our ancestors, which coalesce into a journey down into Egypt – and then, 430 years later, a dramatic Exodus from Egypt – are the various codes of law at the heart of the *Torah*, whose purpose is to regulate the social order. In fact, that's the whole point of the *Torah* – and of the complex odyssey of our forebears, from the time Abraham and Sarah left their land, their kindred, and their home: to journey towards a particular piece of God's earth – the land of Canaan – where they will establish a new society.

Yes, it's very obvious – and yet, we never really consider the implications – for at least two main reasons. Firstly, because reading the *Torah* narrative as we do, year after year, retracing the steps of our ancestors, of the slaves, of the wanderers in the wilderness, and then, just as they are about to enter the land, returning to the beginning again – to Creation – that new society is always a future promise beyond. Secondly, despite the fact that our forebears did, in fact, enter the land and establish a social order – albeit, failing, repeatedly, to follow the laws of justice – they were conquered and exiled again and again, and then spent almost two thousand years living a marginal and vulnerable existence in other people's lands. In other words, our experience as a people has, for the most part, not been about empowerment at all, but rather been about being disempowered – and worse, being persecuted and oppressed.

And so, until the establishment of the modern State of Israel in May 1948, being a Jew was synonymous with being a victim at the mercy of those in power. And so, generation after generation, we have read the *Torah*, not as a self-determining people, with responsibilities and obligations towards others, not as a people with power, but rather, as the vulnerable and the marginal. And so, we haven't really understood the reminder, 'for you were strangers in the land of Egypt' – because we have never forgotten – we have still been the victims. And so, we have, for the most part, failed to notice, that the *Torah* is addressing those with the power and the means to act for good or ill – because, from the perspective of our historical experience, we have, for the most part, been powerless.

But with the establishment of a Jewish state in our ancient homeland, a substantial section of the Jewish people now does have power. And yet, we do not seem to have caught up with this new reality: neither the Jews who live there – the new 'Israelis' – nor the Jews who still live as minorities in the diaspora. In a sense, the Jewish people have become *two* peoples – an empowered people in Israel, and a diaspora people, living in other people's lands. But, of course, we are not prepared to see the Jewish people, as two peoples – for understandable reasons, because we share the same inheritance, the same history, and, crucially, the same very recent trauma: the *Sho'ah*. And most of us are not prepared – neither Jews in Israel nor Jews in the diaspora – for these shared reasons – to acknowledge, not only that a Jewish state *means* Jewish power, but that since 1967, in particular, the State of Israel has exercised power over the lives of others, who are not Jews – the Palestinians in the occupied territories.

Now, there is nothing wrong with having power. One of the most unique and valuable aspects of the *Torah* is that rather than deny the reality of power, the various codes of the *Torah* regulate the exercise of power and insist that those who occupy powerful positions in society exert their power responsibly and ethically, especially in relation to the most vulnerable and marginal.

By reading the accounts of the reigns of the monarchs of the kingdoms of Israel and Judah in the books of the Bible that follow the Five Books of Moses, and in particular, the prophets, who railed against injustice, in the weekly *Shabbat haftarah* portion, we learn that ethical government was very rare. Isaiah, Jeremiah, Micah and Amos raised their voices against the corrupt and oppressive rulers of their day. They were not afraid to speak out – on the contrary, they saw it as their duty as servants of the Eternal One to challenge the abuse of power; when they held the rulers of the people to account and exhorted the wealthy to share their riches, they did so in the name of God, the liberator of the oppressed and the guardian of the needy. Let me just remind you of a few verses from Isaiah.[1]

Wash yourselves clean; put your evil doings away from My sight.

---

1 Isaiah 1:16-17 and 5:7-8.

Cease to do evil; / learn to do good. Devote yourselves to justice; aid the wronged. Uphold the rights of the widow; defend the cause of the orphan.

For the vineyard of the God of Hosts is the House of Israel, and the seedlings He lovingly tended are the men of Judah. And He hoped for justice, but, behold, injustice; for equity, but behold, iniquity! / Ah! Those who add house to house and join field to field, till there is room for none but you to dwell in the land!

Pesach is a moment, when Jews all over the world, in the diaspora and in Israel, celebrate the liberation of our ancestors from tyranny and oppression: 'For you were strangers in the land of Egypt'; remembering that 'we were strangers' is what this festival is all about. But why? Why do we need to remember? We read in the first code of law included in the *Torah, Mishpatim*, the code that is inserted into the account of the Revelation of the Eternal at Mount Sinai, at Exodus chapter 22, verse 20:

> *V'geir lo-toneh v'lo tilchatzeinu; ki geirim heyitem b'eretz Mitzrayim*
> A stranger you shall not wrong or oppress, *for you were strangers in the land of Egypt.*

And a short passage in *K'doshim*, the 'Holiness Code' in Leviticus chapter 19, verses 33 to 34, makes clear the context for the injunction:

> When a stranger resides with you in your land, you shall not wrong him. / The stranger who resides with you shall be like a citizen amongst you, and you shall love him like yourself, *for you were strangers in the land of Egypt*: I the Eternal am your God.

Why the need to remember? Because once settled 'in your land' there is the danger of becoming forgetful … So, what would Isaiah and Jeremiah and Micah and Amos be saying to the government of Israel today? What would they say about the on-going occupation of the West Bank and the continuing domination of another people against their will? What would they say about house demolitions in East Jerusalem and the destruction of Palestinian neighbourhoods to make room for the ever-expanding Jewish settlements? Would they not call the government to account and rail against injustice? I'm sure we know the answers to these questions – and we also know that, if the prophets were around, the Israeli government would probably make strenuous efforts to silence them – just as it has taken steps to silence the individuals and groups working for human rights and justice in Israel today – chief among them: Rabbis for Human Rights, Physicians for Human Rights, Lawyers for Human Rights, the Israel Religious Action Centre, and *B'tzelem*, the Human Rights organisation that takes its name from the verse in the *Torah*, which states that each human being is created *b'tzelem Elohim* – 'in the image of God'.[2]

Those who defend or excuse the actions of the Israeli government often argue that they 'love' Israel and what they are trying to do is protect the Jewish state and ensure its security and survival. Well, I love Israel – and have done ever since I lived on a small *kibbutz* in the Western Galilee for seven months in 1978-79. My efforts are directed towards protecting the Jewish state and helping to make it more secure. I want Israel to survive – and thrive. I also want Israel to be much more Jewish – a really *Jewish* state: a state that is governed by Jewish values; by the ethical imperatives we find in the *Torah* and in the words of the prophets – which is the only way that it will become fully secure and live in peace with the Palestinians and all the other states of the region. I have quoted from Isaiah – and Micah expresses very similar sentiments[3] – but let's give the last word to Amos[4] – or rather to the Eternal One who spoke through him:

> Are you not like the Ethiopians to Me, O Israelites? declares the Eternal. Did I not bring Israel up from the land of Egypt, and also the Philistines from Caphtor, and the Arameans from Kir? / Behold, the Eternal God has His eye upon the sinful kingdom: I will wipe it off the face of the earth! But I will not wholly wipe out the House of Jacob, declares the Eternal. / For, behold, I will give the order and shake the House of Israel through all the nations – as one shakes [sand] in a sieve, and not a pebble falls to the ground. / All the sinners of my people shall perish by the sword, [those] who boast, never shall the evil overtake us or come near us.

---

2 Geneses 1:27.
3 Micah 1:1; 3:1-3; 3:9-12.
4 Amos 9:7-10.

The prophets did not mince their words! And we should not either. Yes, Israel is surrounded by enemies – but the greatest threat it faces is not from Iran or Hamas or Hezbollah – however dangerous these forces of anti-Israel hatred may be. The greatest threat Israel faces is from the forces of injustice within. Surely, the time has come for those who love and support Israel to speak out, so that, in the words of Amos: 'Justice rolls down like waters, and righteousness like an ever-flowing stream',[5] and we may yet see two sovereign democratic nations, Israel and Palestine, flourishing side by side and living in peace – *bimheirah b'yameinu* – speedily in our own day. And let us say: Amen.

---

5 ibid. 5:24.

AFTERWORD

A Prayer for Peace
between Israelis and Palestinians

As my sermons on Israel and Palestine indicate, I write within the context of being a congregational rabbi. Like all congregational rabbis, my core work includes teaching, pastoral care, officiating at life cycle ceremonies and leading *Shabbat* and festival services. In September 2000, in response to the outbreak of the second intifada, I wrote a prayer for peace between Israelis and Palestinians, which I recite during *Shabbat* morning services, after the *Torah* is read. As one-time militant turned peace activist, Nawaf Suf, put it, holding the arm of Rabbis for Human Rights activist, Rabbi Arik Ascherman, as we sat in his living room, 'you cannot live without hope'. Having shared my personal relationship to Israel, and explored Jewish teaching in an effort to articulate an approach to the conflict between Israelis and Palestinians that honours the needs of both peoples, I offer this prayer as a simple expression of hope:

El Malei Rachamim, God Full of Compassion, who heals the broken-hearted and binds up their wounds, we ask You to show all Your children the way of love and compassion, so that hatred ceases to scar their lives.

Eyn Chayyim, Source of Life, we call upon You to send Your abundant blessings into every home, Israeli and Palestinian, so that new hope may overcome old fears.

Adonai Tzadik, Righteous One, who exhorts us to pursue Justice, we fervently pray that a spirit of righteousness may prevail, so that both peoples find the courage to reach a just settlement of their differences.

Oseh Shalom, Maker of Peace, who teaches us to be seekers of peace, we entreat You now to spread Your tabernacle of *shalom* over all the inhabitants of Your land, and to support the peacemakers among both peoples in their efforts to walk the path of reconciliation, so that a just peace may reign supreme at last – *bimheirah b'yameinu*, speedily in our own day.

And let us say: Amen.

APPENDIX

Choosing the B'rit – Covenant

This is the text of the Kol Nidrey sermon I gave at Radlett and Bushey Reform Synagogue in September 1996, when I mentioned that I was going to officiate at the 'Covenant of Love' ceremony for two women. It was the beginning of the end of my relationship with the Reform Synagogues of Great Britain[1]. I resigned the following year.

It is a great honour to be invited to address you on this special evening of *Kol Nidrey*. It is also a particular pleasure for me, personally. In an important sense I began my rabbinic training at Radlett. Even before I attended my first lecture at Leo Baeck College in October 1984, the preceding summer term I began teaching at the *cheder* – rather green around the ears and just one week ahead of the class! I continued teaching for a further three years and one of the joys of returning to Radlett is meeting up again with my former students. It was also in the presence of this community that I read the *Torah* for the first time and delivered my first sermon on *Shabbat Lech L'cha* in October 1985. And it was at Radlett, too, that I worked as a 'junior warden' under the gentle guidance of Dani Kornhauser and learnt about the 'stage-management' dimension of religious services.

I came to Radlett in the first place because of Rabbi Barbara Borts, my mentor and friend, whose vibrant dynamism has been a fundamental influence on my rabbinate. I return here because of Rabbi Alexandra Wright, my co-worker and also my friend, whose integrity and passion for righteousness are a continual source of inspiration for me. If all three of us got together, we would make quite a *Beit Din*!

I return here to offer some reflections for *Yom Kippur*. This evening is the beginning of a long day and I want to start at the very beginning. What do we need to have with us before we sit down to participate in one of the High Holy Day services? A *machzor* to follow the prayers. Perhaps, a cushion or a sweater – especially for

---

1 Now called the Movement for Reform Judaism.

Yom Kippur afternoon when one can feel quite low. I often think that it wouldn't be a bad idea if synagogues issued their members with a Glossary of Terms – a small booklet listing all those key words that only seem to come up a few times a year, with some easy to understand explanations. Words like: sin, transgression, repentance, atonement, redemption, salvation. I don't intend to imply by this suggestion that we don't know what these words mean in a literal sense, but what do they mean to us as Jews, as Reform Jews, today, in the context of our lives?

If I were putting a 'glossary' together, one of the first items I'd want to include is covenant – *b'rit* in Hebrew – and that's the word I want to talk about this evening. Covenant – an old-fashioned term from the world of legalese. A covenant is an agreement. The Hebrew word *b'rit* or *b'ris* is more familiar – at least in the context *of b'rit milah*, circumcision. But interestingly, when it comes to the ritual for welcoming an eight-day-old Jewish boy into the covenant, the *b'rit* part tends to be subsumed by the *milah*. We may talk about going to a *b'ris*, but what we tend to focus on is the act of circumcision – particularly when we are present witnessing the ritual. How many of us reflect on the meaning of our people's covenant with God when the *mohel* is practising his craft?

Like *Shabbat*, circumcision is a sign of the covenant; it is not the covenant itself. Indeed as Rabbi Lawrence Hoffman demonstrates in his new book, *Covenant of Blood, Circumcision and Gender in Rabbinic Judaism*[2], if the act of circumcision was the covenant, half the Jewish people would not be part of it. So what is the meaning of *b'rit*? What is this Jewish 'agreement' all about? On *Rosh Ha-shanah*, the second *Torah* reading was from Deuteronomy chapter 29 in the *parashah, Nitzavim*. That passage takes us back to the wilderness at the end of the forty years of wandering, when we are told everyone 'stood' together 'ready to enter the covenant of the Eternal your God, with its sanctions, which the Eternal your God makes with you today'[3]

The text then goes on to explain further:[4]

Through it God confirms that you are His people and that He is

---

2 The University of Chicago Press, 1996.
3 Deuteronomy 29:11.
4 ibid. 29:12.

your God, as God has said and as God swore to each of your ancestors in turn, to Abraham, to Isaac and to Jacob.

As the people stood together ready to enter the covenant with God, they were reminded that God was fulfilling the agreement made with their ancestors – that they were 'standing' there 'today' because of the promises which God had made with the patriarchs 'yesterday'.

But what has this agreement confirmed over 3000 years ago got to do with us? A naïve question? You've probably heard the official explanation many times. The passage closes with the words:[5]

Not only with you do I make this covenant, with its sanctions, with those who are with us today, standing before the Eternal our God, but with those, too, who are not present this day.

According to commentators down the centuries, that means us: all the generations of Jews. What is more, the notion of 'time' is actually irrelevant. In the words of Abraham Joshua Heschel:[6]

Sinai is both an event that happened once and for all, and an event that happens all the time ... The day of giving the Torah can never become past; that day is this day, every day.

Indeed, that's the spirit in which we are supposed to experience the reading of the Ten Commandments on *Shavuot* as well as the readings from Deuteronomy and Exodus on *Rosh Ha-Shanah* and *Yom Kippur* which relate the events at Sinai. But the question is, do we? Do we feel that we are part of a covenant with God, today, and every day?

Which brings me back to circumcision. Around four years ago, while working as a congregational rabbi, I was approached by a family who wanted a *b'rit* ceremony for their son – without the *milah*. They had come to me after having the door closed on them everywhere else in the area. A little startled by the request, I first enquired about their Jewish status. This confirmed, I arranged to go and see them to listen to their story and to talk things through – to make sure they were fully aware of the implications of their deci-

5 ibid. 29:13-14.
6 *Forms of Prayer: Days of Awe*, Vol. 3, RSGB, London, 1985, p.871.

sion. It became clear that they were intelligent people who had actively chosen to be part of the covenant, who were committed to living Jewishly and to bringing their child up as a Jew – that is why they wanted him to have a covenant ceremony. Finally, I explored some of the psychological issues: Don't you want your son to look like you? I asked the father. 'Yes', he replied, 'that's another reason why I don't think the act of circumcision is so important. I'm not circumcised, either.' He was from Argentina. Most of his Jewish male relatives were not circumcised and he claimed that this was true for many Jewish men in Argentina. Originally, it was a way of not being too different. But these same men were active members of the Jewish community. Indeed, he had been a member of a synagogue at home and he wanted to be a member in England, too – with his new family. Recognising their commitment, I agreed to officiate at the b'rit – without *milah* – and at our next meeting we discussed the format of the ceremony. When the day came, the house was packed with family and friends – much like any other b'rit. Needless to say, they joined the congregation.

That experience taught me something very important about the meaning of b'rit – that it is not an abstract theological concept; it comes alive in the context of our lives. Since that time, I have also officiated at two covenant ceremonies for daughters – my own nieces. In all the three cases, the parents were conscious of bringing their children into the covenant between God and the people Israel. The b'rit represents their commitment to live as Jews.

Four years ago, the family who approached me with their unusual request were a special case. In the past year, circumcision has become a live issue. But the problem is that in the heat of the emotions exploding on all sides, the importance of b'rit, of covenant itself, has almost entirely evaporated. A few weeks ago I met a woman who lives a very Jewish life together with her non-Jewish husband, their seven-year-old daughter and their non-circumcised four year old son. They have a Jewish home. They participate in the life of their local progressive synagogue. With the help of their rabbi, the little boy had a b'rit ceremony – without *milah* – when he was a baby. Her family were not thrilled about it, neither were some of her friends. 'Why is it', she asked, 'that some people do absolutely nothing Jewish except circumcise their sons and yet they are seen as maintaining Jewish life, and I'm seen as undermining Judaism? Surely, it's keeping a Jewish home, educating your children to be proud Jews and participating in the life of your synagogue that really matters?'

Whatever one thinks about their decision not to practice *milah*, there can be no doubt that these two families are choosing to part of the *b'rit*. Ironically, they are probably choosing to be part of it more consciously than many other Jews who don't actually go through the process of deciding to circumcise their sons – they just do it. But what about those other Jews – which probably includes most of us? *Yom Kippur* is an opportunity, not only to acknowledge our misdeeds, but to reflect on our lives, to think about what we are doing and why and to ask ourselves what choices we are making for our lives. But my guess is that very few of us feel that we are making any active choices – even in being here this evening. We feel called here, pulled here; perhaps caught here, trapped here. We have to be here. Maybe, against our better judgement. And there is God. Choosing to live Jewishly is one thing. But what does it really mean to be part of covenant with God – to be in a relationship with God? On *Yom Kippur*, in synagogue, it is practically impossible to avoid that question. But search as we might, the clues to answering it are not really here in the services. They begin with us; with our own lives; with our own relationships; with the covenants we make with those we love.

If we are not sure what it means to be in a covenant with God, the covenant made by two people pledging themselves to one another may serve as a model. Indeed, it is a model that we find both in the Bible and in rabbinic writings. The prophet Hosea proclaims the covenant of God and the people Israel with a beautiful formulation which is recited when laying *t'fillin*:[7]

I betroth you to me forever
I betroth you to me with integrity and justice, with tenderness and love
I betroth you to me with faithfulness
And you will know the Eternal.

Then there is the biblical book, *The Song of Songs, Shir Ha-Shirim* – included in the Bible because Rabbi Akiva, a 2nd century sage managed to persuade his colleagues that what reads like erotic

---

7 Hosea 2:21-22

poetry is really an allegory for the love affair between God and Israel.

In a few weeks' time, I will officiate at the wedding of two women who have been sharing a Jewish home together for three years. They have created the ceremony themselves because there is no official liturgy for same-sex marriages as yet – although a Rabbinic Working Party has just been set up to investigate the issue. Their ceremony draws on many of the elements found in the Jewish marriage service – the k'tubbah, the chuppah, and the two glasses of wine. They have called their wedding B'rit Ahavah, a Covenant of Love – one of the phrases included in the Reform k'tubbah. They have also chosen to express their vows to one another with the words of Hosea because they wish to declare that the covenant they are making is forever, and that it is based on integrity, justice, tenderness and love, and demands faithfulness. Moreover, they have chosen to express their covenant with Jewish language and symbols because they see their marriage as a central feature of their commitment to live together as Jews.

The example of two women consciously devising a ceremony to mark their covenant of love reminds us what we already know about heterosexual marriage but perhaps take for granted because it is more familiar. The point is that the covenant made between two people is the key to what the covenant with God involves; the loving commitment of two individuals for one another is a model for our relationship with God.

And central to this model is the fact that the forging of a covenant revolves around the active choices made by both parties. Just as our ancestors chose to enter into the covenant at Sinai, with the words, na'aseh v'nishma, 'we will do and we will listen',[8] so we, too, must choose. We may be born into the opportunity to live as a Jew, we may experience a covenant ceremony expressing our parents' hopes for our Jewish lives, but, ultimately, every Jew must choose to be a Jew – not just those who undergo 'conversion'. Every Jew – not just those who are married and live in families. While marriage may serve as a model for the covenant with God it is not a substitute for it. The modern orthodox scholar, Irving Greenberg argues that after the Sh'oah, the covenant has become 'voluntary', the relationship between God and Israel is no longer a 'given'; each individual

---

8 Exodus 24:7.

chooses to be part of the covenant.[9] I would say that in an important sense this has always been the case. Towards the end of *Yom Kippur*, we will read again from the *parashah Nitzavim* – this time from Deuteronomy chapter 30, the end of the portion:[10]

> See, I set before you this day life and good, death and evil.....
> I have put before you life and death, blessing and curse.
> Therefore, you shall choose life ...

Therefore you shall choose life – *u'vacharta ba-chayyim*. The word 'you' here is in the singular. We may gather together as a community, but the challenge is to every individual Jew: Choose life! That is perhaps the key message of this day out of life. Today is an opportunity for each and every one of us to make decisive choices for our lives, to covenant ourselves to God or to renew our covenant with God; to commit ourselves to realising our own potential and to restoring our relationships. If it seems a tall order and some of us feel a little sceptical about the prospect of effecting any real changes in our lives, perhaps we need to remember the power of hope in the life of our people and recall the lives of individual Jews that were transformed on *Yom Kippur*. The scholar, Franz Rosenzweig, a colleague of Martin Buber, was on the verge of converting to Christianity when he went to synagogue one *Yom Kippur* and became a committed, believing Jew.[11] More poignantly – and more significantly for Reform Jews this *Yom Kippur* – Rabbi Hugo Gryn, *zichrono livrachah*, may his memory be for a blessing,[12] related how he found God during his 'first *Yom Kippur* in the camps'. Rabbi Gryn wrote later:[13]

> Two contradictory emotions governed much of my inner life: that I was innocent and that I was abandoned. They came to a head during my first *Yom Kippur* in the camps. We knew the date and like many others I fasted and created a little hiding place for myself among stacks of insulation boards. I spent most of the

---

9 *Voluntary Covenant* (1982)
10 Deuteronomy 30: 15-19.
11 The famous story is related by Emil L. Fackenheim in *To Mend the World*. Indiana University Press. 1994.
12 Rabbi Hugo Gryn *z"l* died in July 1996.
13 See: *Churban. The Murder of the Jews of Europe* by Tony Bayfield. Michael Goulston Educational Foundation. The Garden City Press, 1981, page 187-8.

usual working day there – at first reciting bits of remembered liturgy, even singing the *Kol Nidrei*, asking for God's forgiveness for promises made and not kept. But eventually I dissolved into crying. I must have sobbed for hours. Never before, nor since have I cried with such intensity. And then I seemed to be granted a curious inner peace. Something of it is still with me. I believe that God was also crying. And I understand a bit of the revelation that is implicit in Aushwitz. It is about man and his idols. Only I could abandon God. I would like you to understand that in that builder's yard, on that Day of Atonement, I found God. But not the God I had childlishly clung to until those jet streams dissolved over Aushwitz.

Rabbi Hugo Gryn's experience changed the whole course of his life. On that *Yom Kippur* in 1944, he found peace and he discovered God. And he entered into a relationship with God that became a life-long commitment, inspiring his work for understanding and respect between peoples, faiths and races, and within the Jewish community itself. Hugo Gryn's story is deeply moving and it is probably utterly unique. Most of us will never confront such an awesome challenge. And yet the opportunity to find God is also present in the circumstances of our own, less extraordinary lives. And it is present today. All we have to do is to recognise God in our own experience – crying or laughing or simply being here with us. All we have to do is to choose to grasp the opportunity of making the word *b'rit* come alive in our lives.

The gift of *Yom Kippur* lies before us: May each and every one of us find the courage and the honesty to open ourselves to the possibilities which this day holds. And let us say: Amen.

Rabbi Elizabeth Sarah
Erev Yom Kippur – 22nd September 1996
Radlett & Bushey Reform Synagogue

Glossary

Aggadah: lit. 'Tale'. The term given to the corpus of non-legal rabbinic commentary, which takes the form of stories – *aggadot*.

Amora'im: lit. 'Sayers' (Aramaic). The rabbinic 'interpreters', whose commentaries on the first rabbinic code of law, the *Mishnah*, are collected together in the *G'mara* (see *Talmud*).

Ashkenazim: the name given to Jews, descended from mediaeval German Jewish communities. Also used of all Jews of Central and Eastern European origin.

B'rit: lit. 'Covenant'. The word used to describe the binding agreement between the Eternal One and the people Israel, first forged at Mount Sinai.

Bar and Bat Mitzvah: lit. 'Son' and 'Daughter' of the 'Commandment': The age of Jewish responsibility; traditionally, 13 for boys and 12 for girls.

Beit Din: lit. 'House of Judgement'. The name given to the Rabbinic Court, which presides over conversions, adoptions, and issues related to Jewish status.

Beit Midrash: lit. 'House of Study'. One of three traditional names for a synagogue – *k'hillah* in Hebrew. The other two are: *Beit K'nesset* – House of Meeting and *Beit T'fillah*, House of Prayer.

Chasidim: lit. 'Pious ones'. Originally, a movement rooted in the quest to serve God with joy and song, originating in Poland in the 18th century. The *Chasidim* embrace many different groups, each one of which revolves around a 'Rebbe', whose authority derives from being the son of the previous Rebbe, going back to 18th century Poland.

Chavurah/Chavurot: lit. 'Association(s)' – of those 'connected' to one another'. Originating in the United States in the 1970s, a *Chavurah* is a group of friends/like-minded people, who celebrate

Shabbat, the festivals, and other key Jewish moments together.

Cheder: lit. Room. One of the traditional names for the synagogue classes attended by Jewish children.

Diaspora: lit. 'Dispersion'. The term refers to the dispersion of Jews and Jewish communities throughout the world.

Elohim: One of the names for God in the Hebrew Bible. Although it designates the singular Deity, the word is a masculine plural of the noun, *Elo'ah*.

Erev *Shabbat*: lit. 'Eve of the Sabbath' In the Hebrew calendar, the day begins in the evening. Consequently, the Jewish Sabbath, which falls on the seventh day of the week, that is on Saturday, begins on Friday evening

G'mara: lit. 'Completion' (Aramaic). The rabbinic commentary on the Mishnah. See *Talmud*.

Haggadah: lit. 'Telling'. The text that relates the Exodus from Egypt, and is read during the Seder, at the beginning of the Festival of *Pesach*. The *Haggadah* combines passages from *Torah*, with rabbinic commentaries, and the first version of it is found in the *Mishnah*.

Haftarah: lit. 'Conclusion'. The scriptural reading, from the second section of the *TaNaKh*, the Hebrew Bible, the *N'vi'im*, the Prophetic books, which is read after the *Torah* is read on *Shabbat* and the festivals.

Halachah: From the Hebrew root, *Hei Lamed Chaf*, to 'go' or to 'walk'. The term is used to designate Jewish law.

Havdalah: lit. 'Distinction'. The name of the ceremony that marks the end of *Shabbat*; the day of rest, and ritualises the distinction between *Shabbat* and the other six days of the week.

Kabbalah: lit. 'Reception', 'Acceptance'. The mystical, esoteric stream of Judaism, which has its roots in the 16th century mystical commentary on the *Torah*, called the *Zohar*, attributed to the 2nd century sage, Rabbi Shimon ben Yochai.

Kabbalat *Torah*: lit. 'Receiving of the *Torah*', is Liberal Judaism's name for a post-*Bar/Bat Mitzvah* learning programme for 13 to 15-year-olds, which concludes with a special service, and the receiving of a certificate by each student to mark the conclusion of their formal Jewish education.

Kiddush: lit. 'Sanctification', from the Hebrew root *Kuf Dalet Shin*, means to 'set apart'. The ritual performed on *Shabbat* and festivals, which involves the blessing of the fruit of the vine.

Kol Nidrey: lit. 'All Vows' (*Kol* - Hebrew; *Nidrey* - Aramaic). The name for the liturgical passage recited at the beginning of the evening service on the eve of *Yom Kippur*, the Day of Atonement.

Kristallnacht: lit. 'Glass-night'. The German name for the 'Night of Broken Glass.' The night of 8th/9th November 1938 that marked the beginning of the violent persecution of the Jews of Europe, which culminated in the murder of six million Jews.

L'Chayyim!: lit. 'To Life!' The Jewish toast.

M'gillah: lit. 'Scroll'. Word often used specifically of *M'gillat Esther* – the Scroll of Esther, read on the festival of *Purim*. Five of the books in the *K'tuvim*, the 'Writings', the third section of the *TaNaKH*, are also produced as scrolls for liturgical purposes and are connected to five of the Jewish festivals and commemorations.

Midrash: lit. 'Commentary', ' Interpretation.' The word is used of collections of rabbinic commentary, which either take the form of exegesis of the law – *halachah* – or stories – *aggadah*. The word *midrash* is also used in the sense of a particular interpretation or commentary - a *midrash*. In the plural – *midrashim*: commentaries, interpretations.

Mishnah: lit. 'Teaching'. The first post-biblical code of Jewish law, edited by Judah ha-Nasi , 'the Prince', the leading sage of his day, c. 200 CE, reflecting the deliberations of the early rabbis – *tanna'im* – who gave themselves the task of interpreting the teachings of the *Torah*. The *Mishnah* takes the form of six 'orders'.

Mitzvah/Mitzvot: lit. 'Commmandment/s'. The term, as used in the *Torah* and subsequent rabbinic usage, designates an obligation – whether ethical or ritual – that is commanded by God.

Parashah: lit. 'Portion' – of the *Torah*. When the practice of reading the *Torah* in an annual cycle was introduced in the 6th century, the rabbis of that time divided the *Torah* into 54 weekly portions (allowing for the fluctuation between 12 and 13 month years).

PaRDeS: This acronym refers to the traditional method of interpreting the *Torah*: *p'shat*, the 'plain' meaning; *remez*, the 'hints' in the text; *d'rash*, the interpretation of gaps in the text; *sod*, the 'hidden' meaning of the text.

Pesach: lit. 'Passover'. The spring-time seven day festival (eight days, among the Orthodox in the diaspora) that commemorates the Exodus from Egypt, c. 1300 years BCE, and begins with the *seder*, and the narration of the Exodus story as found in the *Haggadah*.

Pirkey Avot: 'The Sayings of the Sages'. The collection of the aphorisms of the first rabbis appended to the fourth 'order' of the *Mishnah, N'zikin*. It is traditional to read from *Pirkey Avot* on *Shabbat* afternoon.

Purim: lit. 'lots'. The festival that recalls how Haman cast 'lots' to destroy the Jewish people. Recorded in the Book of Esther, the story is meta-historical, rather than historical. It is customary to dress up and drown out the name of Haman, during the reading of *M'gillat Esther*. It is also customary to exchange gifts and give *tz'dakah* – charity to those in need.

Rosh Ha-Shanah: lit. 'Head of the Year'. The first day of the seventh month, Tishri. Originally, a 'day of blasting' the *shofar* (ram's horn), in the *Mishnah* the first rabbis designated the day as the New Year for years.

Ru'ach: lit. 'Spirit' or 'Wind'. First used in the *Torah* in Genesis chapter 1(:2): 'The *spirit* of God' was hovering over the face of the waters.' The second use of the word is in Genesis chapter 3 (:8), which speaks of, 'The voice of the Eternal God walking around in the garden at the *windy* time of the day.'

Seder: lit. 'Order' (Biblical Hebrew). Plural: *S'darim*. The name given to the 'order' of the ritual on the first night of the festival of *Pesach* (the first two nights among the Orthodox in the diaspora), which involves the narration of the tale of the Exodus, as set out in the *Haggadah,* and includes partaking of edible symbols of slavery and spring-time.

Sephardim: the name of Jews descended from the mediaeval Jewish communities of *Sepharad* – Spain and Portugal.

Shtetl: The *Yiddish* name given to the small Jewish villages that once populated pre-*Sho'ah* Eastern Europe.

Shabbat: The day of rest on the seventh day of the week. The Hebrew root, *Shin Beit Tav,* means to 'cease'. *Shabbat* is the day of rest in memory, both, of God's 'ceasing' from work (Genesis 2:2 and Exodus 20:8-11), and the Exodus from Egypt (Deuteronomy 5:12-15).

Sh'chinah: the Divine Presence. From the Hebrew root, *Shin Chaf Nun,* to 'dwell'. One of the names for God used in *Kabbalah.*

Sh'ma: lit. 'Hear!'. The initial word of a liturgical text comprising three passages from the *Torah:* Deuteronomy 6:4-9; 11: 13-21; Numbers 15:37-41.

Sho'ah: lit. 'Devastation' or 'Catastrophe'. A word with biblical origins, from the Hebrew root, *Shin Aleph Hei,* to 'crash into ruins'. *Sho'ah* is the term preferred by Jews to designate the Nazi genocide of the Jewish people. The word 'Holocaust', which has much greater currency, is a translation of the biblical Hebrew noun, *olah,* 'burnt offering', which denotes one of the sacrifices offered in Temple times.

Shul: lit. 'School'. A *Yiddish* word, related to the German, *Schule,* school. The most common name Ashkenazi Jews use when referring to the synagogue – which reflects the primary role of education in Jewish life.

Siddur: lit. 'Order' (Rabbinic Hebrew). The name given to the 'order' of prayers that constitutes the daily and *Shabbat* prayer book

S'michah: Rabbinic Ordination. From the Hebrew root, *Sameich Mem Chaf,* to 'lay' (hands). The root is first used in the *Torah* in the case of Moses laying his hands on Joshua to indicate that Joshua is to be his successor (Numbers 27:23).

Sukkot: lit. 'huts'. The seven-day Autumn harvest festival that also recalls the wanderings in the wilderness. One of the principal customs is to build a *sukkah*, a temporary hut, and to dwell in it – or at least sit in it – during the festival.

Talmud: lit. 'Learning'. Consisting of the *Mishnah*, the work of the *tanna'im*, edited by Judah ha-Nasi , 'the Prince', the leading sage of his day, around 200 CE, and the *G'mara*, the work of the *amora'im*, the sages, who expounded the *Mishnah*. The *Y'rushalmi* – the Jerusalem *Talmud* – was completed c. 400 CE. The much longer *Bavli* – the Babylonian *Talmud* – was completed c. 500CE.

TaNaKh: An acronym designating the Hebrew Bible, which is divided into three sections: *Torah* ('Teaching' – the Five Books of Moses'), *N'vi'im* (Prophets) and *K'tuvim* (Writings).

Tanna'im: lit. 'Teachers' (Aramaic). The first generation of rabbinic 'teachers', whose teachings are recorded in the *Mishnah*.

Terezin (Czech)/**Theresienstadt** (German): The name of one of the ghettos in which Jews were incarcerated by the Nazis during the *Sho'ah*. Originally, a military fortress and adjacent walled garrison town.

T'fillin: Name given to the two leather straps and boxes bound on the forehead and around the left arm for daily morning prayer. The boxes contain these verses from the *Torah*: Exodus 13:9 and 13:16: Deuteronomy 6:8 and 11:18.

Tikkun Olam: lit. 'Repair of the world.' An expression first used in the Mishnah in the phrase *mip'ney tikkun ha-olam* 'for the sake of *tikkun* of the world', where it concerns the need to maintain social order. In the *Aleynu* prayer, composed around the same time, *tikkun olam*, takes on the meaning of 'repair of the world'. The concept of *tikkun olam* was later developed by the 16th century *kabbalist* – mystical thinker/practitioner – Isaac Luria in Safed in Northern Israel.

Tishah B'Av: lit. 9th day of the month of *Av*. The day that commemorates the destruction of King Solomon's Temple in Jerusalem by the Babylonians in 586 BCE, and also the destruction of the 'second' Temple by the Romans in 70 CE.

Torah: lit. 'Teaching'. The word is used to refer to Jewish 'teaching' in general and to the first books of the Hebrew Bible in particular – the 'Five books of Moses': Genesis, Exodus, Leviticus, Numbers and Deuteronomy. In addition to printed forms of the *Torah* – the *Chumash*, meaning, 'fived' – the *Torah* is also preserved on a scroll, known as the *Sefer Torah*, a consonantal text, without vowels and punctuation, which is kept in the Holy Ark – *Aron Ha-Kodesh*.

Tosefta: lit. 'Additions'(Aramaic). A collection of the teachings of the *tannai'm* that were not included in the *Mishnah*.

Tz'dakah: lit. 'Righteouness' – connected to the word, *tzedek*, 'justice'. The *mitzvah* of giving money and things to those in need.

Yad Va-Shem: lit. 'Hand and Name'. Israel's national *Sho'ah* (Holocaust) commemoration museum and centre in Jerusalem.

YHWH: The consonants designating the name of God, which are an ancient form of the Hebrew root, *Hei Yud Hei*, to 'be'. Since, the Divine name could only be pronounced by the High Priest in the inner sanctum of the Temple on the holiest day of the year, *Yom Kippur*, a substitute word is used, *Adonai*, meaning, literally, 'my lords'. In the printed version of the Hebrew Bible, the vowels of *Adonai* are added to the consonants, YHVH.

Yiddish: rooted in a mediaeval form of German, and including Hebrew and Russian loan words, *Yiddish* was spoken extensively in Eastern European Jewish communities before these communities were wiped out in the *Sho'ah*. Today the language is the vernacular of the *Chasidim*, for whom, Hebrew, 'the holy tongue' may only be used for study and prayer.

Yom Kippur: lit. 'Day of Covering'. The Day of Atonement, which takes place on the 10th day of *Tishri*, the seventh month of the year. *Yom Kippur* completes a ten day period of repentance, which begins on *Rosh Ha-Shanah*, the first day of the New Year.

z"l: Abbreviation of: *zichronah livrachah* – May her memory be for blessing; *zichrono livrachah* – May his memory be for blessing; *zichronam livrachah* – May their memory be for blessing. Used when referring to someone, who has died.

About the Author

Born in South Shields, County Durham in 1955, Elli (Elizabeth) Tikvah Sarah studied Sociology at the London School of Economics (1974-77) and Rabbinics at the Leo Baeck College in London (1984-89), where she received *s'michah* (ordination) and was awarded a distinction for her rabbinic thesis.

A pioneer in the area of lesbian and gay inclusion, in March 2006, she married her partner, Jess Wood at her synagogue, Brighton and Hove Progressive.

Prior to the rabbinate she engaged in feminist activism, research and writing. She edited *Reassessments of 'First Wave' Feminism* (Pergamon Press, 1982), and co-edited, *Learning to Lose – Sexism and Education* (with Dale Spender, Women's Press, 1980) and *On the Problem of Men* (with Scarlet Friedman, Women's Press, 1982).

Since she became a rabbi she has worked as: Rabbi of Buckhurst Hill Reform Synagogue (1989-94), Director of Programmes for the Reform Synagogues of Great Britain and Deputy Director of the Sternberg Centre (1994-97), a Rabbinic Tutor at the Leo Baeck College (1994-2009), Chair of the Leo Baeck College Rabbinic In-Service Training Team (1996-2002), a Lecturer at Leo Baeck College, teaching 'Classical Hebrew' and 'Spirituality' (1997-2002), Rabbi of Leicester Progressive Jewish Congregation (1998-2000) and Rabbi of Brighton & Hove Progressive Synagogue (2000-current). She was Chair of Liberal Judaism Publications (2004-2009) and is Liberal Jewish Chaplain at Sussex and Brighton Universities.

She has also continued to write, and, in addition to monthly articles for *Sussex Jewish News* (2001-current), and, writing a booklet entitled *Compelling Commitments: A New Approach to Living as Liberal Jew* (Liberal Judaism, 2007), has contributed four dozen articles and several poems to various journals and anthologies. She is currently working with Rabbi Rachel Benjamin on producing a booklet for Liberal Judaism on *Celebrating Shabbat*.